The Christmas Kitchen

Also by Lorraine Bodger:

GREAT AMERICAN CAKES
CHRISTMAS DOUGHCRAFTS
GREAT AMERICAN COOKIES
GIFT WRAPS
CHRISTMAS TREE ORNAMENTS
WOMAN'S DAY DOUGHCRAFTS
PAPER DREAMS

with Delia Ephron

CRAFTS FOR ALL SEASONS
GLADRAGS
THE ADVENTUROUS CROCHETER

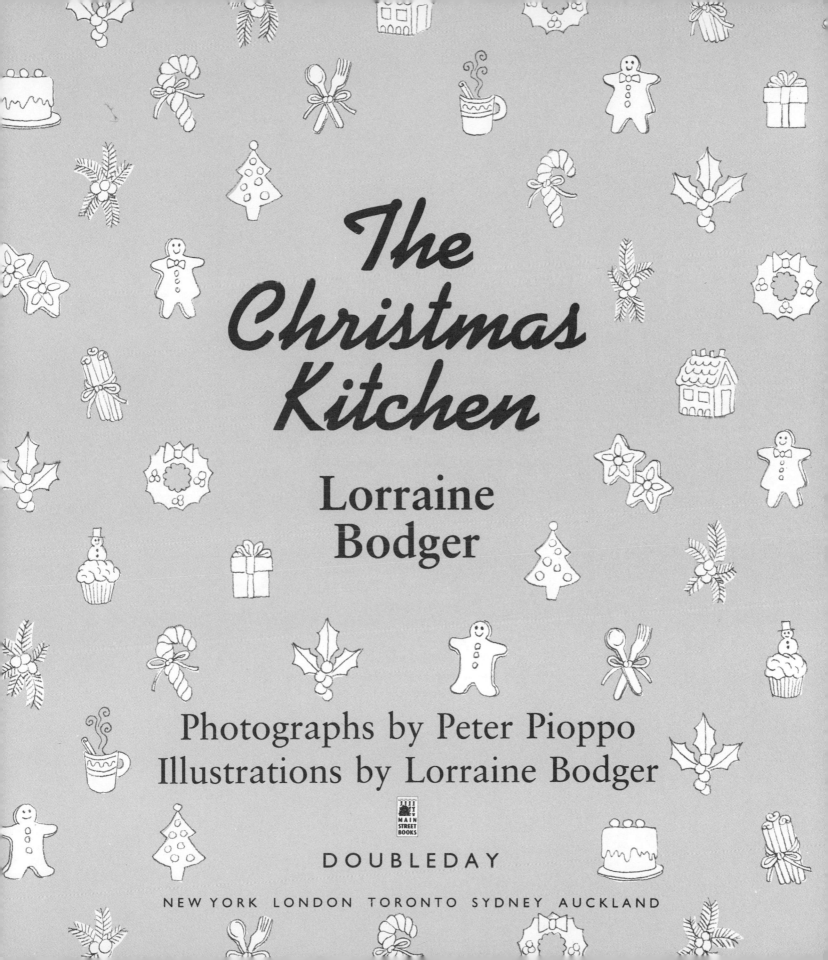

The Christmas Kitchen

Lorraine Bodger

Photographs by Peter Pioppo
Illustrations by Lorraine Bodger

MAIN STREET BOOKS

DOUBLEDAY

NEW YORK LONDON TORONTO SYDNEY AUCKLAND

A MAIN STREET BOOK

PUBLISHED BY DOUBLEDAY

a division of Bantam Doubleday Dell Publishing Group, Inc.

666 Fifth Avenue, New York, New York 10103

MAIN STREET BOOKS, DOUBLEDAY, and the portrayal of a
building with a tree are trademarks of Doubleday,
a division of Bantam Doubleday Dell Publishing Group, Inc.

Library of Congress Cataloging-in-Publication Data

Bodger, Lorraine.
   The Christmas kitchen.
   Includes index.
   1. Christmas cookery.   I. Title.
TX739.2.C45B63   1989   641.5'68   88-31094

ISBN 0-385-42431-0
Copyright © 1989 by Lorraine Bodger

Acknowledgments

I'm grateful for the help I've had from numerous people and I sincerely hope I haven't left too many of them out of the following list. Let me extend my thanks

...to editor John Duff, design director Marysarah Quinn, copy editor Elaine Chubb, and to the late Alex Gotfryd, among others at Doubleday

...to the fine home cooks who donated original recipes: Jenny Snider, Irma de Anchondo and Meredith Nemirov, Diana Calta, Nora Ephron and Marnie Mueller

...to the good friends who told me their Christmas memories: Fritz Mueller, Jane Weiss, Ernie Foster, Angella Baker, Maggie Javna, Delia Ephron, Alison Brown Cerier and others

...to the skilled and talented professionals who were essential to the realization of my ideas and contributed so many terrific ideas of their own: chefs Susan Rosenfeld and Liz Sanchez; photographer Peter Pioppo and his staff; food stylist Bette Friedman

...to the always generous Wm. E. Wright Company, for sending the beautiful ribbons and cords we used in the photography, and to Judy's Chocolate Tree of Hicksville, New York, for supplying plenty of candy canes and peppermint sticks.

And particular thanks to Lowell Bodger, to literary agent Diane Cleaver and to the undaunted friends and relatives who thought they were coming for dinner and ended up taste-testing everything from soup to nuts.

Contents

Introduction 10

CHAPTER 1. Christmas Cookies 12

CHAPTER 2. Christmas Cakes, Pies and Tarts 48

CHAPTER 3. Uncommonly Delicious Fruitcakes 76

CHAPTER 4. Easy Christmas Candies 94

CHAPTER 5. Sweet Holiday Breads, Coffeecakes
            and Tea Loaves 114

CHAPTER 6. Christmas Eve Menus and Recipes 136

CHAPTER 7. Christmas Day Menus and Recipes 156

CHAPTER 8. Holiday Party Menus and Recipes 184

CHAPTER 9. Head-Start Dinners for Busy Days 210

CHAPTER 10. Gifts from Your Kitchen 228

            Index 243

The Christmas Kitchen

Introduction

At Christmas, more than any other time of year, the kitchen is the center of activity, the place where comfort, coziness and hospitality are always found. It may be cold and dark outside, but inside the kitchen it's warm and bright and deliciously fragrant with vanilla and spices, marzipan and chocolate, cranberries, raisins and apples. Everybody's welcome and anyone can join in the pleasure of cooking (and eating) all the wonderful foods we love to prepare for the Christmas season: cookies of all kinds; pies, tarts and fancy desserts; holiday yeast breads and fruitcakes; homemade candies and jars of tasty relishes to give as gifts.

The kitchen plays another essential role, too, since Christmas is the perfect time for lavish entertaining and for getting together with favorite people to enjoy great holiday meals. Spectacular party buffets, family reunions, caroling excursions, cookie swaps, make-ahead suppers for weekend guests, Christmas Eve open house, Christmas morning brunch, Christmas Day dinner—holiday gatherings will be joyous celebrations when good company is matched by delectable food.

This Christmas and for many Christmases to come, you'll find in *The Christmas Kitchen* everything you and your family need for your baking, cooking and entertaining plans: complete menus for each dinner and party (plus strategies that eliminate the confusion and anxiety of preparing for holiday socializing), and step-by-step recipes for delicious new dishes as well as time-honored Christmas specialties. And be sure to check the margins of the book to find your Christmas bonuses—cooking hints, party tips, gift wrap suggestions, decorating ideas and more.

Christmas comes but once a year, but it does come every year, so don't try to do it all in one season—*The Christmas Kitchen* is meant to last through quite a few Christmas seasons. In fact, I hope that over the years you'll gradually bake and cook your way right through this book, and that many of the recipes will become new family favorites and, eventually, old family traditions.

CHAPTER I

Christmas Cookies

This book starts with cookies because Christmas just wouldn't be complete without crunchy, buttery, spicy, marvelous Christmas cookies. You simply can't bake too many Christmas cookies because you'll serve them all the time—to family, friends and holiday visitors, for snacks, dessert and parties. You'll want cookies for the Christmas cookie swap and the holiday bake sale and extras to take with you when you deliver Christmas presents. And your kids will surely want to spend at least one afternoon rolling and decorating sugar cookies and gingerbread Santas. Christmas cookies are so indispensable that you may want to freeze a few kinds of cookies and doughs as a hedge against the days when you don't have time to start from scratch.

In addition to the terrific cookie recipes, there are two very special projects in this chapter: a Gingerbread Cottage and Miniature Cookie Houses (see photographs 1 and 2). Few Christmas decorations captivate a child (or a grown-up) the way a gingerbread cottage or cookie house does, so give yourself the pleasure of making either or both.

Tips and Guidelines

❆ Unless otherwise specified, use sweet (un-salted) butter, all-purpose flour, white granulated sugar, large eggs and ground spices. Nuts and spices should be fresh, raisins and currants should be soft. Vanilla extract must be the real thing—no imitations. The same goes for chocolate—no chocolate-flavored products.

❆ There's no need to sift flour unless the recipe specifically requires it.

❆ Use an electric mixer for creaming and beating.

❆ Use cookie sheets that fit on the oven rack with at least two inches between each edge of the cookie sheet and the adjacent wall of the oven, so the heat can circulate freely.

❆ Always preheat the oven for at least 15 minutes, using an oven thermometer to check the temperature. Bake one sheet of cookies at a time, in the center of the oven, and set your kitchen timer when you put the cookies in. Prepare a second sheet of cookies while the first is baking.

❆ When making batches of cookies, don't wash each cookie sheet every time you reuse it—just scrape off crumbs and wipe with a paper towel. Be sure the cookie sheet is cool before you put more dough on it.

❆ When cookies are done, let them cool as instructed in the recipe, then loosen them all at the same time with a metal spatula and transfer to wire racks, making one layer of cookies. Don't pile up or store the cookies until they are completely cool. You'll find more cookie storage information on page 45.

❆ If you live in an area where there is concern about the use of raw eggs, you may want to consider steering clear of recipes calling for them.

SEE PHOTOGRAPH 2

Double Chocolate Bourbon Cookies

2 cups flour

6 tablespoons unsweetened cocoa powder

¼ teaspoon cinnamon

2 pinches of salt

1 cup (two sticks) butter, room temperature

1 cup (packed) light brown sugar

½ cup bourbon

1 cup miniature semisweet chocolate chips

2 egg whites beaten with two tablespoons water

3 cups finely chopped pecans or walnuts

Makes about 6½ dozen cookies

For chocolate lovers: a brownie-like Christmas cookie, dark and rich, with a zing of bourbon. This cookie is also great when frozen almost solid—try it.

Baking pan: one or two cookie sheets

1. Stir or whisk together the flour, cocoa powder, cinnamon and salt; set aside.

2. In a large bowl, cream the butter until light. Add the brown sugar a little at a time, beating well after each addition. Add the bourbon and blend well.

3. Gradually add the dry ingredients, blending well after each addition. Stir in the chocolate chips. Cover the dough with plastic wrap and refrigerate for two hours. The dough will not become completely firm; it will be sticky but workable.

4. Preheat the oven to 350° F.; grease the cookie sheets.

Shape the dough into balls about one inch in diameter. Roll each ball first in the egg white mixture and then in the chopped nuts. Place on a prepared cookie sheet, leaving ½ inch between balls.

If necessary, return the dough to the refrigerator or freezer periodically to firm up again, especially if the kitchen is warm.

5. Bake for 15–20 minutes, or until the cookies are still soft but have a light crust that you can feel. Let the cookies cool on the cookie sheet for 2–5 minutes and then transfer to wire racks to finish cooling.

SEE PHOTOGRAPH 2

Buttery Gingerbread Santas

Makes about four dozen Santas, each four inches high

5–6 cups flour
2 teaspoons baking soda
2 teaspoons cinnamon
1 teaspoon powdered ginger
½ teaspoon ground cloves
1 teaspoon salt
1 cup (two sticks) butter, room temperature
1 cup (packed) light or dark brown sugar
1 cup unsulfured molasses
2 eggs, beaten
2 teaspoons hot water
2 teaspoons cider vinegar

This is a moister, richer gingerbread cookie than the usual—and still terrific for Christmas tree ornaments; see step 4 for instructions. Decorate the Santas before baking (techniques described on page 32) or decorate baked Santas with simple piping, as shown in the drawing on page 16 and in photograph 2. If you prefer or if you don't have a Santa cutter, use any favorite cookie cutters to make these cookies, such as the teddy bears or gingerbread man shown in the same photograph.

Baking pan: one or two cookie sheets

1. Stir or whisk together five cups of the flour, the baking soda, spices and salt; set aside.

2. In a large bowl, cream the butter and brown sugar. Add the molasses and beaten eggs and blend until smooth. Add the water and vinegar and blend again. (The batter will look broken, but don't be concerned about this.)

3. Gradually add the dry ingredients, blending well after each addition. The dough should be firm but sticky, neither dry nor batter-like; if necessary, blend in some of the remaining cup of flour to get the right consistency.

Divide the dough into quarters, wrap each piece snugly in plastic and refrigerate for two hours, or until firm.

4. Preheat the oven to 350° F.; grease the cookie sheets.

Dust the work surface and rolling pin with flour. Roll out one package of dough at a time, making a rectangle ⅛–¼ inch thick. Cut with a Santa cookie cutter, dipping the cutting edge in flour, if necessary, to keep the dough from sticking. Carefully transfer Santas to a prepared cookie sheet, leaving one inch between them.

If you plan to hang these cookies as tree ornaments, use a plastic drinking straw to punch a hole near the top of each cookie. The holes should remain open during baking; if they don't, punch holes again as soon as you take the cookies out of the oven.

Decorating Icing

Makes about two cups

This recipe may be doubled or halved.

1 pound confectioners' sugar, sifted
   (about 4½ cups)
¾ teaspoon cream of tartar
3 egg whites
   Note: To avoid harmful bacteria, always check the shells of raw eggs and discard any eggs with cracks.
½ teaspoon vanilla extract
Liquid or paste food coloring

Stir the ingredients together in a deep bowl. Beat at high speed for five minutes, or until the icing is firm and holds stiff peaks. If you like, divide the icing among several bowls and color each one with a small amount of food coloring, gradually adding more coloring to get brighter or darker colors. Since this icing dries hard and crisp, it must be kept tightly covered with plastic wrap until you are ready to use it.

Tip: You may store this icing for days in the refrigerator if necessary, but it may lose volume and become soft. When you want to use it again, let it come to room temperature, sift in a spoonful or two of confectioners' sugar and a pinch of cream of tartar and beat at high speed until it is firm.

Leftover dough may be kneaded together, chilled and rolled out two more times; after that, you may want to discard leftovers because the dough will have absorbed too much extra flour from the work surface to produce a tender, tasty cookie. (However, the dough is still perfectly good for making Christmas tree ornaments that will not be eaten.)

5. Bake for 12–15 minutes, until the edges are browned. Let the cookies cool on the cookie sheet for one minute and then transfer to wire racks to finish cooling.

To hang the cookie ornaments, thread short lengths of yarn, cord or narrow ribbon through the holes and tie to the Christmas tree.

OPTIONS: Decorate baked cookies with simple piping (page 19 or 46) or any of the quick and easy decorations described on pages 25 and 39.

Diana's Scandinavian Jam Tots

Makes about five dozen cookies

Diana Calta, an excellent home cook (and mother of one of my closest friends), generously shared the recipe for these melt-in-your-mouth cookies, which she makes every Christmas without fail.

Baking pan: one or two cookie sheets

1 cup (two sticks) butter, room temperature
½ cup (packed) light brown sugar
2 eggs, separated
2 cups sifted flour stirred with two pinches of salt
2 cups finely chopped walnuts
Favorite jam or preserves

1. Preheat the oven to 300° F.
Cream the butter and brown sugar. Add the egg yolks and blend well.

2. Add the flour-salt mixture and blend thoroughly to get a somewhat sticky dough. Chill the dough for one hour, or until firm enough to handle.

3. Dust your hands with flour and roll the dough into balls about one inch in diameter. Dip each ball in the egg white and roll it in the chopped nuts. Place the balls 1½ inches apart on the ungreased cookie sheet and use your flour-dipped fingertip or the flour-dipped back of a ½-teaspoon measuring spoon to make an indentation in each ball.

4. Bake for eight minutes and then take out the cookie sheet and press each indentation again, with your fingertip or measuring spoon. Bake for 12–15 more minutes, or until the cookies are lightly browned and the nuts smell toasty. If necessary, press the indentations again.

Let the cookies cool on the cookie sheet for a minute or two, until slightly firm, and then transfer to wire racks to finish cooling.

When the cookies are cool, fill the indentations with jam or preserves.

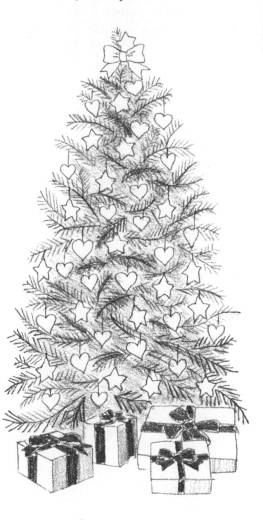

Almond Spritz Cookies

Makes about 4–5 dozen cookies

1 egg plus one egg yolk, room
    temperature
¾ cup superfine sugar
¼ cup ground blanched raw (i.e.,
    untoasted) almonds
    Note: If possible, buy skinless
    (blanched) almonds. If you
    have almonds with skins,
    blanch by putting them in a
    pot of boiling water for a
    minute or two, then draining
    and rinsing well in cold
    water. Pinch off the brown
    skins. Dry first with paper
    towels and then on a jelly roll
    pan in a 300° F. oven, just
    until the almonds are restored
    to crispness but not toasted.
1 teaspoon vanilla extract
½ teaspoon almond extract
2 cups flour
1 cup (two sticks) butter, melted
    and cooled

Spritz cookies are made with a cookie press and an assortment of templates. If you've never made spritz before, it may take you a few tries to get the hang of pressing out just the right amount of dough—but these delicate, almond-flavored cookies are worth the effort.

Baking pan: one or two cookie sheets

1. In a large bowl, beat the egg, egg yolk and sugar until light in texture and pale in color. Stir in the ground almonds, vanilla extract and almond extract.

2. Gradually add the flour, blending well after each addition. Add the melted, cooled butter and blend well again.

Cover the dough with plastic wrap and refrigerate for half an hour.

Meanwhile, preheat the oven to 350° F. and grease the cookie sheets.

3. Attach a wreath, tree or other favorite template to a cookie press. Using a spatula, fill the press half-full of chilled dough; return the remaining dough to the refrigerator.

If you are experienced in working with a cookie press, go ahead and make cookies on a prepared cookie sheet, leaving two inches between cookies. If you are inexperienced, first practice making a dozen or so cookies on the back of any baking pan. When you feel comfortable with the cookie press, scrape the practice dough back into the bowl of dough in the refrigerator and then press real cookies onto a prepared cookie sheet.

Refill the cookie press with chilled dough as needed. Keep your eye on the chilled dough: If it is refrigerated for too long, it may become too stiff to be forced through the press.

4. Bake for 12–15 minutes, or until the cookies are slightly browned around the edges. Do not overbake. Let the cookies cool on the cookie sheet for a minute or two and then transfer to wire racks to finish cooling.

OPTIONS: Because the flavor of these cookies is so light and mellow, don't add decorations that would interfere with the taste—no cinnamon red hots or toasted coconut. Instead, if you want to decorate, simply sprinkle a little colored sugar on the cookies as soon as they come out of the oven.

Another decoration: When the cookies are cool, arrange them close together on a wire rack over waxed paper. Dip a small wire whisk in semisweet chocolate melted with a little water and a few drops of vegetable oil and swing the whisk back and forth above the cookies first in one direction and then another, to make a lattice design. Let the chocolate harden.

COOK'S JOURNAL
Decorating Your Cookies with Simple Piping: Method #1

Spoon *Decorating Icing (recipe on page 16)* into a sturdy plastic zip-lock bag. Snip off a tiny bit of one corner and push the icing down to that corner. Twist the bag tightly closed above the icing and press the icing out through the little hole. You can't make rosettes, but you can pipe straight or curved lines, crisscrossed lines, scallops, squiggles, dots, loops and letters. Practice on waxed paper until you've got the hang of it.

SEE PHOTOGRAPH 2

Christmas Shortbread

1 cup (two sticks) butter, room
    temperature
½ cup superfine sugar
1 teaspoon vanilla extract
2 cups flour stirred with two
    pinches of salt

Makes 34 bars or 16 wedges

Shortbread is a marvel of simplicity. Try the variations, too.

Baking pan: one cookie sheet

1. Preheat the oven to 350° F.

In a large bowl, cream the butter, sugar and vanilla until light and fluffy.

2. Add the flour-salt mixture and beat until thoroughly blended, to make a soft dough.

3. **To make bars:** On a work surface dusted with flour, pat the dough into a rectangle ½ inch thick, four inches wide and about 17 inches long. Use a knife or fluted pastry cutter to cut the rectangle in half lengthwise (two strips, each two inches wide) and then to cut each half into 17 one-inch bars. Use a spatula to transfer the bars to an ungreased cookie sheet, leaving one inch between bars. Use a fork to prick each bar several times.

To make wedges: Dust your hands and an ungreased cookie sheet with flour. Divide the dough in half and pat one half into a ball. Place the ball on the cookie sheet and pat it into a flat disk about ½ inch thick and seven inches in diameter. Use the edge of a plastic ruler—dusted with flour—to mark each disk in eight wedges, cutting about halfway through the dough, and use a fork to prick the dough all over and crimp the edge of the disk. Repeat with the second half of the dough and a second cookie sheet.

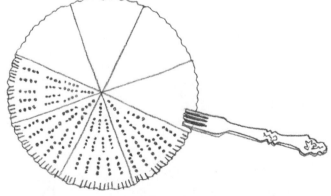

4. Bake bars for 20–25 minutes, or until lightly colored. Do not overbake; the bars should not brown. Let the bars cool on the cookie sheet for one minute and then carefully transfer to wire racks to finish cooling.

Bake disks for 30 minutes, then take the cookie sheet out and cut through the shortbread on the marked lines. Return the shortbread to the oven for five more minutes. Let the wedges cool on the cookie sheet for one minute and then carefully transfer to wire racks to finish cooling.

Variations

To create some delicious shortbread variations, add any of the following to the flour-salt mixture specified in the ingredients list.

Nut Shortbread: ½ cup finely chopped toasted pecans, almonds, walnuts or hazelnuts (see *How to Toast Nuts* on page 40)

Chocolate Chip Shortbread: ½ cup *miniature* semisweet chocolate chips

Orange–Chocolate Chip Shortbread: two teaspoons grated orange rind and ½ cup *miniature* semisweet chocolate chips

Lemon Shortbread: two teaspoons grated lemon rind

DECORATING MEMO
Cookie Ornaments

Cookie ornaments (pages 15 and 24) have an old-fashioned charm that goes beyond the Christmas tree: Tie cookie animals to an evergreen or grapevine wreath; hang cookie Santas from the mantelpiece; line up gingerbread folks on a shelf, molding, windowsill or window ledge.

SEE PHOTOGRAPH 2

Liz's Hazelnut Crescents and Hazelnut Sandwiches

Makes seven dozen crescents or 3½ dozen sandwiches

Liz Sanchez is a professional chef with a special talent for baking, as you will see from this original recipe (and the one on page 29). The crescents are dipped in chocolate and the sandwiches are filled with brandy-flavored apricot jam.

Baking pan: one or two cookie sheets

2 cups flour
¾ teaspoon cinnamon
1 cup (two sticks) butter, room temperature
½ cup confectioners' sugar
1 teaspoon vanilla extract
½ teaspoon almond extract
1⅓ cups finely chopped toasted hazelnuts
  Note: See How to Toast Nuts *on page 40.*

For the crescents:
Chocolate Liqueur Coating (recipe follows)
¼ cup finely chopped toasted hazelnuts for decorating

For the sandwiches:
Apricot Brandy Filling (recipe follows)
Additional confectioners' sugar for dusting

1. Preheat the oven to 350° F. Stir or whisk together the flour and cinnamon; set aside.

2. In a large bowl, cream the butter until light. Add the sugar, vanilla and almond extract and beat well.

3. Gradually add the flour-cinnamon mixture, mixing well after each addition. Add the hazelnuts and mix again.

4. Shape the dough: For each crescent, roll a bit of dough into a ball ¾ inch in diameter and then into a cylinder about two inches long. Place on an ungreased cookie sheet and shape into a crescent. Gently flatten the crescent to ¼ inch thick. Repeat with all the dough, leaving ½ inch between crescents.

For each sandwich, roll two balls of dough, each ¾ inch in diameter; roll each ball into a cylinder about two inches long and place on an ungreased cookie sheet, leaving one inch between cylinders. Gently flatten each cylinder to a little less than ¼ inch thick, keeping the oval shape.

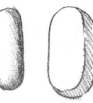

5. Bake for 10–13 minutes, or until the edges are slightly browned. Let the cookies cool on the cookie sheet for five minutes and then remove carefully by hand and place on wire racks to finish cooling.

6. **To complete each crescent:** Dip each end in a little bowl of Chocolate Liqueur Coating, wiping excess chocolate off the underside by gently drawing the cookie across the lip of the bowl. Immediately sprinkle finely chopped hazelnuts on the chocolate and place the crescent on waxed paper. Repeat with all the crescents and let the chocolate set.

Note: As the chocolate cools in the little bowl, it thickens. To thin the chocolate, warm it periodically in the saucepan and, if necessary, add a spoonful of water and stir well.

To complete each sandwich: Spread a little Apricot Brandy Filling on the flat side of one oval cookie and top with a matching oval cookie. Repeat with all the oval cookies. Using a fine strainer, sprinkle the sandwiches generously with confectioners' sugar.

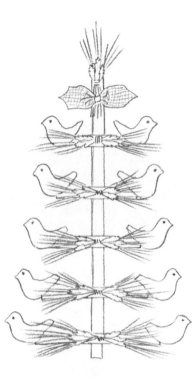

Apricot Brandy Filling

Makes about one cup

If the preserves are chunky, process in a blender or food processor until fairly smooth. Put the preserves and brandy in a small saucepan over low heat and simmer for one minute. Allow to cool for at least five minutes.

1 cup apricot preserves
2 tablespoons brandy

Chocolate Liqueur Coating

Makes about ¾ cup

Put all the ingredients in a small saucepan over low heat and whisk constantly until melted and smooth. Pour into a small, deep bowl. Use while still hot or very warm, reheating and whisking the chocolate in the saucepan as needed.

6 squares (six ounces) semisweet chocolate, chopped
3 tablespoons Triple Sec or Cointreau
3 tablespoons water
1 teaspoon vegetable oil

SEE PHOTOGRAPHS 1 AND 2

Rolled Sugar Cookies

Makes about 5½ dozen cookies, depending on cookie cutters used

4¼ cups flour
1½ teaspoons baking powder
½ teaspoon salt
1½ cups (three sticks) butter, room temperature
1 cup sugar
½ cup (packed) light brown sugar
2 eggs
2 teaspoons vanilla extract

Like the Buttery Gingerbread Santas, these rich, crisp Rolled Sugar Cookies make wonderful Christmas tree ornaments: Use your favorite Christmas cookie cutters to cut them, then bake the cookies and decorate as described on pages 25 and 39 or with simple piping, page 19 or 46. Photographs 1 and 2 show cookies decorated in several different ways.

In addition, this versatile recipe has variations to please every taste—make spice or lemon cookies, cinnamon stars or currant biscuits. If you want to make one of the variations, read the instructions on pages 25–26 before you begin mixing any ingredients.

Baking pan: one or two cookie sheets

1. Stir or whisk together the flour, baking powder and salt; set aside.
2. In a large bowl, cream the butter, sugar and brown sugar. Add the eggs and vanilla and blend well.

3. Add the dry ingredients in four parts, mixing well after each addition. Divide the dough into thirds, wrap each third snugly in plastic and refrigerate for several hours, or until firm enough to roll out.

4. Preheat the oven to 350° F.; grease the cookie sheets.

Dust the work surface and rolling pin with flour. Roll out one package of dough at a time to ⅛ inch thick. Cut with two- to three-inch Christmas cookie cutters. Gather up excess dough and save it for rerolling. Use a spatula to transfer the cookies to a prepared cookie sheet, leaving one inch between cookies.

If you plan to hang these cookies on your Christmas tree, use a plastic drinking straw to punch a hole near the top of each cookie. The holes should remain open during baking; if they don't, punch holes again as soon as you take the hot baked cookies out of the oven.

5. Bake for 8–12 minutes, or until the edges are lightly browned. Let the cookies cool for a minute or two on the cookie sheet and then transfer to wire racks to finish cooling.

If you like, decorate the cooled cookies with simple piping (page 19 or 46) or any of the Quick and Easy techniques described on pages 25 and 39, some of which are shown in photographs 1 and 2.

To hang the cookie ornaments, thread short lengths of yarn, cord or narrow ribbon through the holes and tie to the Christmas tree.

Variations

Sugar Biscuits with Currants: Stir one cup of currants into the dry ingredients; follow steps 2 and 3 as given. Roll out each package of dough to an 8 × 12-inch rectangle, ⅛ inch thick, and use a fluted pastry cutter to cut it in 1½ × 2-inch rectangles. Bake for 12–15 minutes.

Cinnamon Stars: Add two teaspoons of cinnamon to the dry ingredients. Reduce the vanilla to one teaspoon. Make the cookies as directed, using a three-inch star cookie cutter. Before transferring the unbaked cookies to the cookie sheet, brush each one with egg wash (one egg white mixed with one teaspoon water) and sprinkle with cinnamon sugar (one teaspoon cinnamon stirred into ⅓ cup sugar). Bake for 10–12 minutes.

Cinnamon Stars are shown in photograph 12.

QUICK AND EASY
Decorations for Baked Cookies

❋ Mix one egg white with one teaspoon of water; brush mixture on one cookie at a time and sprinkle with colored sugar, multicolored nonpareils (tiny dots) or colored (or chocolate) sprinkles.

❋ Paint a design or greeting on each cookie, using an artist's brush and thin confectioners' sugar glaze (see page 118) tinted with paste food coloring.

❋ Spread thin confectioners' sugar glaze (page 118) on one cookie at a time. While still tacky, press candies, nuts, chocolate chips, finely shredded coconut, glacé cherries, etc., into the glaze.

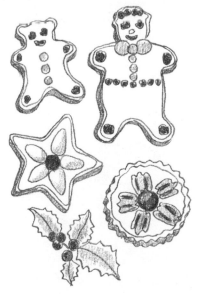

Spice Cookies: To the dry ingredients add one teaspoon cinnamon, ½ teaspoon each powdered ginger and ground allspice and ¼ teaspoon ground nutmeg. Make and bake the cookies as directed.

Lemon Cookies: Omit brown sugar and use instead 1½ cups white sugar. Reduce vanilla to one teaspoon; when adding the vanilla, add also one tablespoon grated lemon rind and one tablespoon fresh lemon juice. Make and bake the cookies as directed.

SEE PHOTOGRAPH I

Candy Cane Cookies

Makes about three dozen cookies

These pink and green cookies are big, rich and delightfully chewy (unless you overbake them slightly, and then they are delightfully crisp). They make an especially attractive addition to any Christmas cookie assortment.

Baking pan: one or two cookie sheets

3½ cups flour
2 teaspoons baking powder
½ teaspoon salt
1 cup (two sticks) butter, room temperature
1¼ cups sugar
2 eggs beaten with two teaspoons vanilla extract
Red and green liquid food coloring

1. Stir or whisk together the flour, baking powder and salt; set aside.
2. In a large bowl, cream the butter and sugar. Add the egg mixture a little at a time, beating well after each addition.
3. Gradually add the dry ingredients, blending well after each addition. Put half the dough in another bowl.

Add eight drops of red food coloring to one bowl of dough and eight drops of green to the second bowl. Mix each thoroughly to get pink and light green doughs. (If you like, add another drop or two to make slightly darker pink and green.)

Flatten each ball of dough, wrap snugly in plastic and refrigerate for 30 minutes, until slightly firm. Don't overchill the dough; it should be firm but flexible.

4. Preheat the oven to 350° F.; grease the cookie sheets. Take the dough out of the refrigerator.

Lightly dust your hands and work surface with flour. Roll a one-inch-diameter ball of pink dough and one of green dough. Roll each ball to a rope about six inches long and ⅜ inch in diameter. Cross the pink and green ropes in the middle and spiral them together from the middle to the ends. Press the ropes together lightly at each end.

Transfer the twist to the cookie sheet and shape it into a candy cane. Repeat to make more cookies, rechilling the dough if necessary. Leave 1½ inches between cookies on the cookie sheet.

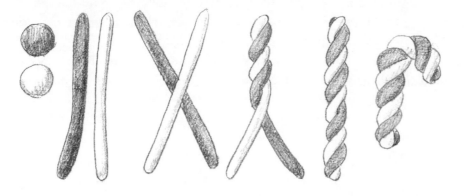

5. Bake for 12–14 minutes, until very lightly browned on the edges. The cookies will be a bit soft on top when they come out of the oven, but they become crisper as they cool. Let them cool on the cookie sheet for two minutes and then carefully transfer to wire racks to finish cooling.

OPTIONS: Candy Cane Cookies do not have to be pink and green, of course. You might prefer pink and white (uncolored dough), green and white or pink and yellow.

You might also enjoy making other shapes of cookies using the twisted ropes of dough—try rounds, S shapes or U shapes.

CHRISTMAS MEMORIES FROM FRIENDS
Christmas in Bavaria

Two weeks before Christmas, I would go with my father to buy our tree at the Christmas market, a sort of winter outdoor fair, wooden booths strung together with boughs and lighted candles. There were trees, ornaments, chocolates, cookies, little gifts—it was very romantic and beautiful, especially when it was snowy. We carried our tree home and kept it outside until the week before Christmas, when my parents would take it into the Christmas Room and decorate it. We weren't allowed to see it until Christmas Eve.

On Christmas Eve we would walk into the darkened Christmas Room. Each person had a little table where his or her presents would be piled up and covered with a napkin. There was a plate of cookies for each person, too—little butter cookies with jelly on top, black and white cookies, gypsy cookies, oatmeal cookies, all baked by my mother. But the most exciting thing was the tree, beautifully decorated and glowing with real lighted candles.

Chocolate-Marzipan-Mocha Layered Bars

Makes 50 bars

A delectable combination of flavors makes an unusual bar cookie to serve with tall glasses of milk or steaming mugs of coffee.

Baking pan: one 10½ × 15½ × 1-inch jelly roll pan

For the bottom layer:

2½ cups flour
½ cup unsweetened cocoa powder, sifted
1 teaspoon baking powder
¼ teaspoon salt
1 cup (two sticks) butter, room temperature
1 cup sugar
2 eggs
1 teaspoon vanilla extract

For the middle layer:

1 eight-ounce can or one seven-ounce tube almond paste, room temperature
2 tablespoons butter, room temperature
½ cup sugar
1 egg white
1 teaspoon vanilla extract
3 eggs

1. Preheat the oven to 350° F.; grease the jelly roll pan.

To make the bottom layer, first stir or whisk together the flour, cocoa powder, baking powder and salt; set aside.

In a large bowl, cream the butter and sugar. Add the eggs and vanilla and beat well. Gradually add the dry ingredients, blending well after each addition. Dip your fingertips in cold water and pat the dough evenly into the prepared pan. Use a rubber spatula dipped in cold water to smooth the dough.

2. Make the middle layer: In a large bowl, beat the almond paste, butter, sugar, egg white and vanilla until smooth. Add the eggs and beat until thoroughly blended. Spread the mixture over the dough in the jelly roll pan.

3. Bake for 20–25 minutes, until the top is lightly browned and a toothpick inserted in the center comes out clean. The top will be slightly puffy but it will flatten as it cools.

Let the layers cool completely in the pan on a wire rack.

4. When the layers are cool, make the mocha frosting: Melt the chocolate with the cream and coffee powder in a small saucepan over very low heat, whisking constantly. Pour the frosting over the cooled layers and spread it evenly with a metal spatula or the back of a spoon. Sprinkle with the chopped almonds.

Let the frosting set for half an hour and then cut into bars. Remove the bars carefully from the pan.

Chocolate Sandwiches with Mint Buttercream Filling

Makes three dozen sandwiches

Taking off from a favorite flavor combination, chef Liz Sanchez has come up with another terrific original recipe (see page 22 for Liz's Hazelnut Crescents and Hazelnut Sandwiches), this time for rich chocolate cookies with a lightly minted, chocolate-chip-studded filling.

Baking pan: one or two cookie sheets

1. Stir or whisk together the flour, baking powder and salt; set aside.
2. In a large bowl, cream the butter until light. Add the melted chocolate and beat well. Add the sugar and beat again.
3. Add the eggs and vanilla and beat well.
4. Gradually add the dry ingredients and beat until well blended. Refrigerate the dough for one hour.

For the mocha frosting:
4 ounces (one bar) sweet cooking chocolate, chopped
¼ cup heavy cream
2 teaspoons powdered instant coffee
Note: To make powdered instant coffee, put several teaspoons of instant coffee granules in a plastic bag and crush with a rolling pin. Measure the powdered coffee as needed.
⅓ cup finely chopped toasted almonds
Note: See *How to Toast Nuts* on page 40.

2½ cups flour
1½ teaspoons baking powder
½ teaspoon salt
1 cup (two sticks) butter, room temperature
3 squares (three ounces) unsweetened chocolate, melted and cooled
1½ cups sugar
2 eggs
2 teaspoons vanilla extract
Mint Buttercream Filling (recipe follows)

5. Preheat the oven to 350° F.; grease the cookie sheets.

Roll the dough into one-inch balls and place on a prepared cookie sheet, leaving two inches between balls.

6. Bake for five minutes and then flatten each ball with the back of a spoon to form a round cookie about ⅛ inch thick. Bake for another 3–5 minutes, or until the centers of the cookies are not shiny. Be careful not to let the bottoms burn. Let the cookies cool on the cookie sheet for five minutes and then transfer to a wire rack to finish cooling.

7. To make each sandwich, spread Mint Buttercream Filling on the flat side of one chocolate cookie and top with another chocolate cookie. Press the cookies lightly so the sandwich holds together.

OPTIONS: If you prefer, fill the sandwiches with any other favorite buttercream—vanilla, chocolate or mocha, for example. Or, to make double the number of cookies, don't make sandwiches at all; simply frost each cookie with a bit of Mint Buttercream Filling (or other buttercream) and scatter chocolate sprinkles on top.

Mint Buttercream Filling

Makes about two cups

½ cup (one stick) butter, room
    temperature
2½ cups confectioners' sugar,
    sifted
½ teaspoon peppermint extract
¼ teaspoon vanilla extract
3 tablespoons milk or cream
½ cup miniature chocolate chips

Beat the butter and sugar together until smooth. Add all the remaining ingredients except the miniature chocolate chips and beat again. Stir in the chips.

SEE PHOTOGRAPHS 2 AND 11

Cranberry-Orange Tartlets or Apple-Mince Tartlets

Makes 24 gem-size tartlets

The procedure for making these bite-size pastries is simple: Make and bake the tartlet shells; make the filling or fillings and spoon into the cooled shells.

The dough makes 24 tartlet shells and each filling recipe makes enough for 24 shells. Choose one filling or, if you can't make up your mind, make two recipes of dough and one recipe of each filling for a total of 24 Cranberry-Orange Tartlets and 24 Apple-Mince Tartlets.

Baking pan: one or two gem muffin pans

1. To make the dough, cream the butter, the cream cheese, sugar and salt until light; add the flour and blend well. Divide the dough in half, wrap each half snugly in plastic and refrigerate for two hours, or until firm.

Preheat the oven to 400° F. Take one package of dough out of the refrigerator and divide into 12 balls of equal size. Press one ball of dough into each cup of the ungreased gem pan, evenly lining the bottom and sides of each cup. If you have a second gem pan, repeat the process with the second package of dough.

Bake the unfilled dough cups for 12–15 minutes, until the edges are slightly browned. Let them cool in the pan on a wire rack and then remove carefully from the pan.

If you have only one gem pan, repeat the process with the second package of dough.

2. **To make the Cranberry-Orange Filling:** First grate the rind from the two oranges. Put all the rind plus the juice from one of the oranges into a saucepan with the cranberries, sugar and cinnamon.

For the dough:
½ cup (one stick) butter, room temperature
1 three-ounce package of cream cheese, softened
1 tablespoon superfine sugar
Pinch of salt
1 cup flour

For the Cranberry-Orange Filling:
2 medium navel (seedless) oranges
1 cup whole cranberries
½ cup sugar
Dash of cinnamon

For the Apple-Mince Filling:
½ cup prepared mincemeat
1 large tart apple, peeled, cored and cut in small dice
  Note. When coring the apple, be sure to remove *all* the seeds and hard matter.
¼ cup finely chopped walnuts or pecans
2 tablespoons (packed) light or dark brown sugar
1 tablespoon butter
1 teaspoon fresh lemon juice

QUICK AND EASY
Decorations
for Unbaked Cookies

Brush each unbaked cookie with egg wash (a mixture of one egg white and one teaspoon of water). While the egg wash is still wet, do one or more of the following, then bake according to the recipe.

❈ Sprinkle with colored sugar or nonpareils.

❈ Firmly press cinnamon redhots, raisins, currants, chocolate chips, whole or chopped nuts, etc., into the cookie.

❈ Cut small shapes and strips of dough and press them gently onto the cookie.

Carefully peel the second orange with a knife, removing all the white membrane. Halve the orange and cut out any fibers from the core. Chop the flesh in small dice, add the diced orange to the saucepan and stir the mixture well.

Bring the mixture to a simmer. Cover and cook for seven minutes, stirring occasionally, until the cranberries have popped. If the filling is still loose, uncover and cook down, stirring, until the liquid is syrupy. Refrigerate the filling until completely cool; it will thicken as it cools. Put a heaping teaspoon of filling in each baked tartlet shell.

3. **To make the Apple-Mince Filling:** Stir the ingredients together in a small saucepan and cook over very low heat, stirring constantly, for about five minutes, or until the sugar is dissolved and the apples are soft but not mushy. Be careful not to let the filling burn; add a little water or apple juice if necessary. Let the mixture cool. Put a heaping teaspoon of filling in each baked tartlet shell.

OPTIONS: Try other fillings with these tartlet shells—lemon curd (page 230) sprinkled with chopped toasted almonds, chocolate pudding topped with miniature chocolate chips, any favorite jam or marmalade.

1. **Gingerbread Cottage,** shown with decorated **Rolled Sugar Cookies** and **Candy Cane Cookies**

2. Miniature Cookie Houses, shown with cookies, clockwise from center: **Cranberry-Orange Tartlets;** gingerbread man made with **Buttery Gingerbread Santa** dough; **Christmas Shortbread; Liz's Hazelnut Crescents; Buttery Gingerbread Santas; Rolled Sugar Cookies; Liz's Hazelnut Sandwiches; Double Chocolate Bourbon Cookies;** teddy bears made with **Buttery Gingerbread Santa** dough

3. Clockwise from top right: **Chocolate-Cherry Fruitcake with Bittersweet Chocolate Glaze; Tipsy Dark Fruitcake;** sliced **Almond-layered Fruitcake; Buttermilk-Pecan Fruitcake; Sherry Fruitcake**

Diagrams and instructions for creating these fruitcake decorations and others are found in Chapter 3.

4. Clockwise from top left: **Christmas Trifle**; **Christmas-Comes-But-Once-a-Year Chocolate Cake**; bowl of **Caramel Sauce**; **Apple Tart with Candied Cranberries and Caramel Sauce**; **Buttermilk-Spice Cupcakes with Brown Butter Frosting**; **Prune-Apricot Custard Tart with Sweet Lemon Crust**

In the center: **Bûche de Noël with Chestnut Buttercream Filling and Mocha Silk Frosting**

5. Clockwise from top left: **Cranberry Spiral Bread with Vanilla Glaze; Spiced Pear and Cherry Kuchen; Santa Lucia Buns; Honey-Pecan Crescents**

6. Clockwise from top right: **Panettone di Natale; Mexican Three Kings Bread; Lattice Coffeecake with Orange-Almond Filling**

7. Clockwise from top left: In the red box, **Christmas Sugarplums** and **Colorful Marzipan Fruits**; in the blue box, **Brown Sugar Butter Crunch with Toasted Almonds** and **Holiday Assortment of Truffles**; in the green box, **Pastel Peppermint Patties** and **Chocolate-dipped Meringue Kisses**
In the center: individually wrapped squares of **Old-fashioned Chocolate Pecan Fudge**

SEE PHOTOGRAPH 2

Miniature Cookie Houses

Makes three cookie houses with bases

These adorable little houses (each is about 5½ inches high) are wonderful additions to your Christmas decorations. Try placing them on your mantelpiece on a bed of Christmas greenery or perhaps nestled in fluffy cotton batting at the base of a tabletop tree.

Each house is made up of individual cookies that are first decorated with colored sugar and candies and then fastened together with icing. Copy the decorations shown in photograph 2, if you like, or alter them by substituting different candies—or go to town inventing your own candy designs.

Instructions are for making one house, for which you will cut and bake one base, two sides, two front/back pieces and two roof pieces. To make three houses, simply cut and bake triple the number of pieces.

Like the Gingerbread Cottage (page 38), Miniature Cookie Houses are decorations that are not really meant to be eaten after the holidays. They'll be stale and dusty by then, and anyway, the hardened Decorating Icing might be difficult to chew. If you want to try preserving them for next year, pack in boxes with plastic foam peanuts under and around each house. Seal with tape and store in a cool, dry, pest-free place (no mice, roaches, ants, etc.). Good luck.

Tip: Unless you can clear a whole day for making the cookie houses, it's a good idea to make and bake the parts on one day and then to decorate the parts, assemble the houses and finish the decorations on a second day.

4½–5 cups flour
2 teaspoons baking powder
½ teaspoon salt
1 cup (two sticks) margarine, room temperature
2 cups sugar
2 eggs
2 tablespoons milk
2 teaspoons vanilla extract
Decorating bag with coupler *OR* three decorating bags
Icing tips: #5 and #7 round tips; #27 star tip
Egg wash (one egg white mixed with one tablespoon of water)
1–2 recipes of *Decorating Icing (page 16)*
   Note: Substitute water for the vanilla; double the recipe if you are making three or more houses.
Colored sugar (turquoise, pink, red and/or green)
Assorted candies (depending on which houses you are making): licorice allsorts; candy canes; gumdrops; candy-coated chocolates; silver dragées; pastel-colored wafers; jelly beans; lozenge-shaped candies

Christmas Touches

A small evergreen tree decorated with sugar cookie angels and stars . . . an Advent calendar for the children, to help them count the days till Christmas . . . decorating the dollhouse for Christmas—and displaying it in the living room . . . hollowed-out orange halves filled with lemon sherbet, served with an assortment of Christmas cookies . . . jars of all sizes wrapped in Christmas calico and bright ribbon, filled with greens and striped candy sticks . . . a little wreath on every bedroom door

Baking pans: two cookie sheets or jelly roll pans

1. Make the cookie dough: Stir or whisk together 4½ cups of the flour, the baking powder and salt; set aside. Cream the butter and sugar until light; add the eggs, milk and vanilla and beat well. Gradually add the dry ingredients and blend to form a smooth ball of dough. If the dough is sticky, add just enough of the remaining flour to eliminate the stickiness. The dough should not be dry. Divide the dough in half, wrap each ball in plastic and refrigerate for several hours, or until firm enough to roll.

2. Meanwhile, cut cardboard templates for the base and the three parts of the cookie house, following the measurements on page 37.

Remember: When you assemble and decorate the houses, you will also need a decorating bag with coupler (or three decorating bags); #5, #7 and #27 tips; one or two recipes of Decorating Icing and the candies specified in the ingredients list.

3. Preheat the oven to 350° F. On a flour-dusted cookie sheet or the *back* of one jelly roll pan, roll out one ball of dough to ⅛–¼ inch thick.

For each house, cut out one base, two front/back pieces, two sides and two roof pieces: Lay out the cardboard patterns on the dough, leaving 1½ inches between them; the layout will depend on the size of your cookie sheet and how many houses you are making. Use a sharp knife to cut around each template, removing excess dough as you cut; wipe the knife frequently. Repeat the rolling and cutting process to make the remaining pieces.

If you want some little trees for the front of your cookie house, cut with a small cookie cutter and place on the cookie sheet.

4. Bake both sheets of cookies at the same time, for 10–15 minutes, removing pieces when they are done. (It is preferable to overbake the cookies by a minute or two than to underbake them, since you want them to be quite firm; the cookies may brown, but this is perfectly acceptable.) Transfer immediately to a wire rack to cool completely.

5. Decorate the front, sides and roof pieces of each house, following the example in the drawing or in photograph 2, or improvising your own design. Do the piping with a decorating bag filled with Decorating Icing and fitted with a *#5* or *#27* tip.

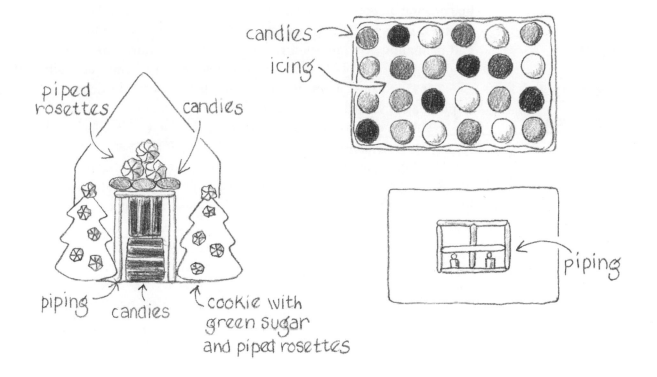

If you like, make tiny candles in the windows with bits of red licorice string; add a bit of yellow food coloring to some icing and use a #5 tip to pipe flames on the candles.

6. Apply colored sugar to the front, back and sides (not the roofs): Working on one piece at a time, brush egg wash on the cookie (being careful not to touch the piping or decorations) and sprinkle immediately with colored sugar. Tap gently to shake off excess sugar. Repeat for all pieces and set aside to dry for half an hour.

Note: If you are adding little trees to the cookie house, brush each tree with egg wash and sprinkle with green sugar.

7. Change to the #7 icing tip and assemble each house on one of the bases:

❄ Arrange front, back and two sides on the base, to get an idea of how to position the house.

❄ Pipe a thick line of icing along bottom edge of back; pipe a thick line of icing on bottom and back edges of one side. Keeping the positioning in mind, press pieces together on the base. Hold in place while icing sets and then allow icing to dry for a few minutes. Reinforce *inside* the house by piping more icing along joint and along base. Let icing set again.

❄ Pipe icing on bottom and back edges of second side piece; press in place against back; reinforce. Let icing set.

❄ Pipe icing on bottom edge and just inside side edges of front; press in place against side pieces; carefully reinforce. Let icing set.

❄ Pipe icing along slanting edges of front and back and top edges of sides; press roof pieces in place. Hold while icing sets and then pipe a line of icing between roof pieces at the peak. Let icing dry for a few minutes.

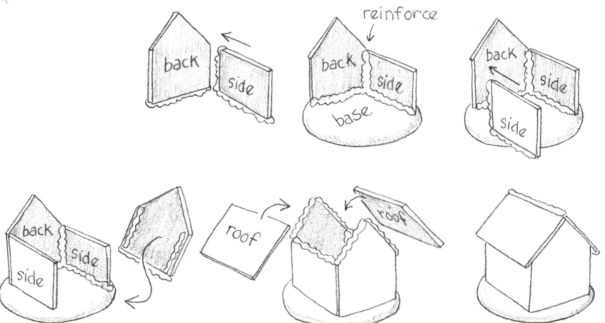

8. When the icing is firm, do all the finishing on the houses and bases, referring again to photograph 2 for guidance.

❋ With #27 icing tip, pipe rosettes or lines of icing along joints on sides of house.

❋ With #27 tip, pipe rosettes or a line of icing along roof peak and finish it according to the design you have chosen. *Remember:* If you are placing candies in the icing along the roof peak, work quickly because icing dries quickly.

❋ With #27 tip, pipe rosettes or lines of icing on roof edges to conceal joints between roof and front, roof and back.

❋ Finish bottom edge of house and/or base according to the design you have chosen—with snowdrifts of icing or large or small rosettes. If you are sprinkling icing with colored sugar or silver dragées or adding trees or gumdrops, do it quickly before icing dries.

❋ Add any additional elements (little trees, candy cane poles with gumdrop tops, a path, etc.), using icing to attach them to house or base.

Let all icing dry thoroughly.

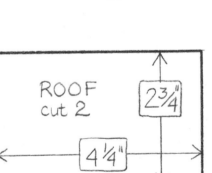

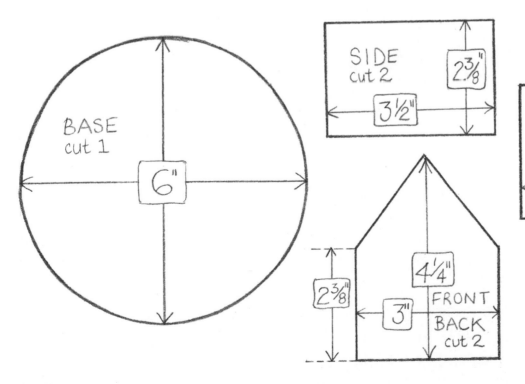

BASE
cut 1

6"

SIDE
cut 2

2 3/8"

3 1/2"

ROOF
cut 2

2 3/4"

4 1/4"

2 3/8"

4 1/4"

FRONT

3"

BACK
cut 2

SEE PHOTOGRAPH I

Gingerbread Cottage

Makes one cottage in a winter setting

5¾ cups flour
1½ teaspoons baking soda
1 tablespoon cinnamon
1 tablespoon powdered ginger
1 cup (two sticks) margarine,
    room temperature
1 cup (packed) light or dark
    brown sugar
1 cup dark corn syrup
2 eggs
Cookie cutters: one-inch-diameter
    flower; 1½-inch heart;
    ½-inch heart; four-inch
    Christmas tree; three-inch
    Christmas tree
2 round cake boards (18-inch
    diameter)
    Note: Buy these sturdy
    cardboard rounds wherever
    cake decorating supplies are
    sold.
White glue
Decorating bags, couplers
Icing tips: #5 and #7 round tips;
    #27 and #30 star tips

Delight the children in your family with this enchanting cottage, complete with evergreen trees and a peppermint fence. The procedure for making the cottage is perfectly straightforward, though it does take time to bake the gingerbread parts, "glue" them together with Decorating Icing (on a sturdy cake board base) and decorate with more icing and lots of candies. Give yourself a couple of afternoons for completing the project.

Note: Refer to photograph 1 for guidance when you do the icing and candy decorations on the cottage.

Tip: This is not the kind of gingerbread house you can eat when the holidays are over. It's pretty stale by then, and besides, the Decorating Icing will have become rock-hard. However, if you want to store the cottage for use next year, pack it carefully in a large box with bubble wrap or other padding all around. Stash it in a cool, dry, pest-free spot (no mice, roaches, ants, etc.) and hope for the best.

Baking pans: two cookie sheets or jelly roll pans

1. Make the gingerbread dough: Stir or whisk together the flour, baking soda and spices; set aside. Cream the margarine and sugar until light; add the corn syrup and eggs and beat until thoroughly blended. Gradually add the dry ingredients, blending until you have a ball of smooth dough. Divide the dough in half, wrap each half in plastic and chill overnight.

2. Meanwhile, make these preparations: Cut cardboard templates for the four parts of the Gingerbread House, following the patterns on pages 46–47. Have ready the required cookie cutters (see ingredients list). Glue the two cake boards together with white glue and weight with books; let the glue dry for several hours.

Remember: When you assemble and decorate the cottage, you will also need: decorating bags and couplers; #5, #7, #27 and #30 tips; three double recipes of Decorating Icing; candies specified in the ingredients list.

3. Preheat the oven to 375° F.

Roll and cut the dough to make the parts of the cottage (one front, one back, two sides, two roof pieces): Dust flour on an ungreased cookie sheet or the *back* of an ungreased jelly roll pan and roll out one ball of dough to ¼ inch thick. Lay out some of the cardboard patterns on the dough, leaving one inch between them; the layout will depend on the size of your cookie sheets. Use a sharp knife to cut around each one, removing the excess dough as you cut; wipe the knife frequently. Run the knife around each piece a second time to clean up rough edges. On the second cookie sheet, with the second ball of dough, repeat the rolling and cutting process to make the remaining pieces.

Remember: You will need two roof pieces, two sides, one front and one back.

Knead all the excess dough into a ball and reserve for cutting any pieces that do not fit on the cookie sheets in this batch.

4. Bake both sheets of gingerbread at the same time, for 12–13 minutes. (It is preferable to overbake by a minute or two than to underbake; the pieces must be quite firm for assembling.) Immediately run a long spatula under each piece—very carefully, to avoid breakage—and let cool for a few minutes on the cookie sheet. Transfer to wire racks to cool completely.

5. Clean off the cookie sheets, rinse in cold water and dry them. Knead the remaining dough together until smooth. If there are any more large pieces (parts of the cottage) to be cut, dust one cookie sheet with flour, roll out leftover dough to ¼ inch thick and cut out the pieces.

3 double recipes (about 12 cups) of *Decorating Icing (page 16)* *Note:* Substitute water for the vanilla extract.
Assorted candies and other decorations: cinnamon redhots; sesame-honey bars; candy-coated chocolates; jelly beans; lozenge-shaped candies; candy canes; chocolate-covered raisins; round peppermints
Green food coloring
Green sugar

QUICK AND EASY
More Decorations for Baked Cookies

❋ Melt semisweet chocolate with a few drops of vegetable oil and enough water to thin it to the consistency of heavy cream. Drizzle on cookies in a lattice pattern.

❋ Spread melted chocolate on cookie, top with slivered almonds, crushed peppermint candy, a few silver dragées or other decoration.

❋ Scatter miniature chocolate chips on hot cookies; the chips will melt just enough to adhere.

COOK'S JOURNAL

How to Toast Nuts

Spread whole or chopped nuts—usually almonds, walnuts, pecans or hazelnuts—on a jelly roll pan or other pan with sides (nuts tend to slide off a cookie sheet) and place in a preheated 350° F. oven for 5–10 minutes. When the nuts smell toasty and a *cooled* nut is crisp and crunchy, the nuts are ready; watch carefully to avoid burning. Let the nuts cool in the pan on a wire rack.

Note: After toasting whole hazelnuts, remove as much of the papery brown skins as possible by rubbing a few nuts at a time between your palms or in a rough napkin or dish towel.

Knead the remaining dough again and roll out to ⅛ inch thick, on a table or counter. Using the cookie cutters specified in the ingredients list, cut out the following: four large trees and eight small trees; 50 small flowers; one large heart with a small heart cut from the center; several small hearts. Use a fluted pastry cutter to cut ten shutters, each about ½ × 1½ inches (make ten so you can choose the prettiest four pairs to use on the cottage). Transfer all the pieces to the second cookie sheet, leaving one inch between pieces. Cut the trunks off the trees and discard.

6. Bake large pieces for 12–13 minutes, then loosen, let cool and remove as described in step 4.

Bake the second cookie sheet (trees and small pieces) for five minutes, then remove the small trees, 25 of the flowers and all the hearts and shutters; transfer to wire racks to cool. Return the cookie sheet to the oven for 1–3 more minutes, until the large trees are done; remove the large trees and transfer to wire racks to cool.

Return the cookie sheet to the oven and let the remaining 25 flowers bake for several minutes more, until they are dark brown; remove and let cool on wire racks.

7. When the front, back, side and roof pieces are cool, use a metal spatula to spread a very thin layer of Decorating Icing on the back of each, to act as reinforcement. Let the icing dry completely.

8. Fit a decorating bag with the #5 tip and fill with Decorating Icing. Decorate the front, side and roof pieces as shown in the drawing (and in photograph 1), attaching each small cookie and candy by piping a bit of icing on the back and pressing in position. (*Note:* Using tweezers makes placement much easier.)

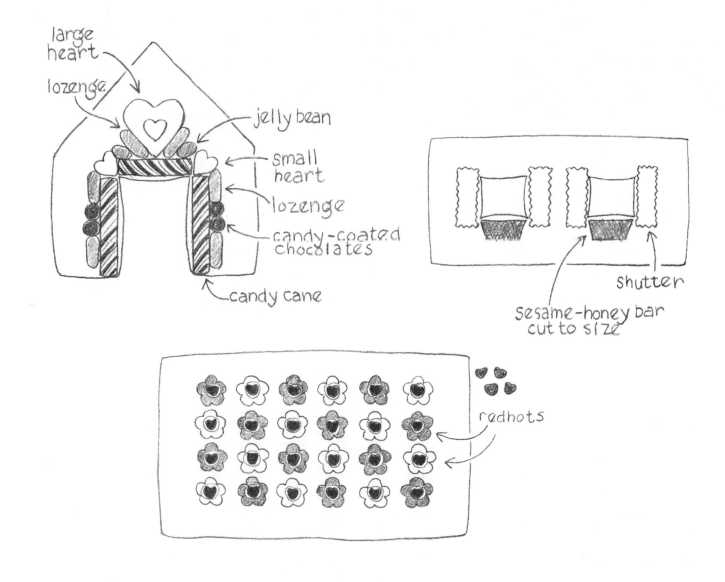

THE CHRISTMAS PANTRY CHECKLIST

Cookie-baking Supplies

If you keep your pantry and refrigerator stocked with these essentials (and some special items), you'll be prepared to bake a batch of Christmas cookies whenever the Christmas spirit moves you.

❅ Sweet butter (regular sticks, not whipped or in tubs)

❅ Sugars: white granulated; superfine; light brown; dark brown; confectioners'

❅ Molasses

❅ All-purpose flour

❅ Baking powder, baking soda

❅ Salt

❅ Large eggs

❅ Extracts: vanilla; almond; peppermint

❅ Chocolate chips (miniature, regular)

❅ Baking chocolate (unsweetened, semisweet); unsweetened cocoa powder

❅ Instant coffee

❅ Spices: cinnamon; ground nutmeg; powdered ginger; ground allspice; ground cloves

❅ Nuts: almonds; walnuts; pecans; hazelnuts

❅ Raisins, currants

❅ Decorations: sprinkles; colored sugars; colored dots

❅ Liquid and paste food coloring

Use the #5 tip to pipe the curlicues and dots on the shutters, above the windows and on the front.

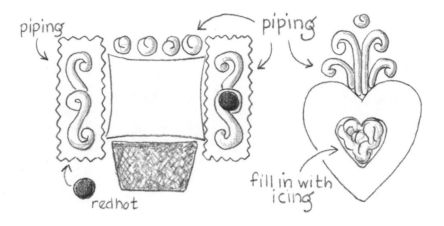

9. Draw a 5¾ × 7-inch rectangle on the cake board as shown.

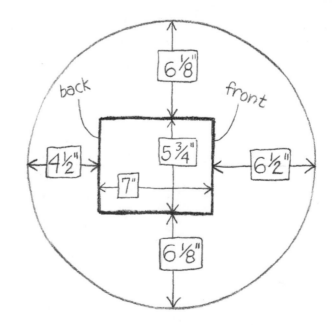

Change to the #7 icing tip and put the house together with piped icing:

❋ Pipe a thick line of icing along bottom edge of back piece; pipe a thick line of icing on bottom and back edges of one side piece. Press together in place on the pencil lines. Hold in place while icing sets and then allow icing to dry for a few minutes. Reinforce *inside* the cottage by piping more icing along joint and along cake board. Let icing set again.

❋ Pipe icing on bottom and back edges of second side piece; press in place; reinforce. Let icing set.

❋ Pipe icing on bottom edge and just inside side edges of front piece; press in place against sides; carefully reinforce. Let icing set.

❋ Pipe icing along slanting edges of front and back and top edges of sides and press roof pieces in place. Hold in place while icing sets and then pipe a line of icing between roof pieces at the peak.

Let icing dry and harden for two hours.

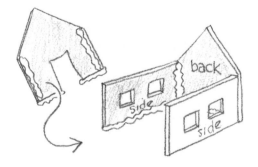

Gift Wraps for Cookies

❋ Center a round cake board on a large square of cellophane (buy cellophane in a party or gift wrap store). Cover board with a pretty paper doily and arrange several layers of cookies on the doily. Bring the cellophane up, twist closed and secure with a twist tie. Overwrap the twist with ribbon and make a bow. (*Note:* The same idea works well with a round tray, round wooden or acrylic cutting board, small pizza pan or pretty china plate.)

❋ Pack cookies in an attractive, sturdy container—shiny gift wrap box, glass bowl, brand-new baking pan, straw or wicker basket or the traditional cookie tin or cookie jar. Line the container with tissue paper or plastic wrap that you can bring up and fasten over the cookies to protect them. Tie with ribbon, cord or yarn; trim with holly leaves, a shiny ornament or a candy cane, as shown in the drawing.

10. Meanwhile, prepare the trees: Mix 1½ cups of green-tinted icing. Spread a thin layer of green icing on each tree. Put the remaining green icing in a decorating bag with a #27 tip and pipe an outline on each tree. Let dry.

With white icing and a #27 tip, pipe white rosettes on one tree at a time, topping the center rosettes with redhots. Set aside to dry.

11. Use white icing and a #30 icing tip to put the finishing touches on the house. (Photograph 1 will be helpful for completing steps 11, 12 and 13.)

❋ Window boxes: On each box pipe three rosettes and top with two candy-coated chocolates; top each candy with another rosette and a redhot.

❋ Side joints (four): Pipe a row of rosettes along each joint.

❋ Roof joints, front and back: Build up each edge with two thick lines of piping. Decorate front edges with green lozenges (use tweezers to put the candies in place). Pipe a generous rosette on the tip of each line of piping.

❋ Roof joint, peak: Have ready 12 or 13 one-inch pieces of candy cane. (*Note:* Candy canes are easy to break if you score them first with a serrated knife.) Now build up the roof peak with three thick lines of piping—two side by side and the third on top. Gently push the pieces of candy cane into the icing. Let dry for a few minutes and then pipe a little rosette on each piece.

12. While the icing on the cottage dries, make the path: Spread a ½-inch-thick layer of icing in front of the doorway; working quickly, press chocolate-covered raisins in the icing. With #30 tip, pipe five little spirals of icing on each side of the path and top each spiral with a round peppermint. Pipe a large rosette on each peppermint and sprinkle with green sugar. When the rosettes are completely dry, blow or brush away excess sugar.

13. Finish the area surrounding the house, working on one side of the house at a time.

❄ Prepare candy cane hoops for the fence: Scoring first with a serrated knife, break off the top section of each cane to make a U-shaped piece about 1¼ inches high; discard the straight pieces. You will need 18 hoops, nine for each side of the house.

❄ With white icing and a small spatula, spread a ½-inch-thick layer of icing from the path all the way around to the back of the house, from the house to the edge of the cake board. Immediately press four small trees and two large trees in position, using toothpicks to prop them up while the icing dries, if necessary. Press nine candy cane hoops in place. Repeat on the other side of the house.

❄ With a #30 icing tip, pipe white rosettes around the perimeter of the cake board.

Let the icing dry for 24 hours.

COOK'S JOURNAL

Cookie Storage

❄ Store cookies in containers with close-fitting lids.

❄ Keep different flavors of cookies in separate containers so the flavors don't mix.

❄ Never store soft cookies and crisp cookies in the same container.

❄ Cookies generally freeze well in plastic containers or zip-lock bags. To defrost, spread them in one layer on a wire rack and let them come to room temperature. If necessary, crisp them in a 325° F. oven for a minute or two; let them cool before eating.

COOK'S JOURNAL

Decorating Your Cookies with Simple Piping: Method #2

For doing somewhat fancier—but still simple—piping, you'll need a ten- or 12-inch decorating bag (disposable plastic ones are convenient), a coupler, a #2 round tip and a #27 star tip. Follow the manufacturer's instructions for assembling the bag, coupler and either tip.

Fold the bag down as shown and fill half-full of *Decorating Icing (recipe on page 16)*. Twist the bag tightly closed above the icing. Hold the bag closed with one hand and with the other hand press out the icing and guide the flow from the tip. Before piping on cookies, practice on waxed paper with either tip; switch tips (the coupler makes this easy) and practice again.

To make dots or rosettes, hold the bag perpendicular to the waxed paper or cookie; to make lines, loops, letters and scallops, hold it at a 30-degree angle to the waxed paper or cookie.

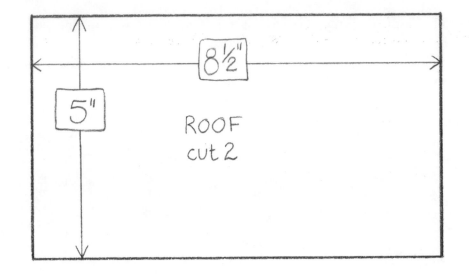

ROOF
cut 2

8½"

5"

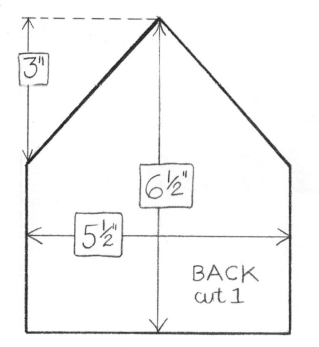

3"

6½"

5½"

BACK
cut 1

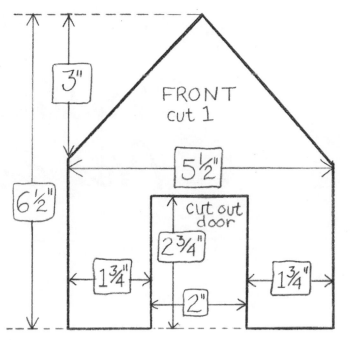

3"

FRONT
cut 1

6½"

5½"

cut out
door

2¾"

1¾"

1¾"

2"

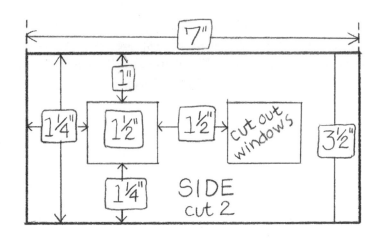

7"

1"

1¼"

1½"

1½"

cut out
windows

3½"

1¼"

SIDE
cut 2

CHAPTER 2

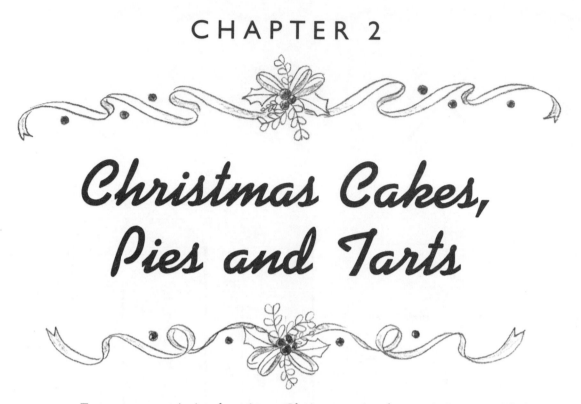

Christmas Cakes, Pies and Tarts

Extravagance is in the air at Christmas, in the excitement and the pace, the lights and gifts and glitter and, of course, the marvelous food. This is the time of year to splurge on just about everything, including dessert. So what will you serve as the grand finale of your holiday dinner or party? Any of these delicious cakes, pies or tarts—from the simplest (traditional Pumpkin Pies with Walnut-Crumb Crusts) to the most elaborate (Christmas-Comes-But-Once-a-Year Chocolate Cake)—will do justice to your Christmas celebration.

Tips and Guidelines

❋ Unless otherwise specified, use sweet (unsalted) butter, all-purpose flour (don't sift unless the recipe specifically requires it), white granulated sugar and large eggs. Cake flour, used in two recipes in this chapter, is not to be confused with self-rising flour.

❋ Be sure that perishables, including nuts and dried fruit, are fresh and wholesome.

❋ Use real ingredients—real vanilla extract, real chocolate, real lemons, real heavy cream. No imitations or substitutions.

❋ Use an electric mixer for creaming, blending, mixing and beating, except where hand-beating or using a food processor is indicated.

❋ For successful baking, use the correct size of baking pans and prepare them as indicated in the recipe. Preheat the oven for at least 15 minutes and always check the temperature with an oven thermometer—oven thermostats are often incorrect. Place cake pans in the center of the oven (unless otherwise specified) with room for heat to circulate around them, and do not open the oven door until the end of the baking period.

❋ Toothpicks or wooden skewers are essential for testing doneness: Insert a toothpick or skewer in the center of the cake (or midway between the inner and outer walls of a tube cake pan) and withdraw it; when the cake is done, the toothpick or skewer will be clean, with no batter or crumbs sticking to it.

❋ Hot cakes, pies and tarts—whether in or out of their pans—must be cooled on wire racks so air can circulate all around them.

❋ If you live in an area where there is concern about the use of raw eggs, you may wish to consider avoiding recipes calling for them.

¾ cup cake flour

¾ teaspoon baking powder

¼ teaspoon salt

5 eggs, room temperature, yolks and whites separated into two large bowls

¾ cup sugar

1 teaspoon vanilla extract

Chestnut Buttercream Filling (recipe follows)

Mocha Silk Frosting (recipe follows)

Angelica and red glacé cherries for decoration

SEE PHOTOGRAPH 4

Bûche de Noël with Chestnut Buttercream Filling and Mocha Silk Frosting

Makes one roll about ten inches long

The Bûche de Noël (or Yule log) is a Christmas classic, a cake rolled with buttercream filling, covered with frosting textured to look like bark—with a characteristic knothole perched on top. You'll find this particular combination of light cake with rich, chestnut-flecked buttercream and mocha frosting incredibly delicious.

Note: Have ready a clean linen or other lint-free dish towel and a wire rack or cookie sheet larger than the jelly roll pan.

Baking pan: one 10½ × 15½ × 1-inch jelly roll pan

1. Preheat the oven to 400° F.; prepare the pan by greasing it, lining the bottom and sides with waxed paper and greasing the waxed paper.

Remember: Have ready a linen dish towel and a wire rack or cookie sheet larger than the prepared jelly roll pan.

Sift together the flour, baking powder and salt; set aside.

2. Beat the egg yolks until thick and pale. Gradually add six tablespoons of the sugar, beating well after each addition; the mixture should fall in a thick ribbon when the beaters are lifted. Add the vanilla and beat again.

3. With clean, dry beaters, beat the egg whites until foamy. Gradually add the remaining sugar, beating constantly, until the whites stand in firm, glossy, moist peaks. Fold a third of the whites into the yolk mixture to lighten it; fold the rest of the egg whites into the lightened yolk mixture.

4. Using a fine strainer, gradually sift the dry ingredients into the egg mixture, folding them in gently but thoroughly. Spread the batter evenly in the prepared pan, making sure to get it into the corners. Put the pan in the oven immediately.

5. Bake for 10–12 minutes, or just until the cake is golden on top and a tester inserted in the center comes out clean. Do not overbake.

Working quickly, cover the pan first with the dish towel and then with the *inverted* wire rack or cookie sheet. Turn over the pan, towel and rack to turn out the cake. Remove the jelly roll pan and then peel off the waxed paper.

Slide the towel and cake onto the counter or table; the cake is wrong side up. Cut off any crisp edges, fold one end of the towel over the short end of the cake and roll up the cake in the towel. Place the rolled cake seam side down on the wire rack to cool completely.

CHRISTMAS MEMORIES FROM FRIENDS

Christmas at Home in Barbados

There is no other time of year when all ten children with their wives and husbands and their 15 children and *their* wives and husbands and *their* eight children all meet in our large airy home in Barbados. So much to do! Drapes to hang, upholstery to be finished, tables to polish. It's hustle, bustle in the kitchen—ham just out of the oven, freshly baked coconut bread, Christmas Black Cake, traditional Jug-Jug. All hands are working, but they never seem to be enough because everything must be done before we go to church.

At 4:45 A.M. the air is so still that one can hear the waves lapping at the shore, footsteps hurrying along the street to St. Peter's. Inside St. Peter's, an air of expectation, excitement almost. Dark and light faces of all ages are filled with awe. At 5 A.M. the same Christmas service is repeated—and has been for many years—and I enjoy it now as much as I did the first time I understood it. It is time to say to one and all— Merry Christmas!

THE CHRISTMAS PANTRY CHECKLIST

Cake-baking Supplies

Cake-baking generally takes some planning, but you'll be ahead of the game if you keep your refrigerator and pantry stocked with the basics.

❉ Sweet butter (regular sticks, not whipped or in tubs)

❉ Sugars: white granulated; superfine; light and dark brown; confectioners'

❉ Light corn syrup

❉ All-purpose flour, cake flour

❉ Baking soda, baking powder

❉ Salt

❉ Large eggs

❉ Milk, heavy cream, buttermilk, evaporated milk

❉ Vanilla extract, almond extract

❉ Baking chocolate (unsweetened and semisweet); unsweetened cocoa powder

❉ Instant coffee

❉ Spices: cinnamon; powdered ginger; ground nutmeg; ground cloves

❉ Nuts: almonds; walnuts; pecans; hazelnuts

❉ Raisins, currants

❉ Lemons

6. Unroll the cooled cake, leaving it on the towel; don't worry about the cake looking deflated—it will perk up soon. Spread ½ cup of Mocha Silk Frosting evenly over the cake, all the way to the edges. Spread two cups of Chestnut Buttercream Filling over the thin layer of mocha frosting, pushing a generous amount into the curved end.

buttercream spread into curved end

Roll up again, without the towel but using the towel to help roll. Place the cake seam side down on a cake plate or tray. Use a small spatula to remove any excess filling from the ends and seam edge. Refrigerate for an hour to firm the filling.

7. Trim and discard (or eat) a thin slice from one end of the chilled cake; cut and reserve a wedge from the other end, as shown in the drawing. Spread a little of the leftover chestnut buttercream on the top center of the cake and press the reserved wedge on it to make the "knothole."

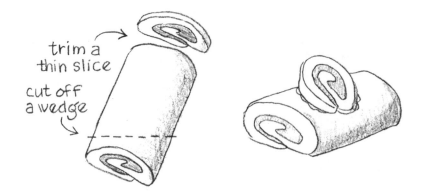

trim a thin slice

cut off a wedge

Now frost the entire cake with the remaining Mocha Silk Frosting, building the frosting up around the sides of the knothole (do *not* cover the top of the knothole) and working the frosting as far under the roll as possible. Repeatedly draw a narrow metal spatula lengthwise through the frosting to simulate the rough texture of bark.

8. Snip pieces of angelica into leaf shapes and cut glacé cherries in half to make the decorations for the log; press into place as shown in photograph 4. Keep the cake refrigerated until serving; it is much easier to slice when cold and firm.

Before serving, surround the cake or the cake plate with holly and a few cranberries.

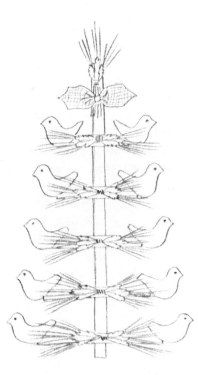

Chestnut Buttercream Filling

Makes 2½–3 cups

1. Combine the superfine sugar, egg yolk, salt, vanilla and 2½ tablespoons of the cream and beat for eight minutes at medium speed.

2. In a large bowl, without washing the beaters, cream ½ cup of the butter until light. Add the yolk mixture a little at a time, beating well after each addition. Gradually add two cups of the confectioners' sugar, beating well after each addition. Set the basic buttercream aside.

3. In a food processor or blender, purée the chestnuts with the remaining two tablespoons of butter, 4½ tablespoons of cream and ⅓ cup of confectioners' sugar.

4. Stir the chestnut purée into the basic buttercream, blending thoroughly. If necessary, thin with a little more cream to bring it to a very spreadable consistency.

½ cup superfine sugar
1 egg yolk
　　Note: To avoid harmful bacteria, be sure to use an egg with no cracks in the shell.
Pinch of salt
1½ teaspoons vanilla extract
7–8 tablespoons heavy cream
½ cup (one stick) plus two tablespoons butter, room temperature
2⅓ cups sifted confectioners' sugar
30 whole cooked chestnuts (from a jar or can)

1¾ cups confectioners' sugar

3 tablespoons unsweetened cocoa
   powder

2 teaspoons powdered instant
   coffee
   Note: To make powdered
   instant coffee, put a few
   teaspoons of instant coffee
   granules in a plastic bag and
   crush with a rolling pin.
   Measure out as needed.

⅓ cup (5⅓ tablespoons) butter,
   room temperature

1½ tablespoons light corn syrup

1 teaspoon vanilla extract

2–4 tablespoons heavy cream

*Walnut-Crumb Crusts (recipe
   follows)*

4 eggs

2 cups (one-pound can) pumpkin
   purée

1 cup (packed) light brown sugar

1 teaspoon cinnamon

½ teaspoon powdered ginger

¼ teaspoon ground cloves

¼ teaspoon salt

2 cups half-and-half or
   evaporated milk

½ cup heavy cream

1 tablespoon confectioners' sugar

Mocha Silk Frosting

Makes about 1½ cups

Sift together and then stir the sugar, cocoa and coffee. Add the butter, corn syrup, vanilla and two tablespoons of cream and beat for a minute at medium speed. Add just enough of the remaining cream to make the frosting easy to spread.

Pumpkin Pies with Walnut-Crumb Crusts

Makes two nine-inch pies

Smooth, dense filling in a buttery, crunchy crust, with sweetened whipped cream on top—this is the simple but perfect pie that pumpkin pie lovers crave.

Baking pans: two nine-inch glass pie pans

1. Preheat the oven to 425° F. Prepare the Walnut-Crumb Crusts in the pie pans as explained in the recipe that follows.

2. In a large bowl, beat the eggs until well blended. Add the pumpkin, brown sugar, spices and salt and beat again. Add the half-and-half or evaporated milk and beat until thoroughly blended. Carefully ladle half the pumpkin filling into each prepared pie pan.

3. Bake for ten minutes at 425° F., then reduce the heat to 325° F. and continue baking for 45–50 minutes longer. Pies are done when a knife inserted halfway between the center and the side comes out almost clean and the pies are still slightly undercooked in the center. Let pies cool completely on wire racks.

4. Put the heavy cream and confectioners' sugar in a deep bowl and whip until stiff; do not overbeat. Fit a large rosette tip on a decorating bag and fill the bag with whipped cream. Pipe rosettes of the lightly sweetened whipped cream around the edge of the pie filling and dust the rosettes with cinnamon.

OPTIONS: If you can't manage the piping, drop neat tablespoons of sweetened whipped cream around the perimeter of the pie filling and dust with cinnamon. Offer additional whipped cream for those who aren't satisfied with just a spoonful.

Walnut-Crumb Crusts

Makes two nine-inch pie shells

Stir together the crumbs, ground nuts and sugar. Add the butter and egg white and blend well. Divide the crumb mixture in half and pat each half evenly over the bottom and sides of one pie pan.

1¾ cups fine graham cracker crumbs (about 16 whole crackers)
Note: Make crumbs in a food processor or put a few crumbled crackers at a time in a plastic bag and roll firmly with a rolling pin.
1¼ cups ground walnuts
½ cup sugar
½ cup (one stick) butter, melted
1 egg white

SEE PHOTOGRAPH 4

Christmas-Comes-But-Once-a-Year Chocolate Cake

Makes one four-layer round cake

¾ cup flour
¼ cup unsweetened cocoa
    powder
¼ teaspoon salt
6 eggs, *room temperature*
1 teaspoon vanilla extract
½ teaspoon almond extract
1 cup superfine sugar
6 tablespoons (¾ stick) butter,
    melted, cooled and clarified
½ cup finely chopped blanched
    almonds, toasted
    Note: See Note on page 18
    for blanching instructions; see
    also *How to Toast Nuts* on
    page 40.
Rum Buttercream Frosting (recipe
    follows)
Almond Chocolate Mousse
    (recipe follows); do not make
    mousse until you complete
    step 5)
4 vanilla wafers, ground to fine
    crumbs in food processor
30 *Chocolate-dipped Almonds*
    (recipe follows)

This is an elegant, sophisticated cake that takes a lot of doing—though none of the doing is difficult. And when you're done, you'll have—trust me—a cake that your friends and family will be talking about for months!

The foundation of the cake is four thin layers of chocolate génoise with chopped almonds. The layers are filled with Rum Buttercream Frosting and Almond Chocolate Mousse, and the whole cake is frosted with more mousse and decorated with Chocolate-dipped Almonds and vanilla wafer crumbs. It's quite an extravaganza, but, after all, Christmas does come only once each year.

Baking pan: two nine-inch cake pans

1. Preheat the oven to 350° F.; prepare each pan by greasing it, lining the bottom with a waxed paper circle, greasing the waxed paper and then dusting bottom and sides with flour.

Sift together the flour, cocoa powder and salt; set aside.

2. Eggs achieve greater volume if they are warm when you beat them, so combine the eggs, vanilla and almond extract in a large deep bowl placed in a shallow bowl of hot tap water. Beat with an electric mixer until light and thick and quadrupled in volume.

Add the sugar one tablespoon at a time, beating continuously. Keep beating until the mixture is thick and airy, like soft whipped cream, and a thick rope of batter falls and sits on top of the mixture for a few seconds when you lift the beaters.

3. Use a fine strainer to sift about a quarter of the dry ingredients over the egg mixture; gently fold it in. Repeat with the remaining dry ingredients.

4. Remove one cup of batter to a separate bowl and whisk it with the clarified butter. Stir in the chopped almonds. Return this mixture to the main bowl of batter, ¼ cup at a time, folding it in gently but thoroughly. Divide the batter equally between the prepared pans.

5. Bake for 25–30 minutes, checking after 25 minutes; when the cake is done, the center will spring back if pressed lightly, and the cake will be pulling away from the sides of the pan.

Let the layers cool in the pans on wire racks for ten minutes and then run a knife around each layer. Turn out, peel off the waxed paper and turn right side up on the racks to finish cooling. When cool, wrap individually in plastic and freeze for an hour, or until firm.

6. Meanwhile, make the Almond Chocolate Mousse according to the recipe that follows. (The Rum Buttercream Frosting, listed with the ingredients, should already be prepared.)

7. Split each cake layer in half horizontally to make a total of four thin layers. Put one layer cut side up on a cake plate and tuck strips of waxed paper under the layer to keep the cake plate neat while you assemble and decorate the cake.

Spread the layer first with about ¾ cup of Rum Buttercream Frosting and then with about ¾ cup of Chocolate Mousse. Repeat with the remaining layers (cut sides down), making a stack that ends with Rum Buttercream Frosting. Use the remaining 1¼ cups of Almond Chocolate Mousse to cover the top and sides of the cake.

8. Sift the vanilla wafer crumbs over the top of the cake and then blow crumbs from your palm onto the sides of the cake. Use a generous amount, since the first layer of crumbs will darken as the crumbs absorb moisture from the cake.

Press Chocolate-dipped Almonds around the top edge to complete the decorations (see photograph 4). Serve immediately or freeze until one hour before serving.

Tip: To freeze, put the cake in the freezer *uncovered* for one hour, or until very firm, then cover with plastic wrap; return it to the freezer until one hour before serving.

START WITH STORE-BOUGHT
Ice Cream

Ice cream with a fancy topping is a nice, easy alternative to homemade dessert. Try one of these combinations for a merry ending to a holiday meal.

Toppings for vanilla ice cream:
❊ Chopped candied chestnuts (marrons glacés), chopped semisweet chocolate
❊ Strawberry syrup, frozen strawberries (defrosted), chopped pistachio nuts
❊ Crushed pineapple, toasted coconut

Toppings for chocolate ice cream:
❊ Orange marmalade mixed with a little orange liqueur, chopped toasted pecans
❊ Raspberry syrup, frozen raspberries (defrosted), crumbled chocolate cookies
❊ Chopped bittersweet chocolate, pitted dark cherries (canned) mixed with a little vodka

Toppings for coffee ice cream:
❊ Almond liqueur, crumbled macaroons, chopped toasted almonds
❊ *Caramel Sauce (page 62)* or butterscotch sauce, miniature chocolate chips
❊ Whipped cream, chocolate sauce, chopped toasted walnuts

½ cup light rum
¾ cup sugar
1½ teaspoons light corn syrup
6 egg yolks
  Note: Be sure to use eggs
  with uncracked shells, to
  avoid harmful bacteria.
1 teaspoon vanilla extract
1½ cups (three sticks) butter,
  room temperature

Rum Buttercream Frosting

Makes about three cups

1. Heat the rum, sugar and corn syrup in a saucepan over low heat, stirring gently until the sugar dissolves. Wash down the sides of the pan with a pastry brush dipped in ice water.

Clip a candy thermometer to the side of the saucepan, raise the heat to medium and boil without stirring until the syrup registers 240° F. (soft ball stage). Remove the syrup from the heat and let it cool slightly while you complete step 2.

2. In a large bowl, beat the egg yolks and vanilla until the mixture is pale and thick and falls in a ribbon when you lift the beaters.

3. Add the hot syrup to the yolks by pouring it down the side of the bowl a little at a time, beating it in after each addition. (Pouring down the side of the bowl keeps the syrup from falling directly on the beaters and forming spun-sugar threads.) Let the yolk mixture cool.

4. Add the butter one tablespoon at a time, beating well after each addition. The frosting should be thick and perfectly smooth.

Use this buttercream as soon as possible, or refrigerate it for up to three days if necessary. When you take it out of the refrigerator, let it come to room temperature and then beat until smooth and spreadable again.

Almond Chocolate Mousse

Makes about 3½ cups

1. Scald ½ cup of the heavy cream with the sugar, stirring to dissolve the sugar. Pour the hot sweetened cream over the chopped chocolate in a large bowl and stir until the chocolate is melted and the mixture is smooth. Set aside to cool completely.

2. When the chocolate mixture is cool, whip the remaining 1¼ cups of heavy cream with the almond extract just until stiff; do not overbeat. Fold the whipped cream into the chocolate mixture. Use as soon as possible.

1¾ cups heavy cream
7 teaspoons sugar
8 squares (eight ounces)
    semisweet chocolate, chopped
¾ teaspoon almond extract

Chocolate-dipped Almonds

Makes 35 almonds

Put the chocolate and vegetable oil in a small heatproof bowl in a larger bowl or saucepan holding an inch of very hot water; stir the chocolate until melted and smooth. Remove the bowl of melted chocolate and set it on a cup or glass, tilting it so the chocolate makes a little pool.

Using tweezers, hold each almond on one long side and dip the opposite side into the chocolate so the almond is half dark, half light. Place on waxed paper on a cookie sheet and let the chocolate harden for several hours. Carefully lift the almonds from the waxed paper and refrigerate until needed.

Note: Choose the 30 prettiest almonds for decorating the cake.

1 square (one ounce) semisweet
    chocolate, chopped
¼ teaspoon vegetable oil
35 blanched, toasted whole
    almonds
    Note: See *Note* on page 18
    for blanching instructions; see
    also *How to Toast Nuts* on
    page 40.

SEE PHOTOGRAPH 4

Apple Tart with Candied Cranberries and Caramel Sauce

For the apple filling:
9 medium McIntosh apples
2 tablespoons fresh lemon juice
¼ cup sugar

For the candied cranberries:
1 cup sugar
⅛ teaspoon salt
⅛ teaspoon baking soda
⅓ cup water
2 cups fresh or frozen whole
    cranberries

For the tart shell:
3 cups flour
¼ teaspoon salt
¾ cup sugar
1 cup (two sticks) cold butter, cut
    in chunks
1 egg plus one egg yolk, beaten
    together
1–2 tablespoons heavy cream

Caramel Sauce (recipe follows)
Whipped cream (optional)

Makes one large tart

The crust of this tart is moist, rich and a bit cakelike, the fruit is soft and retains all of its good apple flavor—a rather substantial dessert, in the German tradition. Easy to make, yet more than a bit special when served with Caramel Sauce.

Tip: If you're in a hurry, omit the candied cranberries, which are there for decoration as much as for taste, and fill in with extra apple slices (step 5).

Baking pan: one 10½ × 15½ × 1-inch jelly roll pan

1. Peel and quarter the apples; carefully cut away the cores and seeds. Cut each quarter in three lengthwise slices. Put the slices in a large bowl, add the lemon juice and sugar and toss gently. Set aside.

2. Make the candied cranberries: In a small saucepan, stir the sugar, salt, baking soda and water over very low heat, stirring constantly and washing down the sides of the saucepan with a brush dipped in cold water, until sugar is dissolved. Do not let the mixture boil.

When the sugar is completely dissolved, bring to a boil without stirring; immediately reduce the heat to very low again and stir in the cranberries. Continue cooking over very low heat for five minutes (do not boil). Turn off the heat and lift out the cranberries with a slotted spoon. Boil the syrup for four minutes to reduce it, then let it cool for two minutes. Return the cranberries to the syrup and stir gently.

Carefully lift the cranberries out of the syrup with the slotted spoon and spread on waxed paper. Separate the cranberries so they dry individually. Set aside.

3. Make the tart dough: In a food processor or large bowl, mix the flour, salt and sugar. Add the chunks of butter and cut them in until the mixture looks like fine crumbs. Add the beaten eggs, process or mix

briefly and then process or stir in just enough heavy cream to hold the ball of dough together; the dough will be soft but not sticky.

4. Preheat the oven to 425° F.

Make the tart shell: Turn the dough into the jelly roll pan, break into pieces and pat it out evenly over the bottom and sides of the pan. (Do not bake yet.)

5. Arrange the apples on the unbaked tart shell in short rows, overlapping the slices. (A toothpick is helpful for moving the apple slices.) Tuck slices on the sides, too, as shown. There will be some space between the rows; these will be filled in with cranberries.

Brush any leftover lemon juice mixture on the apples.

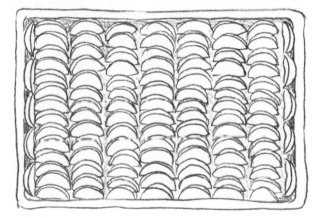

6. Bake the tart for 40–45 minutes, until the tart shell is golden brown and the apples are soft. Put the pan on a wire rack and decorate the hot tart by arranging rows of candied cranberries between the rows of apple slices and/or around the edge of the tart.

Let the tart cool completely, then cut it in squares and arrange the squares on a serving platter. Serve with Caramel Sauce—and for a truly decadent delight, top each sauce-drizzled square of tart with a spoonful of whipped cream.

OPTIONS: If you don't have time to make the Caramel Sauce, serve the tart with sweetened whipped cream, vanilla ice cream or a simple purée of frozen raspberries or strawberries.

COOK'S JOURNAL
Rolled Cakes

The cake used for creating the *Bûche de Noël (page 50)* is also an excellent cake to fill and frost (or glaze) anytime, any way you like. Simply make the cake through step 5, unroll it and spread with the filling of your choice. Roll up again, chill for a short while and then frost or glaze the cake. Add a little decoration if you like.

Fillings: jam or marmalade; thick applesauce; sweetened whipped cream (alone or sprinkled with chopped nuts or chocolate chips); pastry cream; any favorite buttercream; *Double Cream Topping (page 75)*; *Almond Chocolate Mousse (page 59)*; *Old-fashioned Lemon Curd (page 230)*.

Frostings and glazes: Choose a favorite buttercream, glaze or sauce that complements the filling—for instance, chocolate buttercream or *Bittersweet Chocolate Glaze (page 83)* with whipped cream filling, *Orange Glaze (page 118)* or *Caramel Sauce (page 62)* with applesauce filling, *Rum Buttercream Frosting (page 58)* with chocolate filling.

Decorations: confectioners' sugar; chopped nuts; grated or shaved chocolate; toasted coconut; colored sugar; glacé fruit; fresh fruit.

1½ cups sugar
1 teaspoon light corn syrup
¾ cup water
¼ cup (½ stick) butter
1 tablespoon lemon juice
½ cup heavy cream
½ teaspoon vanilla extract
1 tablespoon brandy
1 tablespoon water

CHRISTMAS MEMORIES FROM FRIENDS

The Crèche

Every Christmas the kids in our family—Mary Margaret, Mary Elizabeth, Mary Katherine, Charlie and Greg—would be allowed to set up the crèche, a little house with lots of small Hummel figures to go with it.

First we arranged the house on a table, with straw in and around it. Next came the cows and camels and a donkey, the three Wise Men, Mary, Joseph and a little tiny Baby Jesus. Of course we always bickered over who would get to put Baby Jesus in his cradle. We had a Christmas tree light that we tucked up into the house to make it all glow—as if the star of Bethlehem were shining through the windows. The crèche changed constantly because each time someone would go by, he or she would move things around according to the way he or she thought it ought to be. I wonder who has that crèche now?

Caramel Sauce

Makes 1½ cups

1. In a large saucepan, over low heat, stir together the sugar, light corn syrup, the ¾ cup water and the butter. Continue stirring, washing down the sides of the pan with a brush dipped in cold water, until the sugar is completely dissolved. Do not boil while dissolving the sugar.

2. Clip a candy thermometer to the side of the pan, raise the heat to medium and boil until the thermometer reads 300° F.; watch carefully after the temperature reaches 280° F. Do not stir while boiling, but wash down the sides several times.

3. Turn off the heat and slowly add the lemon juice and heavy cream. (*Important:* Stand back when adding liquid to hot sugar syrup because it may splatter and burn you if you are not careful.) Add the vanilla, brandy and the tablespoon of water and stir gently until thoroughly blended.

You may serve the sauce immediately, while it is still warm, or you may store it in the refrigerator until needed and then reheat it over low heat (do not boil) just before serving.

SEE PHOTOGRAPH 4

Buttermilk-Spice Cupcakes with Brown Butter Frosting

Makes 24 medium cupcakes

Frost and decorate half of these tender, spicy cupcakes to eat right now—and still have a dozen left to stash in the freezer for unexpected guests or to take when you go visiting.

Frost cupcakes one at a time, decorating each one immediately after frosting. The drawings on page 65 will give you some decorating ideas to copy or to use as inspiration for inventing your own Christmas cupcake decorations.

Do not frost the cupcakes you plan to freeze. Simply wrap each unfrosted cupcake in plastic, place all the wrapped cupcakes in one layer on a cookie sheet and freeze. When frozen, place all cupcakes in a plastic bag, seal the bag and return it to the freezer.

Baking pans: two 12-cup medium muffin pans

1. Preheat the oven to 350° F.; line the muffin pans with paper baking cups.

Note: Paper muffin cups produce a higher, neater cupcake than greased and floured muffin pans do.

Stir or whisk together the flour, baking powder, baking soda, spices and salt; set aside.

2. Cream the butter until light. Gradually add the brown sugar, beating well after each addition. Add the beaten eggs a little at a time, beating well after each addition.

3. Add the dry ingredients and buttermilk alternately, in three parts each, beating well after each addition. Stir in the currants if you are using them. Put a scant ¼ cup of batter in each muffin cup.

2 cups flour
¾ teaspoon baking powder
¾ teaspoon baking soda
¾ teaspoon cinnamon
¼ teaspoon ground cloves
½ teaspoon ground nutmeg
¼ teaspoon salt
¾ cup (1½ sticks) butter, room temperature
1½ cups (packed) dark brown sugar
1 egg beaten with two egg yolks
¾ cup buttermilk
¾ cup currants (optional)
Brown Butter Frosting (recipe follows)
Decorations (see drawings, page 65)

4. Bake on two oven racks for 25 minutes, or until a tester inserted in the center of a cupcake comes out clean. Let the cupcakes cool in the pans on wire racks for five minutes and then turn out to finish cooling right side up on the racks.

Frost one cupcake at a time with Brown Butter Frosting (about ⅔ tablespoon frosting per cupcake) and decorate before the frosting sets. Repeat to make only as many cupcakes as needed; wrap unfrosted cupcakes individually in plastic and seal in a plastic bag in the freezer (see instructions at the beginning of the recipe).

Brown Butter Frosting

¼ cup (½ stick) butter
2 cups sifted confectioners' sugar
7 teaspoons heavy cream
2 teaspoons vanilla extract
1 tablespoon hot water
Pinch of salt

**Makes one generous cup, more than enough to frost
24 cupcakes**

Melt the butter in a small saucepan over low heat and cook until lightly browned. Transfer to a large bowl, add the remaining ingredients and stir to blend. Beat until the frosting is smooth; at this point it will be too thin to spread on the cupcakes. Cover the frosting with plastic wrap and set aside for a few minutes; as it cools completely, it will thicken to a proper spreading consistency.

The surface of the finished frosting hardens quickly, so either use the frosting right away or lay a piece of plastic wrap directly on the surface to prevent a crust from forming.

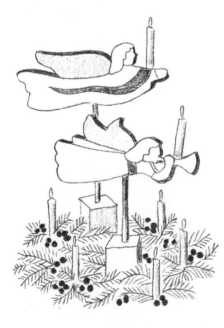

licorice string bow, green sugar

Slivers of glacé cherries with tiny candle

crushed peppermint candy

whole almonds and cinnamon redhots

marzipan snowman with candy cap and coconut snow

swirled frosting flower with frosting leaves

Christmas tree cookie

sugar cube "gift" with icing "ribbons"

red and green icing lattice

mixed candied peel and cinnamon redhots

sliced strawberries topped with glacé cherry

sliced gumdrop flower

Rich Holiday Pound Cake

Makes one tube cake or two loaves

2½ cups flour
1 teaspoon baking powder
¼ teaspoon salt
1 cup (two sticks) butter, room
    temperature
½ pound (one 8-ounce package)
    cream cheese, softened
2½ cups sugar
5 eggs, separated
2 teaspoons vanilla extract

Crisp on the outside, tender on the inside—an absolutely delicious pound cake. It's so good that I usually want it pristine and unadorned, but I must confess it is equally delicious with sauces and ice cream and other goodies. See OPTIONS at the end of the recipe for serving suggestions and QUICK TAKES (page 66) for more pound cake desserts.

Baking pan: one 10½-inch tube pan, three inches deep, _OR_ two 8½ × 4½ × 2½-inch loaf pans

1. Preheat the oven to 350° F.; grease and flour the baking pan or pans.

Stir or whisk together the flour, baking powder and salt; set aside.

2. Cream the butter and the cream cheese until light and smooth. Gradually add two cups of the sugar, blending well after each addition.

3. Add the egg yolks and vanilla and beat well.

4. Add the dry ingredients a little at a time, blending well after each addition.

5. With clean, dry beaters, beat the egg whites until frothy; add the remaining ½ cup of sugar and continue beating until the egg whites hold firm, glossy, moist peaks. Fold a third of the egg whites into the batter to lighten it; fold the rest of the egg whites into the lightened batter. (The lightened batter is still quite thick, so folding in the rest of the egg whites takes some energy.) Pour the batter into the prepared tube pan or divide it equally between the two prepared loaf pans.

6. Bake either tube or loaves for 55–60 minutes, or until a cake tester inserted in the center of the cake comes out clean. The top of the cake will be golden and the cake will be pulling away from the sides of the pan. Let the cake cool in the pan on a wire rack for five minutes and then turn out to finish cooling right side up on the rack. Serve warm or cold.

QUICK TAKES
Pound Cake Desserts

Plain pound cake—homemade or store-bought—is amazingly versatile and can easily be transformed into impressive desserts. Cut pound cake in slices and garnish each slice as described.

❋ Top with a small scoop of fruit sherbet and a few defrosted frozen raspberries or strawberries.

❋ Brush with rum, add a small scoop of rum-raisin ice cream and drizzle with _Bittersweet Chocolate Glaze_ _(page 83)._

❋ Serve with _Caramel Sauce (page 62),_ whipped cream and chopped toasted pecans.

❋ If slightly stale, toast each slice and top with jam, fruit sauce or _Old-fashioned Lemon Curd (page 230)._

OPTIONS: If you'd like to make your plain (uncut) pound cake a little fancier, try one of these suggestions:

❄ Drizzle generously with Orange Glaze (page 118); before the glaze sets, garnish with fine slivers of orange and lemon peel, chopped toasted almonds or rum-soaked raisins.

❄ For a holiday look, drizzle generously with Vanilla Glaze (page 118); before the glaze dries, sprinkle the cake with red or green sugar and decorate with flowers and leaves made of red and green glacé cherries.

❄ Make a two-tone glaze: Drizzle generously with Vanilla Glaze and let the glaze dry; drizzle a little less generously with Bittersweet Chocolate Glaze (page 83), making sure that white glaze shows between the chocolate drizzles.

QUICK AND EASY
Decorations for Cakes, Pies and Tarts

Cakes, pies and tarts should be festively decorated when presented as holiday desserts. Choose a decoration appropriate to the flavor and appearance:

❄ Whole, chopped or slivered nuts
❄ Grated or chopped semisweet, bittersweet or white chocolate
❄ Slivers of orange or lemon zest
❄ Candied ginger or glacé fruits cut in attractive pieces
❄ Piped vanilla whipped cream dusted with cinnamon or nutmeg
❄ Piped chocolate whipped cream topped with chocolate coffee beans or chocolate chips
❄ Toasted coconut
❄ *Colorful Marzipan Fruits (page 100)*
❄ Angelica "leaves" and red glacé cherries
❄ Frosted grapes (dipped first in egg white and then in sugar)

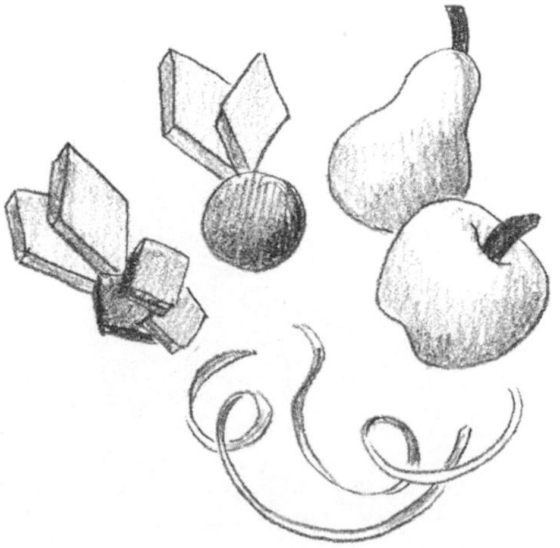

SEE PHOTOGRAPH 4

Christmas Trifle

Makes one trifle, about 10–12 servings

3 ten-ounce packages frozen
    raspberries
Simple Sponge Cake (recipe
    follows)
Cream sherry
1 jar (12 ounces) seedless
    raspberry jam
    Note: If you can find only
    raspberry jam *with* seeds,
    strain it and discard the
    seeds.
Vanilla Custard (recipe follows)
¾ cup heavy cream
2 tablespoons sugar
⅓ cup slivered almonds, toasted
    Note: See *How to Toast Nuts*
    on page 40.

Trifle is a marvelously festive English dessert, a combination of cake, sherry, jam, fruit and vanilla custard—with whipped cream and nuts on top. If you've never had trifle made from scratch, you're in for a treat.

The most attractive presentation for trifle is to layer it in a straight-sided, two-quart glass bowl, but it will taste just as sinfully rich and delectable no matter what you put it in. Eat the trifle as soon as possible, since it becomes soggy (though still tasty) after a few hours.

Note: For photograph 4, we made *two* recipes of Christmas Trifle, layering it in a larger bowl. You might like to do the same when you're giving a large party.

1. Defrost the raspberries and put them in a large strainer set over a bowl. Let them drain for 30 minutes. Set aside 30 of the best-looking raspberries (from the top of the strainer) for decorating the trifle.

2. If the sponge cake is uneven on top, trim it flat. Split the cake in half horizontally to make two thin layers and brush the cut sides with sherry to moisten (not soak) them. Spread the cut sides with most of the raspberry jam; you may not need all the jam. Cut each layer in 25 squares.

3. Line the bottom of a two-quart glass bowl or other pretty bowl with one third of the cake squares, jam sides up. Arrange half of the remaining drained raspberries over the cake. Spread half of the Vanilla Custard over the raspberries. Repeat the process, making another layer of cake squares, raspberries and Vanilla Custard; you will have one third of the cake left over.

Top the custard with the remaining cake squares, jam sides *down*. Refrigerate until needed, but keep in mind that the longer the trifle stands, the more the layers merge and lose their distinct flavors and textures.

4. Just before serving, whip the cream with the sugar and spread about a third of it over the trifle. With the remaining whipped cream, pipe large rosettes or drop large spoonfuls around the edge of the trifle bowl. Decorate with the reserved raspberries and sprinkle with slivered almonds, as shown in photograph 4.

Simple Sponge Cake

Makes one square cake

Baking pan: One 8 × 8 × 1½-inch cake pan

3 eggs, room temperature
¾ cup sugar
Pinch of salt
1 teaspoon vanilla extract
¾ cup cake flour mixed with
    ½ teaspoon baking powder

1. Preheat the oven to 350° F.; grease the baking pan, line bottom and sides with waxed paper and grease the waxed paper.
2. Beat the eggs until frothy. Add the sugar, salt and vanilla and continue beating until thick and pale and tripled in volume.
3. Using a fine strainer, sift the dry ingredients over the egg mixture a little at a time, folding them in. Pour the batter into the prepared pan.
4. Bake for 30 minutes, or until the top is golden and springs back when pressed lightly. Let the cake cool in the pan on a wire rack for five minutes and then turn out on the rack. Peel off the waxed paper and turn right side up to finish cooling on the rack.

Vanilla Custard

Makes about two cups

½ cup sugar
Pinch of salt
3 tablespoons cornstarch
2 cups milk
3 egg yolks
2 teaspoons vanilla extract

1. In a saucepan, stir together the sugar, salt and cornstarch. Gradually add the milk, whisking until the mixture is smooth. Stir in the egg yolks.
2. Bring the mixture to a boil over medium heat and boil for one minute, stirring constantly. Remove from the heat and stir in the vanilla.
3. Strain into a bowl, cover the surface directly with plastic wrap and let the custard cool in the refrigerator.

SEE PHOTOGRAPH 4

Prune-Apricot Custard Tart with Sweet Lemon Crust

For the tart shell:
1⅔ cups flour
¼ teaspoon salt
1 tablespoon grated lemon rind
⅓ cup sugar
½ cup (one stick) plus one
    tablespoon cold butter, cut in
    small chunks
2 egg yolks beaten with
    1½ tablespoons fresh lemon
    juice

For the filling:
8 pitted whole prunes, cut in half
    lengthwise (16 halves), each
    half flattened to a neat oval
1¼ cups brandy
28 dried apricot halves
    Note: Buy packaged apricots,
    which have a tart-sweet
    flavor; the fancier apricots,
    sold loose by the pound, tend
    to be too sweet for this tart.
½ cup plus two tablespoons half-
    and-half
1 egg
2 tablespoons sugar
¼ teaspoon vanilla extract
Pinch of salt
Nutmeg (optional)

*Double Cream Topping
    (page 75; optional)*

Makes one ten-inch tart

Here's a true winter tart, made with dried fruit that is first softened gently in brandy and then baked in light custard in a tender, lemony shell.

Baking pan: one ten-inch tart pan with removable bottom

1. Make the tart dough by hand or in a food processor fitted with the metal chopping blade.

By hand: Stir the flour, salt, grated lemon rind and sugar together in a bowl. Add the chunks of butter and cut them in with a pastry blender until the mixture looks like coarse meal or finely ground nuts. Add the egg yolk mixture and stir briskly with a fork until the dough holds together in a ball.

In a food processor: Put the flour, salt, grated lemon rind and sugar in the bowl and process for a few seconds to blend. Add the chunks of butter and process just until the mixture looks like coarse meal or finely ground nuts. Pour the egg yolk mixture evenly over the ingredients in the bowl and process just until they form a ball that rides on top of the blade.

Pat the dough into a flat round, about six inches in diameter, and refrigerate for one hour.

2. Meanwhile, put the prunes in a small saucepan with ½ cup of the brandy, and the apricots in another saucepan with the remaining ¾ cup of brandy. Simmer uncovered for five minutes, then turn off the heat and cover each pan. Let the fruit steep for 15 minutes, stirring occasionally, to absorb the remaining brandy. Drain and place on paper towels to dry.

3. Make the custard mixture: Whisk or beat together the half-and-half, egg, sugar, vanilla and salt; set aside in the refrigerator.

4. Preheat the oven to 425° F.

When the tart dough is chilled, make the tart shell by either rolling or patting it out as described below. Reserve excess dough for patching the partially baked shell.

To roll: On a lightly floured surface, roll out the dough to a 13-inch circle, about ¼ inch thick; lift it carefully and center it over the tart pan; press it into the pan, making it slightly thicker at the corners and sides. Pinch off the excess dough just below the edge of the pan. Prick the dough all over with a fork.

To pat: Break the dough in pieces and use your fingertips or the heel of your hand to press dough into the tart pan, using just enough to make a layer ¼ inch thick on the bottom of the pan and slightly thicker at the corners and sides. Pinch off the excess dough just below the edge of the pan. Prick the dough all over with a fork.

Refrigerate the unbaked shell for ten minutes.

5. Bake the shell for five minutes at 425° F., then reduce the temperature to 400° F. and bake for 10–15 more minutes. The shell should be almost completely baked—dry-looking and lightly browned on the bottom, medium brown on the sides.

If the shell is cracked, patch it immediately (while very hot) by smearing bits of the reserved raw dough into the cracks; there must be no unfilled cracks (especially at the angle of the sides and bottom) or else the custard filling will leak out. Let the tart shell cool on a wire rack.

Reduce the oven temperature to 375° F.

COOK'S JOURNAL
Cake Storage

❊ Unfrosted cake layers, pound cakes and fruitcakes will keep well at room temperature for several days if snugly wrapped in plastic and then aluminum foil. If you are not planning to eat the cake for a while, or there is leftover cake you're tired of looking at, wrap snugly and freeze.

❊ After serving, cakes frosted with buttercream should be refrigerated in a cake preserver or on a plate covered with an inverted bowl. For longer storage, chill the cake uncovered in the freezer until it is firm, then wrap well and return to the freezer.

❊ Cakes with whipped cream or pastry cream filling and frosting must be kept refrigerated for safety's sake. For longer storage, cakes with whipped cream filling and frosting (but not pastry cream filling and frosting) may be chilled uncovered in the freezer until firm, then wrapped and returned to the freezer. Defrost unwrapped in the refrigerator overnight.

ENTERTAINING NOTEBOOK

Dessert Party

Take out your prettiest lace tablecloth, cake stands, tulip glasses and coffee cups and invite guests for an after-dinner party, to indulge in a luxurious array of large and small sweets.

Depending on how many guests are expected, your dessert menu might include one magnificent chocolate cake, one rich pound cake, a fruit tart or pie, a selection of small pastries (petit fours, lemon or custard tarts, etc.), a generous variety of Christmas cookies and at least one fruitcake. In addition, provide some fresh fruit—for instance, a bowl of strawberries, cubed pineapple and sliced kiwi, flavored with a light fruit liqueur. A little ribbon-tied basket of lovely chocolates and marzipan fruits completes the picture.

Champagne is an ideal accompaniment, and of course you'll offer tea and coffee.

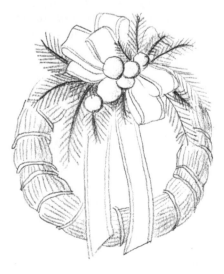

6. Arrange 15 of the prune halves and all the apricot halves in the tart shell as shown in the drawing. (There may be one or two extra prunes and/or apricots.) Pour the custard mixture slowly and evenly into the tart shell, taking care not to disarrange the fruit. Sprinkle with a little nutmeg, if desired.

7. Place the tart on a cookie sheet on the lowest shelf of the oven and bake for 22–24 minutes, or until the custard is set. Let the tart cool in the pan on a wire rack.

Lift out the tart on the removable bottom and use a long spatula to loosen it from the bottom. Carefully slide it onto a perfectly flat platter. Refrigerate until serving.

Serve with Double Cream Topping, if desired.

Old-fashioned Burnt-Sugar Gingerbread with Double Cream Topping

Makes one sheet cake (24 squares)

A tender, spicy, melt-in-your-mouth gingerbread cake made with caramel syrup, served with a sweet topping that tastes like crème fraîche but is much easier to make. Makes a great snack on a winter afternoon, accompanied by hot apple cider.

Note: There are two ways to make caramel syrup—either by cooking sugar and water until the water evaporates and the sugar caramelizes, or by cooking dry sugar until it melts and then adding water. This cake uses the dry sugar method. Be sure you don't actually burn the sugar; "burnt sugar" is just the traditional name for the dry-cooked sugar used in caramel syrup.

Baking pan: one 9 × 13 × 2-inch sheet cake pan

1. Preheat the oven to 375° F.; grease and flour the sheet cake pan.

Make the caramel syrup: Put the ½ cup of sugar in a six- or seven-inch skillet over low heat. Cook, stirring constantly, until the sugar melts and turns first golden and then dark amber; this will happen just as the sugar begins to boil. (If the sugar starts to smoke, immediately lift the skillet off the burner for a few seconds.) Remove the skillet from the heat and let the sugar cool for one minute.

Now you will add water to hot sugar syrup, which can cause the very hot liquid to spatter and burn you, so stand well back from the pan and use a long-handled spoon for stirring: Very carefully add the boiling water *one tablespoon at a time*, stirring gently. The mixture will get sticky and lumpy.

Return the skillet to low heat and cook the syrup for several minutes, stirring constantly, until most of the lumps dissolve and the syrup becomes less sticky. Turn off the heat and continue stirring until

For the caramel syrup:
½ cup sugar
½ cup boiling water

For the batter:
2 cups flour
2½ teaspoons baking powder
½ teaspoon baking soda
2 teaspoons cinnamon
2½ teaspoons powdered ginger
1 teaspoon ground cloves
½ teaspoon salt
½ cup sugar
½ cup (packed) dark brown sugar
½ cup (one stick) butter, room temperature
2 eggs beaten with one teaspoon vanilla extract
¾ cup milk

Double Cream Topping (recipe follows)

DECORATING MEMO

A Cook's Tree

Steal a corner of the dining room, kitchen or front entry and install a second Christmas tree—a special, smaller tree decorated in honor of the cook of the house:

A "sweet" tree might be trimmed with sugar cookie ornaments, cookie cutters, tiny tartlet pans, bundles of cinnamon sticks tied with red ribbon, tissue-wrapped Italian macaroons, gold foil–wrapped candies, little baskets of orange kumquats; tie a pretty lace shawl around the tree base.

A "savory" tree can be decorated with dried chili peppers, nuts (in their shells) tied with red string, brightly colored plastic kitchen gadgets, small wooden spoons, garlands made of pasta strung on yarn; use red bandannas to conceal the base of the tree.

the syrup is completely liquid. Pour the caramel syrup into a measuring cup and set aside to cool. You should have ½–⅔ cup of syrup.

2. Stir or whisk together the flour, baking powder, baking soda, spices and salt; set aside.

In another bowl, stir together the white and brown sugar; set aside.

3. In a large bowl, cream the butter until light. Gradually add the sugar, beating well after each addition.

4. Add the eggs a little at a time, beating well after each addition. After the eggs have been incorporated, continue beating at medium speed for three more minutes.

5. Add the caramel syrup a little at a time, beating continuously.

6. Add the dry ingredients and the milk alternately, in three parts each, blending well after each addition. Pour the batter into the prepared pan.

7. Place the pan on a cookie sheet on the middle shelf of the oven and bake for 24–26 minutes, or until a tester inserted in the center of the cake comes out clean.

The cake may be cooled in the pan on a wire rack for ten minutes and then carefully turned out to finish cooling, or it may be left to cool completely in the pan on a wire rack and then served straight from the pan. In either case, garnish each square with dollops of Double Cream Topping.

OPTIONS: Squares of gingerbread can be topped with applesauce or apple butter, plain or vanilla-flavored sweetened whipped cream, vanilla ice cream or custard sauce (try Warm Custard Sauce, page 201); garnish with currants or dark raisins or chopped toasted walnuts or pecans. If you prefer, frost the whole cake with any good vanilla buttercream and sprinkle with raisins or chopped nuts.

Double Cream Topping

Makes about three cups

This makes enough topping to put very generous dollops (¼ cup each) on 12 squares of cake or smaller dollops (two tablespoons each) on 24 squares. The recipe may be doubled.

In a deep bowl, whip the heavy cream with the sugar and vanilla, until stiff. Fold the whipped cream into the sour cream.

1 cup heavy cream
¼ cup confectioners' sugar
½ teaspoon vanilla extract
1 cup sour cream, stirred until
  smooth

Christmas Touches

Greenery tucked among the plates and cups on the shelves of your sideboard or hutch . . . small red and white candles set with florist's clay in tiny tartlet tins—one candle per tin . . . chocolate-dipped strawberries . . . bunches of dried flowers, tied with ribbon bows, hanging upside down in the kitchen . . . a split of champagne waiting for guests in the guest room.

CHAPTER 3

Uncommonly Delicious Fruitcakes

Over the years I've made a discovery about Christmas fruitcake: I like the cake as much as the fruit (and sometimes more than the fruit). So the recipes in this chapter reflect my new approach: fruitcakes with more cake. And I've also found that fruitcakes are much better when you pick and choose specific fruits and nuts to enhance specific cakes, instead of tossing in every fruit and nut in the cupboard. When you match the fruits, nuts and cakes, each fruitcake will have a delicious character all its own; each one will be a happy marriage of ingredients.

There's another way these fruitcakes diverge from the traditional: They are not made months ahead and left to ripen into family jokes. Except for Almond-layered Fruitcakes and Tipsy Dark Fruitcakes, which ripen for only a week, these cakes are meant to be baked and enjoyed immediately or frozen for future meals and gifts.

Tips and Guidelines

❄ Unless otherwise specified, use sweet (unsalted) butter, unsifted all-purpose flour, white granulated sugar and large eggs. Don't use imitations of or substitutions for real vanilla extract, chocolate, lemon juice, heavy cream, etc.

❄ In fruitcakes, the quality of the dried fruit and nuts is extremely important. It is best to buy nuts in bulk, from a popular gourmet or health food store where they have rapid turnover and fresh merchandise. Taste before buying—if the nuts taste stale or rancid, don't buy. Dried fruit and candied fruit can be bought in bulk, too, but it is not essential, since the quality of packaged fruit is generally good; just be sure the fruit is soft and succulent, not hard and dry.

❄ When toasted nuts are required, spread nuts on a jelly roll pan (more convenient than a cookie sheet because the nuts can't slide off) and place in a preheated 350° F. oven for 5–10 minutes; watch carefully to be sure they don't burn. When the nuts smell toasty and a *cooled* nut is crisp and crunchy, the nuts are ready. A note on hazelnuts: After toasting, remove the papery brown skins by rubbing a few nuts at a time between your palms or in a rough dish towel.

❄ Candied fruit and peel used in the cakes should be chopped down to ¼-inch dice. This will help prevent the fruit and peel from sinking to the bottom of the cake during baking.

❄ Use an electric mixer for creaming, blending and beating to make the basic cake batter. When adding fruits and nuts, however, I find it is easier to mix by hand.

❄ Because most of these fruitcakes are more cakelike than traditional ones, it is important to use the pan indicated in the recipe; don't substitute another size. Prepare the pans as instructed and preheat the oven for at least 15 minutes, using an oven thermometer to check the temperature. Place filled cake pans in the center of the oven (unless otherwise specified) with room for the heat to circulate freely around them. Do not open the oven until the end of the baking period.

❋ Use toothpicks or wooden skewers to test for doneness: Insert the pick in the center of the cake (or midway between the inner and outer walls of a tube cake pan) and withdraw it; if the cake is done, the toothpick or skewer will be free of batter and crumbs, although there may be some sticky fruit clinging to it.

❋ Hot cakes—in or out of the pans—must be cooled on wire racks to allow air to circulate freely around them.

❋ It is not essential to decorate your fruitcakes, but it does give them a special Christmas look. To create an allover design, paint the top of a cake with light corn syrup and press decorative elements onto the corn syrup—toasted coconut, chopped and whole nuts, fruit left over from the baking, etc. For a more specific design, arrange the elements on the top of a cake, then lift each one, brush light corn syrup on the back and replace in position on the cake.

Illustrations of decorations follow each recipe, where applicable, and can also be found on page 89 and in photographs 3 and 11.

❋ If you prefer, follow exactly the same decorating procedure using a thick or thin confectioners' sugar glaze (see Glazes for Coffeecakes, page 118) instead of corn syrup, but work quickly because the glaze dries quickly.

❋ All the cakes in this chapter can be frozen for long-term storage, so consider making your gift cakes early in the season. Defrost and decorate them just before gift-wrapping.

❋ If you live in an area where there is concern about the use of raw eggs, you may want to consider passing up any recipes calling for them.

mixed peel
toasted coconut

pecans   glacé oranges,
angelica

SEE PHOTOGRAPH 3

Almond-layered Fruitcakes

Makes two loaves

Ribbons of rich almond paste run through every slice of these moist, golden loaves. A very special holiday treat.

Baking pan: two 8½ × 4½ × 2½-inch loaf pans

1. Preheat the oven to 300° F.; grease and flour the loaf pans.

Combine the peel, raisins and ¼ cup of the flour in a large bowl and toss well to coat; set aside.

In another bowl, stir or whisk together the remaining flour, the baking soda, spices, salt and orange rind; set aside.

2. In a third bowl, cream the butter and sugar until light. Add the eggs one at a time, beating well after each addition.

3. Add the dry ingredients and yogurt alternately, in three parts each, blending well after each addition. Stir in the fruit, peel and raisins.

Measure the batter; there will be about nine cups.

4. Divide the almond paste into four equal parts. Dust your work surface and rolling pin with confectioners' sugar and roll out each part to an 8 × 4-inch rectangle.

Put one sixth of the batter (about 1½ cups) in each loaf pan and smooth it out. Cover the batter in each pan with a rectangle of almond paste. Add another sixth of the batter (about 1½ cups) to each pan, smooth it and top with another rectangle of almond paste. Spread about 1½ cups of the remaining batter over the almond paste in each pan. (Any excess batter may be baked in a small loaf pan, on the same oven rack as the two almond-layered cakes.)

5. Bake for 2½–3 hours, or until a tester inserted in the center of each cake comes out free of batter (although it may have some sticky almond paste clinging to it), the tops of the cakes are firm and the cakes are pulling away from the sides of the pans. Let the cakes cool completely in the pans before turning them out.

1½ cups mixed candied peel, chopped down to ¼-inch pieces
1½ cups dark raisins
1½ cups light raisins
3¾ cups flour
1 teaspoon baking soda
½ teaspoon cinnamon
½ teaspoon ground nutmeg
½ teaspoon ground allspice
½ teaspoon salt
1 teaspoon grated orange rind
1 cup (two sticks) butter, room temperature
2 cups sugar
4 eggs
1¾ cups plain (unflavored) yogurt
2 eight-ounce cans or two seven-ounce tubes almond paste
Confectioners' sugar

Four Delicious Hard Sauces

Hard sauce, the traditional accompaniment for warm fruitcake (and plum pudding, too), is served cold or at room temperature and melts on the warm cake to form a soft sauce. The best hard sauce is made with good, strong flavoring, in order to counteract the cornstarchy taste of confectioners' sugar.

Here are the basic instructions for making hard sauce: Cream ½ cup (one stick) sweet butter until light; gradually beat in 1½ cups confectioners' sugar to make a firm paste. Beat in the flavorings listed for any of the sauces below. Each recipe makes about 1¼ cups.

Pack the finished hard sauce into a jar or crock and store in the refrigerator; before serving, remove from the refrigerator to soften slightly.

Vanilla Hard Sauce: three teaspoons vanilla extract; four teaspoons water

Lemon Hard Sauce: one teaspoon grated lemon rind; two tablespoons fresh lemon juice

Spiced Hard Sauce: two tablespoons brandy; ¾ teaspoon cinnamon; ¼ teaspoon powdered ginger; pinch of ground cloves

Coffee Hard Sauce: one tablespoon brandy; one tablespoon instant coffee dissolved in two tablespoons hot water; ½ teaspoon vanilla extract

6. Wrap each cake in a double layer of cheesecloth that has been dampened in brandy or cognac. Overwrap each cake first with plastic and then with aluminum foil. Let the cakes ripen in the refrigerator for one week, occasionally dampening the cheesecloth with more spirits.

OPTIONS: You may, of course, use three cups of either light or dark raisins instead of a combination of both.

After the cakes have ripened—and before serving them or giving them as gifts—decorate with whole blanched almonds (see *Note* on page 18 for blanching instructions) and mixed candied peel, following the suggestions on page 89 and referring to the drawings below and to photograph 3.

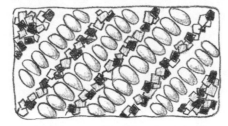
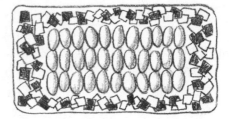

Carrot-Pineapple Fruitcakes

Makes two loaves

A flavorful fruitcake, moist and rough-textured. You can't exactly taste the pineapple, but you'll know it's there. Top the cake with Vanilla Glaze or Brown Butter Frosting and decorate with candied pineapple and glacé cherries (see OPTIONS at the end of the recipe).

Baking pans: two 9½ × 5½ × 2¾-inch loaf pans

1. Preheat the oven to 350° F.; grease and flour the loaf pans.
Stir or whisk together the flour, baking powder, baking soda, spices and salt. Add the walnuts and stir; set aside.

2. In a large bowl, cream the margarine and white sugar. Add the brown sugar gradually, beating until the mixture is light.

3. Add the egg mixture a little at a time, beating well after each addition. Gradually add the dry ingredients, mixing at low speed or by hand.

4. Stir the carrots into the batter, ½ cup at a time. Add the crushed pineapple and blend thoroughly. Fill the prepared pans with equal amounts of batter.

5. Bake for 55–60 minutes, or until a cake tester inserted in the center comes out with a few moist crumbs clinging to it. Let the cakes cool in the pans on wire racks for five minutes and then turn out to finish cooling on the racks.

OPTIONS: Spread each loaf with Vanilla Glaze (page 118) or Brown Butter Frosting (page 64) and decorate with candied pineapple and red and green glacé cherries as shown in the drawings.

3 cups flour
3 teaspoons baking powder
1 teaspoon baking soda
2 teaspoons cinnamon
½ teaspoon ground nutmeg
½ teaspoon ground cloves
½ teaspoon salt
2 cups chopped walnuts
1 cup (two sticks) margarine, slightly softened
¾ cup sugar
¾ cup (packed) dark brown sugar
4 eggs beaten with one teaspoon vanilla extract
2 cups peeled and grated raw carrots
1½ cups well-drained crushed pineapple (one 20-ounce can) *Note:* Put the crushed pineapple in a strainer and press out the excess liquid.

COOK'S JOURNAL
Plump Fruit

Raisins and other dried fruit tend to dehydrate and harden when stored for long periods. Bring them back to their former plumpness by simmering them for a few minutes in water, brandy, wine or fruit juice. Don't overcook or they will become mushy.

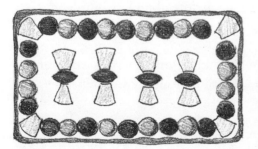

SEE PHOTOGRAPH 3

Chocolate-Cherry Fruitcake with Bittersweet Chocolate Glaze

2¼ cups flour
1½ teaspoons baking powder
½ teaspoon salt
1 cup chopped red glacé cherries
½ cup (one stick) butter, room temperature
1½ cups sugar
4 eggs
1 teaspoon vanilla extract
4 squares (four ounces) semisweet chocolate, melted and cooled
¾ cup milk
¾ cup miniature semisweet chocolate chips
Bittersweet Chocolate Glaze (recipe follows)
Red and green glacé cherries for decoration

Makes one tube cake

Chocolate Cherry Fruitcake is a bit more like pound cake than ordinary fruitcake, though it has plenty of cherries (and chocolate chips) in the batter. Glazed and decorated with red and green cherries, it's an impressive dessert for a party.

Note: You must use *miniature* chocolate chips for this recipe; do not substitute regular-size chips.

Baking pan: one ten-inch fluted tube pan, 3¾ inches deep (Bundt pan)

1. Preheat the oven to 350° F.; grease and flour the tube pan.

Stir or whisk together the flour, baking powder and salt. Add the chopped red cherries and mix well with your hands, separating the bits of cherry. Set aside.

2. In a large bowl, cream the butter and sugar. Add the eggs, one at a time, beating well after each addition. Add the vanilla and blend well.

3. Stir in the melted chocolate.

4. Add the dry ingredients and the milk alternately, in three parts each, blending well after each addition. Stir in the chocolate chips. Pour the batter into the prepared tube pan.

5. Bake for 60–70 minutes, or until a tester inserted in the cake comes out free of batter (the tester may have some sticky cherry clinging to it). Let the cake cool in the pan on a wire rack for ten minutes and then turn out to finish cooling rounded side up on the rack.

Spoon or pour Bittersweet Chocolate Glaze on the cake and decorate with whole red and green glacé cherries before the glaze hardens. (See photograph 3 for guidance.)

OPTIONS: If you prefer, omit the glaze and cherries and simply serve the cake with vanilla or coffee ice cream or lightly sweetened vanilla or chocolate whipped cream.

Bittersweet Chocolate Glaze

Makes about $1\frac{1}{3}$ cups

2 ounces (two squares) unsweetened chocolate, chopped
$\frac{1}{4}$ cup ($\frac{1}{2}$ stick) butter
6 tablespoons heavy cream
$1\frac{1}{2}$ cups sifted confectioners' sugar

1. Melt the chocolate and butter in the top of a double boiler over an inch or two of hot water (brought to a boil and turned off) or in a bowl over a saucepan with an inch or two of hot water. Stir until melted and smooth.

2. Add the cream and confectioners' sugar and whisk until smooth. The glaze will thicken as it cools, so leave it over the hot water until you are ready to use it.

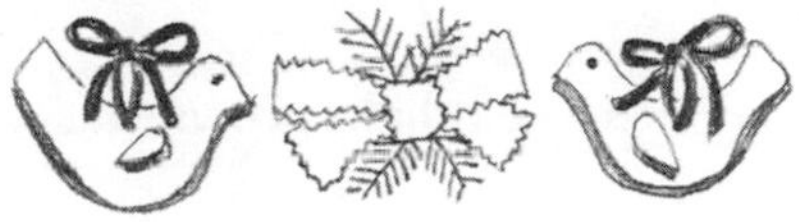

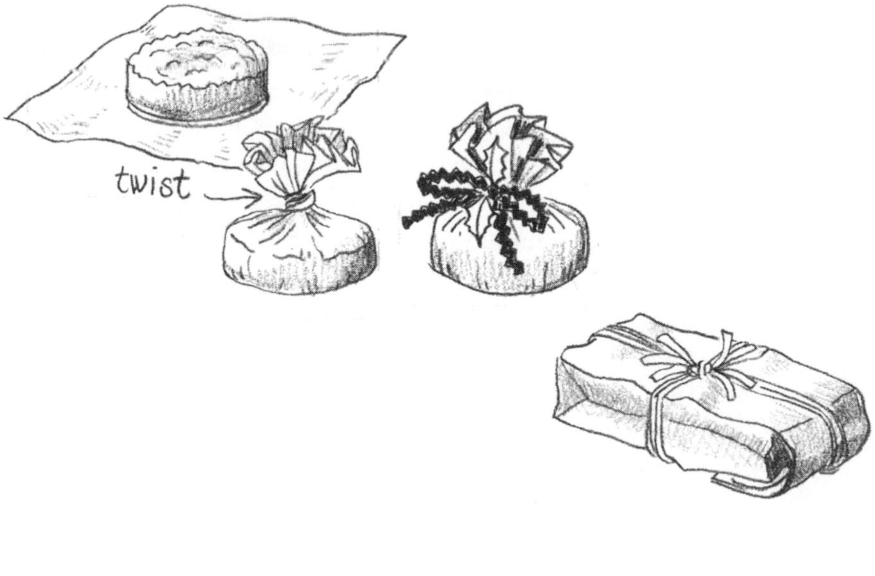

Gift Wraps for Fruitcakes

Note: Before gift-wrapping, wrap fruitcake snugly in two or three layers of plastic.

❄ Make a bed of packing straw or tissue paper in a pretty basket with a handle; tuck the fruitcake in the basket and tie a big ribbon bow on the handle.

❄ Place a round fruitcake on a cake board on a big square of red or green cellophane; bring up the cellophane, twist and secure with a twist tie. Overwrap the twist tie with several long strands of rickrack, tuck in a bit of holly and make a bow.

❄ Wrap fruitcake in brown wrapping paper; tie with calico craft ribbon.

❄ Slip a loaf of fruitcake into a gold or silver bottle bag, turn the end under and tape it neatly out of sight. Tie with silver or gold cord, shiny red ribbon or green gingham ribbon.

60 whole pitted prunes, chilled
2 cups brandy
4 cups flour
4 teaspoons baking powder
2 teaspoons cinnamon
½ teaspoon salt
2 cups chopped pecans
1 cup (two sticks) butter, room
    temperature
2 cups (packed) light brown sugar
6 eggs
2 teaspoons vanilla extract
½ cup seedless raspberry jam
    Note: If you can find only
    raspberry jam *with* seeds,
    strain it and discard the
    seeds.
Milk
Confectioners' sugar

ENTERTAINING NOTEBOOK
Candles

Few things transform a room as easily and magically as glowing candles. They make everyone look wonderful and they lend warmth, intimacy and festivity to any occasion. And there are so many varieties of candles and candle holders that you can always find the right style for your decor. One warning: Don't use scented candles, which interfere with the taste of food and the pungent smell of the Christmas tree—and give headaches to many allergy-prone people.

Brandied Prune Fruitcakes

Makes two rings

Smooth, even-textured cake studded generously with pecans and brandied fruit. Though it's not the kind of fruitcake that needs a lot of time to ripen, Brandied Prune Fruitcake does taste even better on the second day.

Baking pans: two nine-inch fluted tube pans, 3¾ inches deep (kugelhopf pans)

1. Preheat the oven to 325° F.; grease and flour the tube pans.
    Cut each prune in four or five pieces. (This is a sticky business, but if you keep the prunes chilled they will be firmer and easier to cut.) Put the chunks of prune in a saucepan with the brandy and simmer partially covered for ten minutes. Let stand while you make the batter.
    Stir or whisk together the flour, baking powder, cinnamon and salt. Stir in the pecans and set aside.

2. In a large bowl, cream the butter and sugar. Add the eggs one at a time, beating well after each addition. Add the vanilla and jam and beat again.

3. Drain the prunes, reserving the brandy. Add enough milk to the brandy to make ¾ cup liquid.

4. Add the dry ingredients and the brandy mixture alternately to the egg mixture, in three parts each, blending well after each addition. Stir in the prunes. Divide the batter equally between the prepared tube pans.

5. Bake for 75–85 minutes, or until a tester inserted in the center of the cake comes out clean. Let the cakes cool in the pans on wire racks for five minutes and then turn them out to finish cooling (rounded sides up) on the racks.
    Sift confectioners' sugar generously over the cooled cakes.
    Tip: Do not cut the cake until it is completely cool and use a plain sharp knife, not a serrated cake knife.

Orange-Hazelnut Cake

Makes one 10½-inch tube cake

This mellow and fragrant cake gets its elegant flavor from oranges in three forms—grated rind, marmalade and liqueur—and lightly toasted hazelnuts. It's a perfect light treat to serve holiday visitors who drop in for late dessert and small cups of espresso.

Baking pan: one 10½-inch tube pan, three inches deep

1. Preheat the oven to 350° F.; grease and flour the tube pan.
   Stir or whisk together the flour, baking powder, baking soda and salt; set aside.

2. In a large bowl, cream the butter. Add the sugar gradually, beating well after each addition. Add the beaten eggs gradually, beating well after each addition. Add the marmalade and orange rind and blend well.

3. Add the dry ingredients and the Grand Marnier alternately, in three parts each, blending well after each addition. Stir in the chopped nuts. Pour the batter into the prepared tube pan.

4. Bake for one hour, or until a tester inserted in the cake comes out clean. Let the cake cool in the pan on a wire rack for ten minutes. Run a knife around the cake to loosen it from the pan and then turn out to finish cooling rounded side up on the rack.

No decorations are necessary on this cake, but if you like, drizzle with Orange or Lemon Glaze (page 118) and sprinkle with slivers of orange zest before the glaze dries.

3 cups flour
3 teaspoons baking powder
½ teaspoon baking soda
½ teaspoon salt
¾ cup (1½ sticks) butter, room temperature
1½ cups sugar
3 eggs beaten with one teaspoon vanilla extract
6 tablespoons orange marmalade
1 teaspoon grated orange rind
¾ cup Grand Marnier
2 cups hazelnuts, toasted, skinned and chopped coarsely
Note: For toasting instructions, see *Tips and Guidelines*, page 77.

CHRISTMAS MEMORIES FROM FRIENDS

A Doctor's Christmas

When I was little, we lived in a small mill town. My dad was the family doctor for many hardworking, but poor, first- and second-generation Americans. They loved and trusted him but they couldn't always pay him—with money. Instead, during the holiday season, we would often open our back door to find huge trays of beautifully prepared food—baked pasta and stuffed cabbage, still-warm holiday breads and nut rolls and best of all, to us children, an amazing variety of sweet and spicy Christmas cookies—tiny pecan pies, anise-flavored pizelles, giant Santas, sticky baklava, delicate vanilla crescents, cream-filled pastry horns.

Lightly Spiced Dark Fruitcakes

2 cups dried figs, stems removed,
  chopped in ¼-inch pieces
1 cup currants
1 cup dark raisins
1½ cups chopped toasted walnuts
  Note: For toasting
  instructions, see *Tips and
  Guidelines*, page 77.
3½ cups flour
2 teaspoons baking powder
1 teaspoon baking soda
1½ teaspoons cinnamon
½ teaspoon ground nutmeg
½ teaspoon ground allspice
½ teaspoon salt
1 cup (two sticks) butter, room
  temperature
1½ cups (packed) dark brown
  sugar
3 eggs
2 tablespoons grated orange rind
1 cup tawny port wine

Makes two loaves

If you're a fan of dark, spicy fruitcakes (like Tipsy Dark Fruitcakes, page 88), you'll love this light-textured, lightly spiced dark fruitcake, too.

Baking pans: two 9½ × 5½ × 2¾-inch loaf pans

1. Preheat the oven to 325° F.; grease and flour the loaf pans.
  In a large bowl, mix the figs, currants, raisins and chopped nuts. Add ½ cup of the flour and mix well with your hands, making especially sure to separate the pieces of fig.
  In another bowl, stir or whisk together the remaining flour, the baking powder, baking soda, spices and salt; set aside.
2. In a third large bowl, cream the butter and sugar. Add the eggs, one at a time, beating well after each addition; continue beating at high speed for another minute or two until the mixture is light and fluffy. Add the grated orange rind and blend well.
3. Add the dry ingredients and the wine alternately, in three parts each, blending well after each addition. Fold the fruit and nuts into the batter. Divide the batter evenly between the two prepared pans.

4. Bake for one hour, or until a tester inserted in the center comes out free of batter (the tester may have some sticky fruit clinging to it). Let the cakes cool in the pans on wire racks for 15 minutes. Run a knife around each cake to loosen it from the pan and then turn out to finish cooling right side up on the racks.

Tip: Do not cut the cake until it is completely cool, and use a plain sharp knife, not a serrated cake knife.

OPTIONS: Decorate the loaves with walnuts, angelica and red glacé cherries, following accompanying drawings and the suggestions on page 89.

THE CHRISTMAS PANTRY CHECKLIST
Nuts and Dried Fruit

At holiday time, keep a supply of unsalted nuts and dried fruits on hand for baking and candy-making and just plain nibbling. Nuts in their shells are fun, too—guests love to sit in front of a fire, cracking open and eating the nuts while they chat.

To maintain freshness, store nuts in the refrigerator or freezer, dried fruits in plastic containers or heavy plastic bags in the pantry.

❊ Almonds
❊ Brazil nuts
❊ Cashews
❊ Chestnuts
❊ Hazelnuts (also called filberts)
❊ Peanuts
❊ Pecans
❊ Pine nuts
❊ Pistachios
❊ Walnuts

❊ Apples
❊ Apricots
❊ Currants
❊ Dates
❊ Figs
❊ Glacé fruits: apricots; red and green cherries; oranges; peaches; pears; pineapple
❊ Peaches
❊ Pears
❊ Pineapple
❊ Prunes
❊ Raisins, light and dark
❊ Miscellaneous: crystallized and candied ginger; angelica; mixed candied peel

SEE PHOTOGRAPH 3

Tipsy Dark Fruitcakes

Makes three loaves

This is a fine example of the traditional dark fruitcake, with the added advantages of being moister, tastier, richer and generally more delicious.

Remember: Begin by making the fruit mixture (step 1) the day before you want to bake the cakes.

Baking pans: three 8½ × 4½ × 2½-inch loaf pans

For the fruit mixture:
¾ cup brandy
1 cup currant jelly
3 cups light raisins
3 cups dark raisins
1½ cups currants
1 cup chopped dates
   Note: Cut dates in ¼-inch
   pieces.
1 cup mixed candied peel,
   chopped down to ¼-inch dice
2 cups coarsely chopped walnuts

For the batter:
1 teaspoon baking soda
½ cup unsulfured molasses
2½ cups flour
½ teaspoon ground allspice
½ teaspoon ground mace
½ teaspoon salt
¾ cup (1½ sticks) butter, room
   temperature
1 cup (packed) dark brown sugar
5 eggs

1. Make the fruit mixture one day before you want to bake the fruitcakes: In a large bowl, stir together the brandy and currant jelly. Add all the fruits and nuts and stir well. Set aside in the refrigerator overnight.

2. Preheat the oven to 300° F.; butter each loaf pan, then line the bottom with kitchen parchment and butter that, too.

Stir the baking soda into the molasses; set aside. Stir or whisk together the flour, spices and salt; set aside.

3. In a large bowl, cream the butter and sugar until light. Add the eggs one at a time, beating well after each addition. Add the molasses and beat again.

4. Gradually add the flour mixture, stirring well after each addition. Add the fruit and nut mixture a little at a time, blending well after each addition. Divide the batter equally among the three prepared pans.

5. Place a shallow pan of water on the bottom shelf of the oven; place the three loaf pans on the middle shelf. Bake for 1½–2 hours, or until a tester inserted in the center of each cake comes out free of batter (although it may have sticky fruit clinging to it), the tops of the cakes are firm and the cakes are pulling away from the sides of the pans.

Let the cakes cool for ten minutes in the pans on wire racks, then turn out, peel off the parchment and finish cooling right side up on wire racks.

6. Wrap each cake in a double layer of cheesecloth that has been dampened in brandy. Overwrap first with plastic and then with aluminum foil. Let the cakes ripen in the refrigerator for a week, occasionally dampening the cheesecloth with more brandy.

OPTIONS: After the fruitcakes have ripened—and before serving them or giving them as gifts—decorate with walnut halves, mixed candied peel and light raisins, following the suggestions on page 89 and the drawings. Photograph 3 shows a decoration made up of apricots, red glacé cherries and angelica.

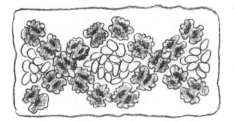 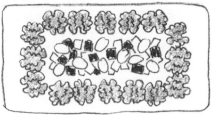

COOK'S JOURNAL
Decorations for Fruitcakes

Decorations can be as simple as a scattering of chopped nuts or as fancy as a design of flowers. Geometric arrangements of nuts and glacé or dried fruits are effective, too. Add decorations just before serving or gift-wrapping the cake; use light corn syrup or confectioners' sugar glaze for attaching decorations to the cakes, as explained in *Tips and Guidelines* (page 78).

❋ On dark fruitcakes, create a dramatic look with brightly colored glacé fruits, light-colored fruits (light raisins, dried apples and pears, crystallized ginger, mixed diced candied peel), light nuts (blanched almonds and Brazil nuts, chopped pistachios, pine nuts) and/or shredded coconut.

❋ On light fruitcakes, use bright or dark fruits (glacé cherries and apricots, dates, dark raisins, dried peaches, prunes), dark nuts (walnuts, pecans, unblanched almonds) and/or toasted coconut.

SEE PHOTOGRAPH 3

Sherry Fruitcakes with Fluffy Apricot Sauce

1 cup light raisins
1 cup diced dried apricots
    Note: Dice apricots in ¼-inch bits.
1¼ cups cream sherry
2½ cups flour
1 teaspoon baking powder
½ teaspoon baking soda
¼ teaspoon salt
1 cup chopped almonds, toasted
    Note: For toasting instructions, see *Tips and Guidelines*, page 77.
½ cup (one stick) butter, room temperature
1½ cups (packed) light brown sugar
2 eggs
1 cup sour cream
Fluffy Apricot Sauce (recipe follows)

Makes two small round cakes

A sweet cake with plenty of sunny raisins, apricots and almonds and a light taste of sherry. Serve alone or with butter for an afternoon snack; pair it with the tart-sweet apricot and whipped cream sauce if you're having it for dessert.

Tip: Wrapped in bright cellophane, these small cakes make charming holiday gifts.

Baking pans: two six-inch round cake pans

1. Preheat the oven to 325° F.; grease and flour the pans.

Put the raisins, apricots and sherry in a saucepan and bring to a boil. Turn down the heat and simmer uncovered for five minutes. Cover and let stand for 30 minutes. Drain the fruit (reserving the leftover sherry) and pat dry on paper towels. If necessary, add enough additional sherry to the reserved sherry to make ¼ cup; set aside.

Stir or whisk together the flour, baking powder, baking soda, salt and chopped almonds; set aside.

2. In a large bowl, cream the butter. Add the brown sugar gradually, beating well after each addition. Beat in the eggs one at a time.

3. Blend in the sour cream and the reserved ¼ cup of sherry.

4. Add the dry ingredients by hand, in four parts. Stir in the raisins and apricots. Divide the batter equally between the two prepared pans.

5. Place the pans on a cookie sheet in the oven. Bake for 75–85 minutes, or until a tester inserted in the center of each cake comes out clean. Let the cakes cool in the pans on a wire rack for ten minutes and then turn out to finish cooling right side up on the rack.

Cut the cake in wedges and serve with Fluffy Apricot Sauce (recipe follows).

OPTIONS: An alternative topping can be made by folding Old-fashioned Lemon Curd (page 230) with whipped cream.

Decorate the cakes with whole almonds and glacé cherries, following the general suggestions on page 78 and the drawings below or photograph 3.

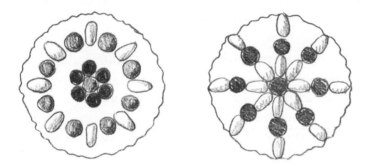

Christmas Touches

Delicious stocking stuffers—a packet of Christmas cookies, marzipan fruits, butter crunch, a miniature fruitcake ... a straw "kitchen" wreath, trimmed with cookie cutters or wooden spoons or tiny tartlet tins ... a collection of glass and china animals with ribbon bow collars, marching across the mantel on Christmas greens ... groups of poinsettias—on the stair landing, flanking the Christmas tree, in the front hall ... Christmas cards framing a doorway.

Fluffy Apricot Sauce
Makes about two cups

In a large bowl, stir together the egg yolks and puréed jam. Beat at high speed for four minutes, or until light and fluffy. In a separate bowl, whip the cream. Fold the cream into the apricot mixture.

2 egg yolks
  Note: To avoid harmful bacteria, check the shells of raw eggs before use; discard any eggs with cracked shells.
6 tablespoons apricot jam, puréed in blender or food processor
½ cup heavy cream

SEE PHOTOGRAPHS 3 AND 11

Buttermilk-Pecan Fruitcakes

4½ cups flour
2 teaspoons baking powder
1 teaspoon baking soda
1 teaspoon salt
3 cups chopped dried pears
  Note: Before chopping, be sure to remove all seeds and hard bits of core in the dried fruit. Cut the pears in ¼-inch dice.
2 cups coarsely chopped toasted pecans
  Note: For toasting instructions, see *Tips and Guidelines*, page 77.
1 cup (two sticks) butter, room temperature
3 cups sugar
4 eggs, separated
2 teaspoons vanilla extract
2 cups buttermilk

Makes two regular and three gift-size loaves

Toasted pecans and tangy dried pears in a buttermilk batter are a sensational combination, my personal favorite of the fruitcake recipes. Serve one cake fresh from the oven and freeze the others (individually wrapped in two layers of plastic plus a plastic freezer bag) for holiday desserts or gift-giving.

Tip: If you prefer (and you have enough pans), omit the regular-size loaves and make eight gift-size loaves, filling each pan two-thirds full of batter and baking on two oven racks, for about 55 minutes.

Baking pans: Two 8½ × 4½ × 2½-inch loaf pans plus three 5¾ × 3¼ × 2-inch loaf pans

1. Preheat the oven to 400° F.; grease and flour the pans.
   Stir together the flour, baking powder, baking soda and salt. Add the dried pears and pecans and stir again. Set aside.

2. In a large bowl, cream the butter and sugar. Add the egg yolks, one at a time, beating well after each addition. Add the vanilla and blend well.

3. Add the dry ingredients and the buttermilk alternately, in four parts each, blending well after each addition.

4. With clean, dry beaters, beat the egg whites until they stand in firm, glossy, moist peaks. Fold a third of the egg whites into the batter to lighten it; fold the remaining egg whites into the lightened batter. Fill each prepared pan two-thirds full of batter.

5. Turn the oven down to 350° F. and put all the pans in the oven, on two racks positioned to divide the oven in thirds. Bake the small loaves for 50 minutes and the larger loaves for 65 minutes, or until a

tester inserted in the center of each cake comes out clean. Ten minutes before the baking is complete, rotate the pans back to front so the cakes on each rack brown evenly. Let the loaves cool in the pans on wire racks for five minutes and then turn out to finish cooling on the racks.

OPTIONS: Decorate the loaves with pecan halves, following the general suggestions on page 78 and the specific designs in the drawings and in photographs 3 and 11.

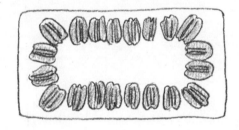

DECORATING MEMO
Decorations Using Candles

Candles make the most impact in groups of three or more. If you don't have enough candle holders, borrow from friends—the more the merrier. Or use bits of florist's clay (or adhesive clay) to hold candles in little dishes, saucers, cups or any other pretty containers. (Don't worry about melted wax; put the candle holder in the freezer for an hour and then lift the wax right off.) Here are some simple ways to use candles in your Christmas decorations (more ideas on page 173):

❋ Arrange fat red and/or white candles of different heights on the sideboard or mantel and surround with greens.

❋ Place white votive candles in clear or red cups around your crèche.

❋ Tie a red-and-green-plaid taffeta ribbon bow at the base of each taper in a candelabrum.

❋ Put candles in a shallow wooden bowl (anchor with florist's or adhesive clay) and fill bowl with cranberries or tiny pinecones.

CHAPTER 4

Easy Christmas Candies

When I was a child, I was completely enthralled by one particular feature of my grandfather's enormous Christmas parties: There were bowls of wonderful candies everywhere—chocolates on the coffee table, peppermints on the piano, candy-coated almonds in the foyer. This was forbidden fruit, no question about it, but I had a six-year-old's confidence that in such a crowd of grown-up guests nobody would notice a small girl in a lace-collared velveteen dress making her way from bowl to bowl, popping sweets into her mouth.

Candy and Christmas do seem to go together—perhaps because the cold, dry weather helps produce perfect candy results, perhaps just because holidays call for special treats and homemade goodies. If you dream of Christmas sugarplums and a Christmas stocking stuffed with butter crunch and fudge, you'll love the easy recipes in this chapter. (So easy, in fact, that you don't even need a candy thermometer for most of the recipes.) Make them for yourself and your Christmas party guests and for truly special gifts—see the gift wrap ideas on page 109 and in photograph 7.

Tips and Guidelines

✼ These candy recipes do not require you to learn any special skills—no tempering of chocolate, no fondant-making, no fancy dipping. The candies here are quite simple to make if you follow the recipes carefully.

✼ Unless otherwise specified, use sweet (unsalted) butter and white granulated sugar. Use high-quality vanilla extract (no imitations), fresh nuts, plump raisins, soft dried fruit.

✼ These recipes were tested with Baker's chocolate and Callebaut chocolate. Chocolates do vary, so I can't guarantee that other brands (for instance, Hershey, Tobler and Lindt) will work for every recipe. In any case, the chocolate you use must be the real thing—no imitations or chocolate-flavored products. Use the best you can afford, whether American or European, and do not substitute semisweet chocolate chips for squares or for sold-by-the-pound pieces of good semisweet chocolate. Store chocolate in a cool, dry place (not the refrigerator).

✼ The safest way to melt chocolate, which burns easily, is in the top pan of a double boiler or a bowl over a saucepan: First chop the chocolate into small pieces. Next put an inch or two of water in the bottom of the double boiler or in the saucepan and bring to a boil; turn off the heat. Cover with the top pan or bowl; water should not touch the top pan or bowl. Add the chopped chocolate and stir until completely melted and smooth. Be sure absolutely no water or steam gets into the chocolate.

✼ Store different kinds of candy in separate containers. If packed together, candies tend to exchange flavors, ruining the tastes of both. Hard candies like butter crunch will become sticky if stored with moist candies like Rum-Walnut Balls.

✼ If you live in an area where there is concern about the use of raw eggs, you may want to consider avoiding recipes calling for them.

Dark Chocolate Raisin-Peanut Clusters

1 pound bittersweet chocolate, chopped, *OR* ½ pound bittersweet chocolate and ½ pound semisweet chocolate, chopped

1 teaspoon vegetable oil

1 cup dark and/or light raisins

1 cup coarsely chopped unsalted peanuts

½ cup finely chopped unsalted peanuts, for topping

DECORATING MEMO

Party Favors

Christmas is a lovely time to revive that childhood tradition—a small favor for each dinner guest, wrapped, ribboned and waiting at each place. The favor should be something small and delightful, a treat rather than a full-fledged gift. You might give chocolates, marzipan, a small ornament for the Christmas tree, a decorated gingerbread Santa, a sachet or pretty hanky, a tiny sewing kit or tool kit, a small puzzle or game.

Makes 60–65 clusters

Making great candy doesn't necessarily involve hard work and dozens of ingredients, as you can see from this recipe. Because there are so few ingredients, use the best quality you can afford—good chocolate, plump raisins, fresh peanuts.

Note: Have ready two cookie sheets or jelly roll pans lined with waxed paper.

Tip: Dampening the pans with a sponge before lining will keep the waxed paper from sliding around.

1. Put the chocolate and vegetable oil in the top pan of a double boiler over an inch or two of hot water (brought to a boil and then turned off) or in a bowl over a saucepan that contains an inch or two of hot water; water should not touch the bottom of the pan or bowl. Stir the chocolate until completely melted and smooth.

2. Add the raisins and peanuts and stir well. Remove the top pan or bowl from the bottom pan.

3. Drop half-tablespoons of the mixture onto the waxed paper, close together; the chocolate will not spread, so 30 clusters should fit on one pan. Immediately sprinkle with finely chopped peanuts. Let the clusters harden in a cool place (not the refrigerator).

Note: If the chocolate mixture thickens while you are spooning it out, put the pan or bowl back over the hot water and stir to warm and loosen the mixture a bit.

4. Lift the clusters from the waxed paper and store them in an airtight container. For gift wrap ideas, see page 109.

White Chocolate Coconut-Pecan Clusters

Makes 34–36 clusters

If you like white chocolate, you'll love these rich, crunchy nuggets. They are favorites of mine and I confess to stashing some in the freezer for late-night cravings.

Note: Before beginning, line two cookie sheets or jelly roll pans with waxed paper; dampening the sheets or pans with a sponge before lining will help the waxed paper stay in place.

Important: White chocolate must be bone-dry when you put it in a pan to melt it; any dampness or water on the cutting board, knife, pot, etc., may cause lumping.

1½ cups unsweetened flaked or shredded coconut
Note: If you can't find unsweetened coconut, make an acceptable substitute by rinsing sweetened coconut in running water. Drain well, pat dry on paper towels and then spread out the coconut to dry some more. (It will dry further when you toast it; it must be bone-dry before using it to make this candy.)
14–16 ounces white chocolate, chopped
1 cup chopped pecans

1. Toast the coconut on an ungreased cookie sheet in a preheated 350° F. oven for 5–10 minutes, until lightly browned and crisp. Watch the coconut carefully, stirring it around several times. Let it cool completely.

2. Melt the white chocolate in the top pan of a double boiler over an inch or two of hot water (brought to a boil and then turned off) or in a bowl over a saucepan that contains an inch or two of hot water; make sure the water does not touch the top pan or the bowl. Take care that no steam or water gets into the white chocolate.

Stir until the white chocolate is completely melted and smooth. Leave it over the hot water.

3. Stir in one cup of the cooled coconut and all the pecans. Drop six half-tablespoons of the mixture on the waxed paper and sprinkle with some of the remaining toasted coconut. Repeat, stirring the white chocolate mixture occasionally, until all the mixture is used up.

4. Put the sheets or pans in a cool place (not the refrigerator) until the clusters have hardened, about two hours. Lift the clusters from the waxed paper and store in an airtight container. For gift wrap ideas, see page 109.

½ pound Baker's or Callebaut
    semisweet chocolate, chopped
⅔ cup heavy cream
1½ tablespoons cognac or brandy
2 tablespoons butter, room
    temperature
Unsweetened cocoa powder
1 container (2¾ ounces)
    chocolate sprinkles (optional)

SEE PHOTOGRAPH 7

Holiday Assortment of Truffles

Truffles are the royalty of homemade candy—small spheres of smooth, flavored chocolate, coated with sprinkles, cocoa powder, chopped nuts or grated chocolate. Simple but elegant; it may surprise you to find out just how simple.

Note: For gift wrap suggestions, see page 109, as well as photograph 7.

Chocolate Truffles

Makes 34–36 pieces

1. Put the chopped chocolate in a bowl. In a saucepan, bring the cream just to a boil and pour it all at once onto the chocolate. Whisk briskly until the mixture is smooth. Add the brandy and whisk again until smooth. Refrigerate for half an hour, until thickened and completely cool.

2. With a rubber spatula or a wooden spoon, stir and mash the butter into the chocolate mixture, bit by bit, until the butter is completely incorporated. The mixture will thicken. Return it to the refrigerator to chill until firm but not hard; the idea is to bring the chocolate to the point at which it is chilled enough to hold a shape but still soft enough to mold easily.

3. Keeping your hands generously dusted with cocoa, shape bits of the chocolate mixture into one-inch balls. (If the chocolate mixture softens too much while you are shaping the balls, chill it briefly in the refrigerator.) Roll each ball in cocoa powder or chocolate sprinkles until it is well coated; roll the sprinkle-coated balls around on waxed paper to set the sprinkles.

Note: Let me warn you that making truffles is almost as messy as making mud pies, and you'll have to wash your hands after every eight or ten balls of chocolate.

As you finish the truffles, set them aside on waxed paper; they will firm up as they rest.

4. Place truffles in paper candy cups and store in layers in an airtight container, with waxed paper between layers. If you want the truffles to have a firm texture, you may keep them in the refrigerator for up to three weeks or in the freezer for up to three months.

The entire assortment of chocolate truffles is shown in photograph 7.

Hazelnut Truffles

Makes about 40 pieces

You'll need about ¾ cup ground toasted hazelnuts for these truffles (see *How to Toast Nuts* on page 40). Make the Chocolate Truffles recipe, adding ¼ cup of the ground toasted hazelnuts when you add the brandy or cognac. Omit the cocoa powder and chocolate sprinkles and instead roll the truffles in the remaining ground hazelnuts.

Orange Truffles

Makes about 36 pieces

Make the Chocolate Truffles recipe, using Cointreau instead of cognac or brandy and adding two teaspoons of grated orange rind when you add the Cointreau. Omit the cocoa powder and chocolate sprinkles and instead roll the truffles in grated white chocolate.

Note: To make grated white chocolate, freeze a four-ounce piece of white chocolate for a few minutes to harden it. Grate half the piece at a time, returning the second half to the freezer until needed.

Mocha Truffles

Makes about 36 pieces

Make the Chocolate Truffles recipe, substituting strong coffee (one teaspoon of instant coffee dissolved in 1½ tablespoons of prepared hot coffee) for the cognac or brandy. Roll each truffle in cocoa powder and gently press a chocolate coffee bean on the top.

Christmas Touches

A Gumdrop Tree—silver-sprayed branches pushed firmly into a basket filled with florist's foam, with a gumdrop on the tip of every branch . . . windows framed with strings of lights and garlands of greenery . . . a tray of Christmas cookies or candies in the foyer to greet guests . . . popcorn balls wrapped in red or green cellophane . . . champagne and chocolate truffles on Christmas Eve.

SEE PHOTOGRAPH 7

Colorful Marzipan Fruits

Makes about 25 pieces

Brightly colored marzipan fruits are so festive and pretty—somehow they suit the holiday perfectly.

There are four steps to making Colorful Marzipan Fruits: making the Basic Marzipan; shaping the marzipan fruits; coloring the marzipan fruits; glazing the marzipan fruits.

For the Basic Marzipan:

2 eight-ounce cans or two seven-ounce tubes almond paste

2 egg whites

   Note: To avoid harmful bacteria, be sure the eggs are not cracked before use.

½ teaspoon almond extract

4–4½ cups confectioners' sugar

For the shaping, coloring and glazing:

Whole cloves

Egg white

Paste food coloring

Vodka or kirsch

½ cup water

¼ cup light corn syrup

Red sugar

1. Make the Basic Marzipan: Break up the almond paste in a large bowl. Add the egg whites and almond extract and mix thoroughly. Add the sugar one cup at a time, kneading well after each addition; add enough sugar to make a solid, heavy "dough." (The mixture is quite sticky and hard to handle at first, but as you add sugar it dries and becomes workable.)

Note: At this point you may store the dough for up to one week by wrapping it in plastic and storing it in a plastic bag in the refrigerator. Bring to room temperature and knead again before using.

2. Shape the marzipan fruits: Break off one-inch balls of marzipan and shape them to look like lemons, oranges, apples, pears and strawberries. (There is enough dough to make five of each fruit.) The drawings, plus the following tips, will help you:

❋ Lemons and oranges: Roll on a fine grater to create a pebbly texture; insert cloves (star-shaped ends up) for the stem ends.

❋ Apples: Indent tops; insert cloves (pointed ends up) to represent stems.

❆ Pears: Insert cloves (pointed ends up) for stems.

❆ Strawberries: Shape little flat marzipan stars to make the caps; attach caps with cloves and a dab of egg white.

3. Color the marzipan fruits: Use a small, soft paintbrush and paste food coloring diluted with a little vodka or kirsch. Mix colors (a gem muffin pan makes a good palette) and paint each fruit completely. Don't forget to paint the strawberry caps green.

Place painted fruits on a wire rack to dry overnight; turn occasionally so they dry evenly.

4. Glaze the marzipan fruits: In a small saucepan, stir together the water and corn syrup to make a glaze. Bring to a boil, remove from the heat and allow to cool until just warm. Brush warm glaze on the red part of each strawberry; sprinkle with red sugar and place on a wire rack to dry overnight. Brush warm glaze on each of the other marzipan fruits and let dry overnight on the wire rack. When the glaze is dry on the strawberries, paint glaze on the strawberry caps; let dry overnight.

5. Put marzipan fruits in paper candy cups and store in an airtight container. You'll find gift wrapping suggestions on page 109.

DECORATING MEMO
Herb and Spice Ornaments for the Christmas Tree

Here's a great project to do with kids on a winter afternoon before Christmas. First ransack the spice shelves for whole bay leaves, peppercorns, mustard seeds, sesame seeds, dried parsley or basil, paprika, powdered ginger, cinnamon sticks, whole nutmegs, whole allspice. To make ornaments, begin by cutting white cardboard or mat board into simple shapes (diamonds, squares, rounds) and punching a hole at the top of each. Plan an herb-and-spice design for each shape, then brush white glue on the cardboard, apply the chosen herbs and spices and let dry. Glue on little ribbon or cord bows, if you like, and thread a bit of ribbon or cord through the hole.

SEE PHOTOGRAPH 7

Christmas Sugarplums

Makes 40–45 pieces

1½ cups sweetened shredded or
  flaked coconut
20–25 pitted dates (about nine
  ounces)
20 pitted prunes (about nine
  ounces)
1 eight-ounce can or one seven-
  ounce tube almond paste
⅓ cup orange marmalade
1½ tablespoons brandy or orange
  juice

These are pleasingly plump little pockets stuffed with bits of rich almond paste and coated with coconut. Be sure to use dates and prunes that are fresh and soft, not old and hard.

1. In a food processor, chop the coconut into small pieces; transfer the coconut to a small bowl and set aside.

Slit each date and prune lengthwise, being careful not to cut it completely in half.

2. Roll small pieces of almond paste (about ½ teaspoon each) into sausage shapes and stuff one into each date or prune. Press the date or prune around the almond paste.

3. Warm the marmalade in a small saucepan over low heat and stir until melted. Strain the liquid into a small bowl and discard the solids. Stir in the brandy or orange juice to make a glaze.

4. Brush the glaze on each filled date or prune and roll in chopped coconut. Store sugarplums in an airtight container, in layers separated by pieces of waxed paper.

The sugarplums are pictured in photograph 7; for more gift wrap ideas, see page 109.

CHRISTMAS MEMORIES FROM FRIENDS

Maple Sugar Candy

My mother always gave my sisters and me a box of maple sugar candy for Christmas. I thought this was the most legitimately Christmasy thing about our Christmas because the candy came from Vermont where there was snow. We lived in Los Angeles, and even though I knew Santa visited us, I could never picture Santa landing on a house with a palm tree in front of it. I remember the maple sugar box exactly. It is probably still the same package, with the candies in alternating red and green papers. It was the richest candy I had ever tasted and I ate each piece in tiny bites—holding each bite in my mouth until it dissolved on my tongue. One piece could last an hour.

Caramel Popcorn Balls

Makes 14 balls

Popcorn balls wrapped in colored cellophane were exciting treats when we were kids, and I still love to nibble them—especially these rich, chewy homemade ones. The wrapped balls look great hanging on the Christmas tree, too, tied with a bit of bright yarn.

Note: Have ready a jelly roll pan or sheet cake pan lined with waxed paper.

½ cup unpopped popcorn
1 cup chopped unsalted peanuts
1 cup (packed) light brown sugar
1 cup light corn syrup
⅓ cup water
1 teaspoon cider vinegar
¼ teaspoon baking soda

1. Pop the corn and put it in a large bowl, discarding any unpopped kernels. Sprinkle the chopped peanuts over the popcorn; set aside for now.

2. Put the remaining ingredients in a saucepan. Stir over low heat until the sugar is completely dissolved, about five minutes, frequently washing down the sides of the pan with a pastry brush dipped in cold water. Clip a candy thermometer inside the pan, raise the heat and bring the mixture to a boil. Boil without stirring until the thermometer reads 250° F. (firm ball stage).

3. Immediately pour the syrup slowly over the popcorn and peanuts, stirring vigorously so the syrup coats the mixture evenly, be sure the peanuts are distributed throughout the mixture.

4. Butter your hands well and, taking the coolest popcorn and peanuts from the top of the bowl, make a 2½–3 inch ball. (Be very careful not to burn your hands with hot syrup.) The ball should hold together but should not be compressed too tightly; shape the ball a second time when it is a little cooler. Place on waxed paper to cool completely.

Repeat to make a total of 14 balls, buttering your hands each time. Wrap individually in plastic.

COOK'S JOURNAL

Winter Fruit Compote

Dried fruits—apples, pears, prunes, apricots, peaches, raisins, etc.—make a rich, comforting dessert when simmered in liquid until the fruits are very soft. The simmering liquid can be orange juice, apple juice, water plus brown sugar and a little lemon juice, or water plus sugar and a little brandy; use just enough liquid to cover the fruits, and season to taste with cinnamon or a dash of ground nutmeg. Serve warm with soft whipped cream and a sprinkling of toasted coconut or chopped nuts.

SEE PHOTOGRAPH 7

Brown Sugar Butter Crunch with Toasted Almonds

¾ cup (1½ sticks) butter
1½ cups (packed) light brown sugar
1½ tablespoons light corn syrup
1 teaspoon vanilla extract
1¾ cups toasted chopped almonds
  Note: See *How to Toast Nuts* on page 40.
1½ cups chopped semisweet chocolate

Makes about one pound

A perennial favorite—crisp, buttery candy loaded with chopped almonds, with a coating of semisweet chocolate and more toasted almonds. This version uses brown sugar, for a deeper, more caramelized flavor.

Note: You will need a 14 × 17-inch cookie sheet.

1. Make the following important preparations: Butter the cookie sheet; set aside. Be sure the nuts are chopped, toasted, cooled and divided into two parts—¾ cup to mix into the candy and one cup for the topping. Have the vanilla on hand, along with the chocolate, which should be chopped in pieces the size of small peas. You'll also need a large glass of ice water and a pastry brush, a candy thermometer, a large metal spatula and a small metal spatula.

2. In a heavy, deep saucepan, melt the butter over low heat. Add the brown sugar and corn syrup and continue stirring gently, occasionally washing down the sides of the saucepan with a pastry brush dipped in ice water, until all the sugar is completely dissolved. It will take 15–20 minutes for the sugar to dissolve. Taste it (carefully—it's very hot) and feel it for graininess; when the sugar is completely dissolved you will detect no graininess at all.

Wash down the sides one final time.

3. Clip a candy thermometer inside the pan and raise the heat to medium. Cook without stirring, until the candy thermometer registers 300° F., about ten minutes, then turn off the heat but do not move the pan or the thermometer. The temperature will continue to rise; remove the pan from the burner when the thermometer registers 310° F. (hard crack stage).

Important: Watch the temperature carefully after it reaches 280° F., because it will rise very quickly.

4. Immediately add the vanilla and ¾ cup of the almonds and stir gently. Pour the mixture onto the prepared cookie sheet and use the large spatula to spread it in an even layer that reaches not quite to the edges of the cookie sheet.

5. Let the candy cool for two or three minutes and then sprinkle the chopped chocolate on it. When the chocolate begins to melt, use first the large spatula and then the small spatula to spread it evenly over the candy. By the time you finish, all the chocolate will be melted. Immediately sprinkle with the remaining cup of almonds and pat the almonds into the soft chocolate.

6. When the chocolate is firm (this will take several hours), break the butter crunch into chunks and store in an airtight container. You may refrigerate it if you like, to keep it fresh for a longer time, but it is not necessary. You'll find Brown Sugar Butter Crunch in photograph 7; see page 109 for gift wrap ideas.

Kids' Christmas Crispies

Makes 24 squares

These are called Kids' Christmas Crispies not because kids can make them but because kids love them. They are a simple and time-honored confection.

¼ cup (½ stick) butter or margarine
1 ten-ounce bag of marshmallows
½ cup dark raisins
½ cup chopped unsalted peanuts
5 cups crisp rice cereal

1. Grease a 9 × 13 × 2-inch sheet cake pan.

Melt the butter or margarine in a large saucepan. Add the marshmallows and cook over low heat, stirring, until thick and syrupy. Turn off the heat. Add the raisins, peanuts and cereal and stir until thoroughly mixed.

2. Working quickly, turn out into the prepared pan, rub a little butter or oil on your hands and press the mixture into an even layer. Let the mixture cool completely, then use a sharp knife to cut 24 approximately two-inch squares. Wrap individually in plastic or store unwrapped in an airtight container. Great for stocking stuffers.

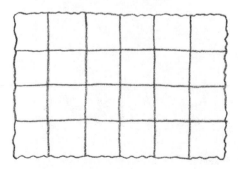

3 egg whites, room temperature
Pinch of salt
¼ teaspoon cream of tartar
¼ teaspoon fresh lemon juice
½ teaspoon vanilla extract
¾ cup superfine sugar
4 squares (four ounces) semisweet
    chocolate, chopped
1 teaspoon vegetable oil
2 containers (1¾ ounces each) of
    colored dots (colored
    nonpareils)

SEE PHOTOGRAPH 7

Chocolate-dipped Meringue Kisses

Makes about 120 kisses

The recipe makes a lot of kisses, but they don't last long, since each is just a single delicious mouthful.

Note: You will need a decorating bag fitted with a #2D (½-inch) star tip.

1. Preheat the oven to 250° F.; grease and flour two cookie sheets or jelly roll pans.

2. In a large bowl, combine the egg whites, salt, cream of tartar, lemon juice and vanilla. Beat until the egg whites hold soft peaks. Add the sugar one tablespoon at a time, beating until the whites are thick and smooth and stand in firm, glossy peaks, and the sugar is completely dissolved.

3. Fit a decorating bag with a #2D (½-inch) star tip and fill with half the meringue mixture. Pipe one-inch-diameter kisses on one prepared cookie sheet, leaving ½ inch between kisses and using up all the meringue in the bag. Repeat with the remaining meringue mixture and the second cookie sheet.

4. Bake both sheets at the same time for 40 minutes. Turn off the oven heat and leave the meringues in the warm oven to dry out completely for four hours (or overnight if it is more convenient).

Gently twist the meringues off the cookie sheets (or remove with a small spatula if necessary) and brush excess flour off the bottoms.

5. Put the chocolate and vegetable oil in the top pan of a double boiler over an inch or two of hot water (brought to a boil and then turned off) or in a bowl over a saucepan that contains an inch or two of hot water; water should not touch the bottom of the pan or bowl. Stir the chocolate until completely melted and smooth.

6. Pour the colored dots into a small bowl. Dip the top of each meringue into the melted chocolate, let excess chocolate drip off and then dip the pointed top in the colored dots. Place the finished kisses in single layers on trays or cookie sheets to let the chocolate harden (about two hours).

Note: If necessary during the dipping process, reheat the water and warm the chocolate to maintain the proper dipping consistency.

Store in airtight containers. Suggestions for gift wraps are on page 109; kisses can be seen in photograph 7.

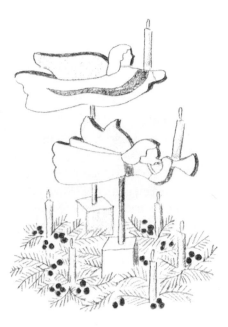

Rum-Walnut Balls

Makes 38–40 pieces

You can't miss the heady taste of rum and the richness of chocolate in these confections. A Christmas classic.

1¾ cups vanilla wafer crumbs
1¾ cups sifted confectioners' sugar
1½ cups ground walnuts
¼ cup unsweetened cocoa powder
3 tablespoons honey
½ cup light or dark rum
Sifted confectioners' sugar for coating

1. In a large bowl, stir together the crumbs, confectioners' sugar, walnuts and cocoa powder until thoroughly blended.

2. Stir the honey into the rum and gradually add the rum mixture to the dry ingredients, mixing first with a spoon and then with your hand; add just enough rum mixture to make a dough that holds together.

3. Roll bits of the dough into balls about one inch in diameter. Dredge lightly in a bowl of sifted confectioners' sugar.

Note: The balls will seem soft at first, but they firm up after a short time.

4. Package the Rum-Walnut Balls in airtight containers and store in the refrigerator for two days to let the flavors mellow. After that, you may keep the balls, refrigerated, for up to two weeks. Gift wrap ideas are on page 109.

SEE PHOTOGRAPH 7

Old-fashioned Chocolate Pecan Fudge

2 cups sugar
½ cup milk
½ cup (one stick) butter, cut in slices
2 squares (two ounces) unsweetened chocolate, chopped
1 tablespoon light corn syrup
1 teaspoon vanilla extract
1½ cups coarsely chopped pecans
16 pecan halves

Makes 16 squares

This is fudge made the old-fashioned way—by careful cooking and beating—and it is as silken and scrumptious as you could possibly want. Individually wrapped pieces of fudge make great stocking-stuffers; a whole batch would be a gift to make any candy-lover swoon.

1. Line the bottom and sides of an 8 × 8 × 2-inch pan with aluminum foil; butter the foil. Set aside.

2. Stir the sugar and milk in a deep, heavy saucepan over low heat until the sugar is dissolved, frequently washing down the sides of the pan with a pastry brush dipped in cold water. Do not boil.

Note: It is difficult to see through the milk to check whether the sugar is fully dissolved, so take your time and be conscientious about stirring. Undissolved sugar will ruin the fudge.

3. Add the butter, chocolate and corn syrup and stir to melt.

4. Clip a candy thermometer inside the saucepan and raise the heat to medium, bringing the mixture to a low boil. Boil until the temperature reaches 240° F. (soft ball stage), watching carefully after the thermometer reaches 220° F. Do not overcook.

5. Remove the pan from the heat and set aside to cool. Don't move or jiggle the pan once you have put it down to cool. When the thermometer reads 110° F., stir in the vanilla and chopped pecans.

Note: It will take over an hour for the chocolate mixture to cool to 110° F.; don't get impatient.

6. Using a wooden spoon, beat the mixture (in the saucepan) until it becomes very thick and stiff, somewhat lighter in color and less shiny; when it is sufficiently beaten, the fudge will *not* stream off the spoon. This may take anywhere from five to 15 minutes, depending on the indoor temperature and humidity.

Note: Once you start beating, don't stop. (Here's where a buddy system helps, since beating the fudge is a strenuous activity.)

Immediately push the fudge into the prepared pan, using a spatula to get as much fudge as possible out of the saucepan without scraping any granulation from the sides of the saucepan. Work quickly to smooth the fudge and push it into the corners of the prepared pan. With the tip of a knife, mark 16 squares and press a pecan half into each square. Let the fudge cool until firm, 20–45 minutes, again depending on the temperature and humidity.

7. Lift the foil and fudge out of the pan. Cut the fudge in squares, on the marked lines; serve immediately or store unwrapped in an airtight container or wrap individually in plastic. The fudge does not have to be refrigerated, but you may do so if you like.

You'll find individually wrapped and tied squares of fudge included in photograph 7; see page 109 for gift wrap suggestions.

Gift Wraps for Candies

If candies are small, you might like to put each one in a paper candy cup before gift-wrapping; if large (like pieces of fudge), consider wrapping individually before gift-wrapping.

❋ Arrange marzipan fruits in a small glass bowl or plate placed on a square of clear cellophane. Bring the cellophane up over the candy, twist it closed and tie with ribbon.

❋ Use the same cellophane trick with candies arranged in a small basket. If the basket has a handle, line the basket with a square of clear cellophane and fill with candies; twist the cellophane closed and tie with ribbon.

❋ Pack layers of candy in a pretty Christmas tin, separating the layers with neatly cut pieces of waxed paper. (Avoid unlined cardboard boxes, which will impart an unpleasant smell and taste to the candy.)

❋ Fill a lidded ceramic box with candies, tie with gold or silver cord and add a bit of holly, a pretty ornament or a few shiny Christmas balls.

❋ Apothecary-style jars with wide mouths make terrific containers for candies that do not crush easily—for instance, *Brown Sugar Butter Crunch with Toasted Almonds (page 104)*, *Chocolate-dipped Meringue Kisses (page 106)*, fruit drops, caramels.

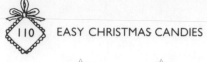

20 dried apricot halves
20 dried pear halves
3½ cups (or more) brandy
½ pound semisweet chocolate, chopped
2 teaspoons vegetable oil
4 ounces chocolate sprinkles

ENTERTAINING NOTEBOOK

Stocking Stuffers for Kids

❊ Candy canes, peppermint sticks
❊ *Old-fashioned Chocolate Pecan Fudge (page 108)*
❊ *Caramel Popcorn Balls (page 103)*
❊ Chocolate Santa
❊ Brightly colored bandanna
❊ Miniature doll, furniture, dishes
❊ Tiny pack of cards
❊ Dominoes
❊ Miniature jigsaw puzzle
❊ Stuffed animal
❊ Small plastic dinosaurs
❊ Hand puppet
❊ Paperback book
❊ Stampers and ink pad
❊ Crayons, felt-tip markers
❊ Little spiral-bound sketchbook
❊ Harmonica
❊ Miniature car, truck, airplane
❊ Kaleidoscope
❊ Prism
❊ Magnifying glass
❊ Horseshoe magnet
❊ Snap blocks

Chocolate-dipped Apricots and Pears

Makes 40 pieces

The apricots and pears must be soaked in brandy for five days and then dried overnight before they are dipped in chocolate, so make your plans accordingly.

1. Simmer the apricots and pears in water to cover, for about two minutes, to soften them slightly. Drain and pat dry on paper towels. Put the dried fruit in one or two large jars and pour in enough brandy to cover the fruit completely. Tilt the jar(s) back and forth so the brandy gets into the nooks and crannies. Leave in a cool place (not the refrigerator) for five days, adding brandy as needed to keep the fruit covered.

2. After five days, drain the fruit (reserving the brandy for another use), dry it with paper towels and then arrange the pears and apricots on a wire rack to air-dry overnight.

3. Next day, when the fruit is dry, place the chocolate and vegetable oil in the top pan of a double boiler over an inch or two of hot water (brought to a boil and turned off) or in a bowl over a saucepan that contains an inch or two of hot water; the bottom of the pan or bowl should not touch the water. Stir until the chocolate is completely melted and smooth. Remove from the hot water.

4. Pour the sprinkles onto a plate; have ready two cookie sheets or jelly roll pans lined with waxed paper.

Hold one end of an apricot or the narrow end of a pear and partially dip the top side in melted chocolate. Gently shake off any excess chocolate, then press the chocolate-dipped part into the sprinkles. Place the fruit on the waxed paper. Repeat until all the fruit has been dipped.

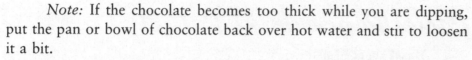

Note: If the chocolate becomes too thick while you are dipping, put the pan or bowl of chocolate back over hot water and stir to loosen it a bit.

5. Leave the cookie sheets or pans in a cool place (not the refrigerator) while the chocolate hardens. When the chocolate is firm, store the fruit in an airtight container, in layers separated by pieces of waxed paper. See page 109 for gift wrap suggestions.

START WITH STORE-BOUGHT
Wreaths

Buy a handsome but unadorned evergreen wreath and decorate it yourself using the elements described below. Attach decorations with short lengths of wire, bright yarn, narrow satin ribbon, thin string or crochet cord.

❉ Romantic wreath: little bunches of baby's breath tied with peach satin ribbon; small white satin balls; gold cords; peach satin ribbon and white lace bow with streamers

❉ Country wreath: red, green, yellow and blue gingham ribbon bows; tiny baskets filled with artificial flowers

❉ Natural wreath: sprays of wheat, dried grasses and dried flowers secured with wire and then tied with plaid taffeta bows; small and medium pinecones, if desired.

SEE PHOTOGRAPH 7

Pastel Peppermint Patties

¼ cup (½ stick) butter, room
    temperature
6 tablespoons light corn syrup
1½ teaspoons peppermint extract
1 pound confectioners' sugar,
    sifted (about 4½ cups)
Red and green liquid food
    coloring
Decorating Icing (recipe follows)

ENTERTAINING NOTEBOOK
Host and Hostess Gifts

Anyone who puts on a big party or entertains guests for a weekend deserves applause. If you're the lucky guest, an appropriate gift will convey your appreciation and make your host and hostess feel marvelous. Here are some suggestions:

❋ Chocolates or after-dinner mints

❋ Wine or liqueur

❋ Pair of tulip glasses and a split of champagne

❋ Gourmet treats such as macadamia nuts, caviar, fancy jams and honeys, pralines, Scotch shortbread, glacé fruits

❋ Homemade cookies, fruitcake, condiment or chutney

❋ Book or record in which your hosts have expressed interest

❋ Photo album

❋ Poinsettia plant

❋ Two or three special Christmas tree ornaments

Makes about 75 patties

These white, pink and light green candies have a lovely old-fashioned look, thanks to the pastel colors and tiny piped decorations.

Note: You will need two decorating bags, #2 round tip and #27 star tip. If you don't know how to use a decorating bag and icing tips, read about simple piping on page 46.

1. Have ready two cookie sheets lined with waxed paper.

Blend the butter, corn syrup and peppermint extract together in a large bowl. Gradually add the confectioners' sugar, mixing with a wooden spoon as long as possible and then kneading in the rest of the sugar with your hands, to make a sugar "dough."

2. Divide the sugar dough in three parts: Leave one part white. Knead a few drops of green food coloring into the second part to make pale green dough and a few drops of red food coloring into the third part to make light pink. Wrap each part in plastic.

3. Working with one color of dough, roll seven or eight ¾-inch balls at a time and place them one inch apart on a prepared cookie sheet. Gently flatten each ball with the bottom of a glass lightly dusted with confectioners' sugar. With your finger, gently rub the top of each patty to smooth it and to dust off the excess confectioners' sugar. Continue making patties until all the dough is used up.

Repeat the process with the other two colors of dough.

4. Divide the Decorating Icing between two bowls. Mix 15 drops of red food coloring into one bowl to tint the icing medium pink and 15 drops of green food coloring into the other bowl to tint it medium-

light green. Fit one decorating bag with a #27 star tip and fill with pink icing; fit the other bag with a #2 round tip and fill with green icing.

Using the star tip, pipe three little pink rosettes in the center of each patty. Using the round tip, pipe a few little green "leaves" around them.

5. Let the patties dry on waxed paper for three hours, then transfer to wire racks to dry overnight. Store in airtight containers.

Peppermint patties are shown in photograph 7; for gift wrap ideas, see page 109.

Decorating Icing

Makes about one cup

Stir the ingredients together in a deep bowl. Beat at high speed for five minutes. Since this icing dries hard and crisp, it must be kept tightly covered with plastic wrap until you are ready to use it.

½ pound confectioners' sugar, sifted (about 2¼ cups)
Heaping ¼ teaspoon cream of tartar
1½ egg whites
   Note: To avoid harmful bacteria, be sure to use eggs with no cracks in the shells.
¼ teaspoon vanilla extract

CHAPTER 5

Sweet Holiday Breads, Coffeecakes and Tea Loaves

Home-baked breads and coffeecakes are a treasured part of Christmas. Cranberries and cherries, pecans and almonds, dates and raisins—the flavors of the season are baked into spirals and loaves and crescents, filling the house with rich aromas that send us straight to the kitchen to beg for the first slice of sweet bread, fresh from the oven.

This chapter offers sweet yeast breads and quick breads for leisurely breakfasts, party brunches and late afternoon snacks and for delicious gifts to take when you call on friends and family during the holidays. Of course, it's terrific when you can serve your sweet bread or coffeecake on the same day you bake it, but at this busy time of year it's a great help to know that most of the breads in this chapter freeze beautifully, so you can bake ahead and have plenty of Christmas treats ready to go at a moment's notice.

Tips and Guidelines

❋ Unless otherwise indicated, use sweet (unsalted) butter, all-purpose flour, white granulated sugar and large eggs. Nuts, fruits and spices should be fresh, never old and stale.

❋ Don't use baking powder that has been opened and standing around for a long time; buy a new can. Check the expiration date on yeast packages and discard outdated yeast.

❋ Flour does not have to be sifted.

❋ Always preheat the oven for at least 15 minutes, using an oven thermometer to check the temperature. Bake yeast or quick breads on the middle rack of the oven, if possible, or—if you must use the middle two racks—stagger the pans so heat can circulate freely.

❋ Beat quick bread batters just until well blended; do not overmix. It's helpful to know that batters made with baking powder can stand for a short while after mixing and will still rise properly when baked.

❋ Test quick breads for doneness with a wooden toothpick or skewer, inserting it in the center of the pan. When the quick bread is done, the toothpick or skewer will come out clean, with no batter or crumbs sticking to it.

❋ Read the special tips and guidelines (below) for baking yeast breads.

Tips and Guidelines for Baking Yeast Breads

❄ The liquid used for activating the yeast must be warmed to a certain temperature, as specified in each recipe; use an instant-reading thermometer to measure that temperature.

❄ Kneading is an important—and enjoyable—step in making most yeast breads: Shape the dough into a ball and place it on a lightly floured surface. Firmly push the heels of your hands into the dough, fold it and give it a quarter turn; repeat, dusting with just enough flour to keep the dough and your hands from sticking. Knead the dough for the full amount of time specified in the recipe, usually 5–15 minutes, until smooth and elastic.

❄ Let dough rise, usually until doubled in bulk, in a dry, draft-free, warm (but not heated) place. The oven (with no heat turned on) is an ideal place if the pilot light doesn't create a lot of heat. If the oven is actually cool, turn the heat on for a few seconds to warm it slightly.

❄ Dough is doubled in bulk when it is high, rounded and puffy and two fingers pressed ½ inch into the dough leave a depression that remains. If the depression fills in again quickly, let dough rise for another 15 minutes and test again.

❄ Punch down the dough by firmly pushing your fist into it so it collapses. This step is usually followed by a short period of time in which you simply leave the dough to rest, which makes it more workable during shaping.

Christmas Stollen

Makes two loaves

Stollen is a traditional German holiday bread, not too sweet, perfect for nibbling when you take time out for a cup of fresh coffee. Make a few stollen and freeze them (wrapped well to prevent them from drying out) to have on hand for gifts or guests.

Baking pan: one cookie sheet

1. Sprinkle the yeast over the warm water and stir with a warm spoon to dissolve the yeast; set aside for a few minutes.

2. Scald the milk and pour it into a large bowl. Add the butter, sugar, mace, salt and lemon rind and stir until the butter melts and the sugar dissolves. Let the mixture cool to lukewarm (110° F. on an instant-reading cooking thermometer). Add the yeast mixture and stir to blend.

3. Add the eggs and beat well.

4. Add two cups of the flour, the almonds, raisins and candied peel and beat to make a batter. Beat in enough of the remaining flour, ½ cup at a time, to make a soft but not sticky dough.

5. Turn the dough out onto a well-floured work surface and knead until smooth and elastic, about five minutes. Sprinkle often with flour to keep the dough from sticking.

Put the dough in a buttered bowl and turn all around to coat with butter. Cover with a clean dish towel and place in a draft-free place (for example, the oven with no heat turned on) to rise until doubled in bulk, about 2½ hours.

2 packages (¼ ounce each) dry yeast
½ cup warm water (105° to 115° F., tested with an instant-reading cooking thermometer)
½ cup milk
½ cup (one stick) butter, room temperature
½ cup sugar
½ teaspoon ground mace
1 teaspoon salt
1 teaspoon grated lemon rind
2 eggs, room temperature
4½–5½ cups flour
¾ cup sliced almonds, toasted
   Note: See How to Toast Nuts on page 40.
¾ cup dark raisins
½ cup mixed candied peel, chopped down to ¼-inch pieces
Confectioners' sugar

Glazes for Coffeecakes

Beat or whisk the ingredients together in the order given, until smooth. If necessary, thin the glaze with a little more liquid. Use as soon as possible. To prevent a crust from forming, store glaze with a piece of plastic wrap pressed directly onto the surface.

Vanilla Glaze (about ⅔ cup): one tablespoon butter, melted; one teaspoon vanilla extract; 2½ tablespoons milk or cream; pinch of salt; two cups sifted confectioners' sugar

Lemon Glaze (about ¾ cup): one tablespoon butter, melted; two tablespoons fresh lemon juice; two teaspoons water; ½ teaspoon vanilla extract; one teaspoon grated lemon rind; 1½ cups confectioners' sugar, sifted

Orange Glaze (about ¾ cup): two tablespoons defrosted frozen orange concentrate; one teaspoon fresh lemon juice; one teaspoon grated orange rind; 1½ cups confectioners' sugar, sifted

Cinnamon Glaze (about ½ cup): 1¼ cups sifted confectioners' sugar; ¾ teaspoon cinnamon; two tablespoons milk

6. Turn the dough out onto a flour-dusted surface and punch down. Cut in half and let rest for ten minutes. Flatten and shape each ball of dough into an 8 × 10-inch oval. Fold each oval almost in half and press the fold to set it.

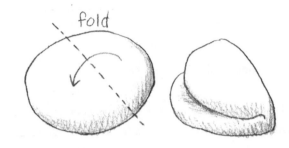

Place the loaves on an ungreased cookie sheet, leaving several inches between them. Cover with the dish towel and return to the draft-free place to let the dough rise a second time, until puffy and almost doubled in bulk, about one hour and 45 minutes.

7. Preheat the oven to 350° F. Bake the loaves for 40–45 minutes, until golden brown. Let the loaves cool on the cookie sheet for ten minutes, then run a spatula under them and slide onto wire racks to finish cooling.

Use a fine strainer to sprinkle confectioners' sugar generously on the loaves. Serve immediately or store in the freezer, wrapped first in plastic and then in aluminum foil.

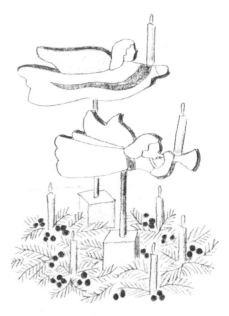

SEE PHOTOGRAPH 5

Spiced Pear and Cherry Kuchen

Makes one round cake

Serve this moist fruit kuchen for breakfast or a holiday brunch. The kuchen is a baking powder cake (no yeast involved), made in the upside-down-cake manner, with the pear slices laid out on the bottom of the pan like the petals of a flower and the cherries filling in the spaces.

Note: Even though the pan is lined with waxed paper, some of the butter and brown sugar may leak out of the pan during baking; do not be concerned about this.

Baking pan: one nine-inch springform pan

1. Preheat the oven to 400° F.; brush a little of the melted butter on the bottom of the springform pan and line the bottom with a waxed paper circle ten inches in diameter.

Add ¼ cup of the melted butter and brush it all over the waxed paper circle and the sides of the pan.

Stir together the brown sugar and the spices; sprinkle the brown sugar mixture evenly over the bottom of the pan.

Remove ⅓ cup of cherries and chop them in halves; set aside.

Peel the pear, quarter it lengthwise and core it carefully. Cut each quarter lengthwise in three slices. Arrange the pear slices and the whole cherries on the brown sugar mixture in the pan, as shown. Set the pan aside.

¾ cup (1½ sticks) butter, melted and cooled
½ cup (packed) light brown sugar
½ teaspoon cinnamon
¼ teaspoon ground nutmeg
¼ teaspoon ground cloves
1 can (16½ ounces) pitted dark sweet cherries, drained
1 ripe Anjou or Comice pear
1½ cups flour
2 teaspoons baking powder
½ teaspoon salt
½ cup sugar
½ cup milk
1 egg, beaten with ½ teaspoon vanilla extract
Confectioners' sugar for decoration

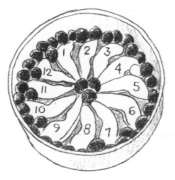

Gift Wraps
for Loaves and Rings

Note: Before gift-wrapping, wrap the loaf or ring snugly in two or three layers of plastic.

❄ Loaves can be tucked into brand-new loaf pans and tied with ribbon—a double present.

❄ Place a ring or round braid on a round plastic or wood cutting board, pretty round tray or round cake board on a large square of cellophane; bring cellophane up and twist closed; secure with a twist tie, then overwrap with ribbon and tie a big bow.

❄ Anchor a loaf or ring with masking-tape loops on an attractive serving plate or platter; tie wide ribbon around the plate and loaf, taping the ribbon on the underside of the plate to hold it in place; make a bow on top and add a sprig of greenery, a little wooden spoon or a big candy cane.

❄ Tuck a loaf into a shiny paper bottle bag, turn the end under and tape neatly on the underside. Tie with ribbon, cord or yarn.

2. In a large bowl, stir or whisk together the flour, baking powder, salt and white sugar.

3. Add the milk, the egg mixture and the remaining butter and beat just until the batter is blended. Carefully spoon the batter over the fruit in the pan and smooth it out with a spatula. Scatter the chopped cherries over the batter and use the spatula to press them into the batter.

4. Place the springform pan on a jelly roll pan or cookie sheet and bake for 40–45 minutes, or until a tester inserted in the center of the cake (but not as far down as the fruit) comes out clean. A small amount of butter and sugar may leak from the springform pan, but don't worry about this.

Let the cake cool in the pan on a wire rack for ten minutes. Cover the pan tightly with an inverted serving platter and turn pan and platter over; the cake will drop onto the platter. Release and remove the side section of the springform pan; the round bottom section of the pan will drop onto the cake. Carefully remove the round bottom section and the waxed paper; if necessary, use a long spatula to loosen any cherries that cling to it.

When the kuchen is just warm (not hot), use a fine strainer to sift confectioners' sugar around the edge, as shown in photograph 5. This is easily accomplished if you mask off the center of the cake with a circle of waxed paper.

Serve the kuchen warm or cool.

SEE PHOTOGRAPH 5

Honey-Pecan Crescents

Makes 24 crescents

These attractive little breakfast rolls are made by rolling triangles of quick-rise yeast dough around a buttery pecan filling.

Note: Honey-Pecan Crescents freeze well if you wrap them individually in plastic; be sure to reheat them after defrosting.

Baking pans: two cookie sheets

1. In a large bowl, stir or whisk together three cups of the flour, the cinnamon, salt, sugar and yeast. In a small saucepan over low heat, stir the milk and butter until very warm (125° to 130° F. on an instant-reading cooking thermometer). Add the milk mixture to the flour mixture and beat well.

2. Add the eggs and beat for three minutes. Stir in as much of the remaining flour as needed to make a soft but not sticky dough.

3. Turn the dough out onto a well-floured work surface and knead for ten minutes, or until smooth and elastic. Sprinkle often with flour to keep the dough from sticking.

Place the dough in a buttered bowl and turn all around to coat with butter. Cover with a clean dish towel and put in a draft-free place (for example, the oven with no heat turned on) to rise until doubled in bulk, about 90 minutes.

4. Turn the dough out onto a flour-dusted surface, punch it down and let it rest for ten minutes. Divide dough in half and roll out each half to a 13-inch circle, about ¼ inch thick. Cut each circle in 12 wedges (see drawing).

4½–5 cups flour
1 teaspoon cinnamon
½ teaspoon salt
½ cup sugar
1 package (¼ ounce) quick-rise dry yeast
1 cup milk
½ cup (one stick) butter
2 eggs, beaten
Honey-Pecan Filling (recipe follows)
Egg glaze (one egg, one tablespoon sugar and one tablespoon milk beaten together)

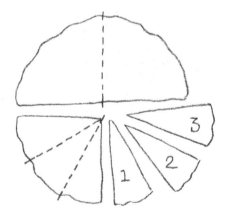

5. Place a tablespoon of Honey-Pecan Filling on the wide end of each wedge and roll up loosely from the wide end, ending with the point underneath. Turn and shape into crescents (as shown in the drawing) and place on ungreased cookie sheets, leaving two inches between crescents.

Tip: Smudge each pointed end firmly onto the cookie sheet to hold the crescent shape while baking.

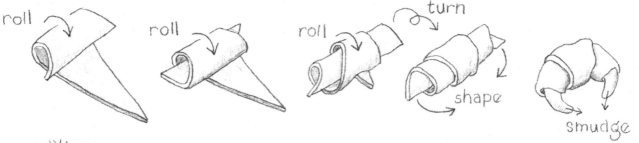

Cover the crescents with clean dish towels, return to the draft-free place and let the dough rise a second time until doubled in bulk, about 75 minutes.

6. Preheat the oven to 375° F. Brush the crescents with egg glaze and bake for 15 minutes. Cool the crescents on the cookie sheets for five minutes and then transfer to wire racks to finish cooling.

OPTIONS: When the crescents are cool, drizzle with any of the glazes on page 118. Or instead of drizzling in an open pattern, thin the glaze a little more, pour a spoonful of thinned glaze on the midsection of each crescent and immediately sprinkle with chopped pecans.

Honey-Pecan Filling

Makes about 1½ cups

½ cup honey
2 tablespoons butter
½ teaspoon vanilla extract
1½ cups finely chopped pecans

Warm the honey in a saucepan over low heat, add the butter and stir to melt and blend. Remove from the heat and stir in the vanilla and chopped nuts. Let the filling cool.

SEE PHOTOGRAPH 5

Cranberry Spiral Bread with Vanilla Glaze

Makes two rings

A beautiful sweet bread, with a ruby-red spiral of cranberry filling and a lattice pattern of vanilla glaze. Fun to make, too—especially when you shorten the rising periods by using quick-rise yeast.

Baking pans: two cookie sheets

1. In a large bowl, stir together 3½ cups of the flour, the yeast, sugar, brown sugar, cinnamon, salt and lemon rind. In a small saucepan over low heat, stir the milk, water and ¼ cup of butter (or margarine) until very warm (125° to 130° F. on an instant-reading cooking thermometer). Add the milk mixture to the flour mixture and stir.

2. Add the eggs and beat for three minutes. Beat in enough of the remaining flour, ½ cup at a time, to make a soft but not sticky dough.

3. Turn the dough out onto a well-floured surface and knead until smooth and elastic, about 15 minutes. Sprinkle often with flour to keep the dough from sticking.

Put the dough in a buttered bowl and turn all around to coat with butter. Cover with a clean dish towel and place in a draft-free place (for example, the oven with no heat turned on) to rise until doubled in bulk, about one hour.

4. Turn the dough out onto a flour-dusted surface and punch down. Cut in half and let it rest for ten minutes. Meanwhile, grease the cookie sheets.

Roll out each ball of dough to a 12 × 15-inch rectangle; brush excess flour from the undersides. On each rectangle spread half of the very soft butter (two tablespoons) and then half the Cranberry Filling (about 1½ cups), working it almost all the way to the edges. Roll up each rectangle from the long side.

6–7 cups flour
2 packages (¼ ounce each) quick-rise dry yeast
½ cup sugar
½ cup (packed) light brown sugar
1 teaspoon cinnamon
1 teaspoon salt
2 teaspoons grated lemon rind
1 cup milk
½ cup water
¼ cup (½ stick) butter or margarine
2 eggs
¼ cup (½ stick) very soft butter for the filling
Cranberry Filling (recipe follows)
Egg glaze (one egg beaten with one tablespoon water)
Vanilla Glaze (page 118), with one extra teaspoon milk

roll

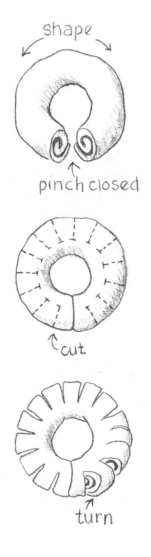

shape

pinch closed

cut

turn

5. Transfer one roll to a greased cookie sheet, placing it seam side down and shaping it into a ring. Dampen the ends and pinch them together firmly. Use scissors to make cuts one inch apart, right through the ring, as shown in the drawing. Turn each slice to the side. Repeat with the second roll, using the second cookie sheet.

Cover each ring with a dish towel and return them both to the draft-free place to rise again until doubled in bulk, about 35 minutes.

6. Preheat the oven to 350° F. Brush the rings with egg glaze.

Bake for 25 minutes, or until the breads are nicely browned. Immediately loosen them from the cookie sheets with a long spatula and slide onto wire racks to cool.

When the rings are completely cool, decorate with Vanilla Glaze, using one of these two methods:

Stir the Vanilla Glaze with a wire whisk. Dip the whisk in Vanilla Glaze and swing it over one bread in a back-and-forth motion to drop threads of glaze in one direction. (*Note:* You may have to thin the Vanilla Glaze a bit more.) Repeat, swinging the whisk in the opposite direction to make crisscross lines. Repeat the procedure on the second bread.

If you find it easier, transfer the Vanilla Glaze to a decorating bag fitted with a round tip and pipe the glaze onto the cake in a crisscross pattern.

Refer to photograph 5 for guidance.

Cranberry Filling

Makes about three cups

½ cup plus one tablespoon sugar
6 tablespoons light corn syrup
½ cup plus one tablespoon water
¾ cup whole cranberries
¾ cup chopped cranberries
1 heaping cup chopped walnuts
1 teaspoon grated lemon rind
 (rind of about 1½ medium-
 large lemons)
3 teaspoons fresh lemon juice

1. In a heavy saucepan stir together the sugar, corn syrup and water. Bring to a boil over medium heat and boil for five minutes, uncovered.

2. Add the cranberries, cover and continue cooking over medium heat for four minutes, stirring occasionally.

3. Remove from the heat and stir in the chopped nuts, lemon rind and lemon juice. Let the filling cool completely.

Date and Honey Loaves

Makes two loaves

Another of my personal favorites—a pretty brown loaf with lots of sweet dates and a distinctively mellow honey taste. Freezes well and does not need to be warmed after defrosting; in fact, it's great cold.

Baking pan: two 8½ × 4½ × 2½-inch loaf pans

1. Preheat the oven to 325° F.; grease and flour the loaf pans.
Put the dates in a bowl. Dissolve the baking soda in the boiling water and pour over the dates. Set aside for 20 minutes or longer, until the batter for the loaf is ready.
Stir together the flour, baking powder, cinnamon and salt; set aside.

2. Cream the butter; gradually add the honey, beating well after each addition. Add the eggs and vanilla and beat again.

3. Gradually add the dry ingredients, stirring by hand after each addition. (Do not beat with an electric mixer.) Add the date mixture and stir until well blended. Pour the batter into the prepared loaf pans.

4. Bake for one hour, or until a tester inserted in the center of each loaf comes out free of batter (although the tester may have some sticky date clinging to it). Let the loaves cool in the pans on a wire rack for five minutes and then turn out onto the wire rack to finish cooling. Do not slice until completely cool.

OPTIONS: Serve with honey butter (sweet butter blended with honey, to taste) or nutted cream cheese (softened cream cheese blended with a little milk or cream and plenty of toasted chopped pecans or walnuts). Toasted slices of Date and Honey Loaf are also delicious spread with Winter Pear Butter (page 233).

2 cups pitted dates, coarsely chopped
1½ teaspoons baking soda
¾ cup boiling water
2½ cups flour
3 teaspoons baking powder
½ teaspoon cinnamon
½ teaspoon salt
½ cup (one stick) butter, room temperature
1 cup honey
2 eggs beaten with one teaspoon vanilla extract

Christmas Touches

In the foyer—a small boxwood tree trimmed with foil-wrapped candies . . . a muffin tin candle holder with one small candle per cup (secured with florist's or adhesive clay), surrounded by miniature shiny balls and velvet leaves . . . a cozy cup of hot chocolate and warm milk, with a spoonful of whipped cream and a cinnamon stick for stirring . . . homemade fruit butter with breakfast.

Marbled Cinnamon Coffeecake with Streusel Topping

Makes one nine-inch round cake

Moist, spicy and quite rich—a real treat on a cold winter afternoon. This is a quick coffeecake, made with baking powder and baking soda rather than yeast, so you can whip it up in a very short time.

Baking pan: one nine-inch springform pan

For the streusel topping:

¼ cup (packed) light or dark
    brown sugar
1½ teaspoons cinnamon
½ cup flour
3 tablespoons butter, cool but not
    cold
½ cup coarsely chopped walnuts
    or pecans, toasted
    Note: See *How to Toast Nuts*
    on page 40.

For the coffeecake:

1¾ cups flour
2 teaspoons baking powder
½ teaspoon baking soda
¼ teaspoon salt
1 cup (two sticks) butter, room
    temperature
1 cup sugar
2 eggs
1 cup sour cream
1 teaspoon vanilla extract
1½ teaspoons cinnamon mixed
    with ⅓ cup sugar

1. Preheat the oven to 350° F.; grease the springform pan.

Make the streusel topping: Stir together the brown sugar, cinnamon and flour; add the butter and cut it in with a pastry cutter until the mixture is crumbly; stir in the nuts. Set aside.

In another bowl, stir or whisk together the flour, baking powder, baking soda and salt; set aside.

2. In a large bowl, cream the butter and sugar. Add the eggs one at a time, beating well after each addition.

3. Add the sour cream and vanilla and beat again.

4. Fold in the dry ingredients a little at a time. Pour two thirds of the batter into the prepared pan. Dot the batter with spoonfuls of the cinnamon-sugar mixture and use a knife to marble it into the batter. Spoon the rest of the plain batter evenly over the marbled batter.

5. Sprinkle the streusel topping evenly over the batter.

6. Bake for 80 minutes, or until a tester inserted in the center of the cake comes out free of batter (the tester may have some cinnamon-sugar clinging to it).

Let the cake cool in the pan on a wire rack. (The cake has a tendency to sink a bit in the center, but that doesn't affect the taste at all.) Run a knife around the cake and then release and remove the sides of the springform pan. Run a long spatula under the cake and slide it onto a serving platter. Serve in wedges, warm or cool.

Ginger-Nut Loaves

Makes two loaves

Crystallized ginger and pecans give these sweet loaves their name. Don't confuse them with gingerbread—these are completely different in flavor and texture, a bit exotic and quite special. A lovely gift. Freezes well.

Baking pans: two 8½ × 4½ × 2½-inch loaf pans

1. Preheat the oven to 350° F.; grease the loaf pans.
Stir together the flour, baking powder, baking soda, powdered ginger and salt; add the pecans and chopped ginger and stir again. Set aside.

2. Beat the brown sugar, eggs and melted butter until smooth and creamy.

3. Add the dry ingredients and buttermilk alternately, in four parts each, stirring well by hand after each addition. (Do not beat with an electric mixer.) Pour equal amounts of batter into the greased loaf pans.

4. Bake for 60–65 minutes, or until a tester inserted in the center of each loaf comes out clean. Let the loaves cool in the pans on a wire rack for five minutes and then turn out onto the wire rack to finish cooling. Serve warm or cool.

OPTIONS: Serve Ginger-Nut Loaf for afternoon refreshment, along with sweet butter, softened cream cheese and a delicate honey. If you have visitors, turn your snack into a real tea party by adding a few treats to the menu—perhaps some little sandwiches (minced ham, egg salad, sliced chicken), a plate of Christmas cookies (Chapter 1) and a rich fruitcake (Chapter 3). Offer dry sherry to your guests, as well as strong tea with milk or lemon.

3¾ cups flour
2 teaspoons baking powder
2 teaspoons baking soda
½ teaspoon powdered ginger
½ teaspoon salt
1 cup chopped pecans, toasted
    Note: See *How to Toast Nuts* on page 40.
⅔ cup finely chopped crystallized ginger
2 cups (packed) light brown sugar
2 eggs, room temperature, beaten
¼ cup (½ stick) butter, melted and cooled
2 cups buttermilk

COOK'S JOURNAL

Fruit for Breakfast

Tempt your family (and your houseguests) with these intriguing combinations:

❋ Apple slices sautéed with raisins and snippets of dried fig

❋ Bananas sautéed in butter and honey (or brown sugar), with a sprinkling of chopped pecans

❋ Orange sections mixed with defrosted frozen blueberries and strawberries

❋ Poached pears topped with a purée of defrosted frozen raspberries

❋ Fruit kebabs of seedless grapes and cubed ripe pineapple

SEE PHOTOGRAPH 6

Lattice Coffeecake with Orange-Almond Filling

Makes one large coffeecake

A great coffeecake to make at any time of year, because it requires no kneading and only one period of rising. It's a simple rectangle of rich, slightly sweet dough topped with a layer of luscious filling and decorated with a pretty lattice of dough strips. This is another of my favorites.

Baking pan: one 9 × 13 × 2-inch sheet cake pan

For the Orange-Almond Filling:
½ cup (one stick) butter
½ cup sugar
¾ cup orange marmalade
1 cup chopped almonds, lightly
    toasted
    Note: See How to Toast Nuts
    on page 40.

For the coffeecake:
½ cup milk
1 package (¼ ounce) dry yeast
⅔ cup butter (one stick plus
    2⅔ tablespoons), room
    temperature
⅓ cup sugar
½ teaspoon almond extract
1 teaspoon salt
4 eggs, room temperature, beaten
4 cups flour

1. Grease the baking pan.
Make the Orange-Almond Filling: Combine the butter, sugar and marmalade in a saucepan. Bring to a boil and simmer for four minutes, stirring; add the chopped almonds and set aside to cool.

2. In a small saucepan, warm the milk to 105°–115° F. on an instant-reading cooking thermometer. Use a warm spoon to stir the yeast into the milk. Set aside for a few minutes.

3. In a large bowl, cream the butter and sugar. Add the almond extract, salt and all but two tablespoons of the beaten eggs (reserve the two tablespoons). Beat until well blended. Add the yeast mixture and one cup of the flour and beat again until creamy, smooth and well blended.

4. With a wooden spoon, beat in the remaining three cups of flour, ½ cup at a time. (If you like, knead in the last ½ cup of flour.) Remove and set aside a little less than one third of the dough.

Roll out the remaining dough to a 9 × 13-inch rectangle and transfer it to the prepared pan. Spread the filling on the dough, almost to the edges.

5. Roll out the reserved dough to a ten-inch-long rectangle, ¼ inch thick, and use a sharp knife or fluted pastry wheel to cut ¼-inch-wide strips. Lay ten strips diagonally across the filling, evenly spaced, cutting to size as needed; brush with the reserved beaten egg. Repeat, laying ten strips in the other direction, to make the lattice. Brush beaten egg on these strips and on any exposed edges of the dough rectangle, too.

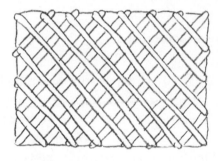

   Cover the pan with a clean dish towel and place in a draft-free place (for example, the oven with no heat turned on) to rise until almost doubled in bulk, about 1¼ hours.

6. Preheat the oven to 400° F. Bake for ten minutes at 400° F., then reduce the heat to 350° F. and bake for 25 minutes more, until golden brown. Let the coffeecake cool in the pan on a wire rack for 15 minutes, then run a knife around it and carefully turn out to finish cooling right side up on the rack.

THE CHRISTMAS PANTRY CHECKLIST

Baking Equipment

❋ Mixing bowls
❋ Measuring cups (flat rim for dry ingredients, pouring spout for liquid ingredients)
❋ Measuring spoons
❋ Mixing spoons
❋ Wire whisks (small, medium)
❋ Spatulas (metal, rubber)
❋ Fine-mesh strainers (small, large)
❋ Four-sided metal grater
❋ Pastry blender
❋ Electric mixer
❋ Food processor (optional)
❋ Rolling pin
❋ Pastry cutter (fluted, plain)
❋ Baking pans (made of shiny, heavy aluminum): round cake pans; loaf pans; cookie sheets; jelly roll pan; muffin tins (gem, medium and large); sheet cake pan; springform pan, tube pans; tart pans (with removable bottoms)
❋ Pastry brushes (½ inch wide, one inch wide)
❋ Oven thermometer, instant-reading cooking thermometer
❋ Timer
❋ Wooden toothpicks and skewers for testing doneness
❋ Wire racks

SEE PHOTOGRAPH 6

Mexican Three Kings Bread

2 packages (¼ ounce each) dry
    yeast
½ cup warm water (105° to
    115° F., tested with an
    instant-reading cooking
    thermometer)
¾ cup milk
½ cup (one stick) butter or
    margarine, room temperature
½ cup sugar
1 teaspoon salt
2 eggs, room temperature
5 cups flour
1 cup chopped walnuts
½ cup chopped red glacé cherries
½ cup chopped green glacé
    cherries
    Note: Cherries should be
    chopped in ¼-inch dice.
*Thick Vanilla Glaze (recipe
    follows)*
Red and green glacé cherries for
    decorations

Makes two braided rings

I think you'll enjoy this braided *pan dulce*—sweet bread—that is chock full of nuts and cherries, topped with a thick layer of vanilla glaze and decorated with "poinsettias" made of additional bright red and green glacé cherries. In Mexico, Three Kings Bread is traditionally served on Twelfth Night, the sixth of January.

Baking pans: two cookie sheets

1. Sprinkle the yeast over the warm water and stir with a warm spoon to dissolve the yeast; set aside for a few minutes.

2. Scald the milk and pour it into a large bowl. Stir in the butter, sugar and salt and let the mixture cool to lukewarm (110° F. on an instant-reading cooking thermometer). Add the yeast mixture and stir to blend.

3. Add the eggs and beat well. Add 2½ cups of the flour and beat to make a smooth batter. Stir in the walnuts and chopped cherries.

4. Beat in the remaining flour by hand, ½ cup at a time, to make a soft but not sticky dough. Turn the dough out onto a well-floured surface and knead until smooth and elastic, about ten minutes. Sprinkle often with flour to keep the dough from sticking.

Put the dough in a buttered bowl and turn all around to coat with butter. Cover with a clean dish towel and place in a draft-free place (for example, the oven with no heat turned on) to rise until doubled in bulk, about two hours.

5. Turn the dough out onto a flour-dusted surface and punch down. Cut in six equal pieces and let rest for ten minutes. Meanwhile, grease the cookie sheets.

Roll each piece of dough into a rope 24 inches long. Braid three ropes together and transfer to a prepared cookie sheet; shape the braid into a ring and pinch the ends together. Repeat with the other three ropes and the second cookie sheet. Cover each ring with a dish towel.

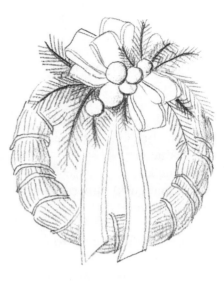

Warm the oven for a few seconds and turn off the heat. Place the rings in the oven to rise a second time, until puffy and almost doubled in bulk, about 1¾ hours.

6. Preheat the oven to 375° F. Bake for 20 minutes, until golden brown. Use a spatula to loosen the braided rings from the cookie sheets, then slide the rings onto wire racks.

While the braids are still very warm, spread Thick Vanilla Glaze (recipe follows) over them. Decorate immediately with red and green glacé cherries, as shown in the drawing at the beginning of the recipe or in photograph 6.

Thick Vanilla Glaze

Makes enough to frost both braided rings

Beat or whisk the ingredients together in the order given, until smooth. If necessary, thin the glaze with a little more liquid. If you must store the glaze, prevent a crust from forming by pressing a piece of plastic wrap directly onto the surface.

2 tablespoons butter, melted
2 teaspoons vanilla extract
6 tablespoons milk or cream
2 pinches of salt
6 cups sifted confectioners' sugar

ENTERTAINING NOTEBOOK

Morning Coffee and Afternoon Tea

When friends drop in for a Christmas shopping breather, a party planning session or just a neighborly chat, they'll welcome a pot of freshly brewed coffee or tea and a pick-me-up snack.

Set the table—kitchen, dining room or living room—with your prettiest cups, plates and napkins and serve your guests thin slices of fruitcake or pound cake, a simple tea loaf, warm coffeecake or cinnamon toast. For more substantial refreshment, add sweet butter, cream cheese, honey, jam or preserves.

SEE PHOTOGRAPH 5

Santa Lucia Buns

Makes 24 buns

2 packages (¼ ounce each) dry
    yeast
½ cup warm water (105° to
    115° F., tested with an
    instant-reading cooking
    thermometer)
⅔ cup milk
½ cup (one stick) butter, room
    temperature
½ cup sugar
⅛ teaspoon chopped saffron
1 teaspoon salt
2 teaspoons grated lemon rind
2 eggs, room temperature
5–5½ cups flour
1 cup dark raisins
Egg glaze (one egg beaten with
    one tablespoon water)
3 tablespoons butter, melted
Additional sugar for sprinkling

If you've never had sweet bread flavored with saffron, don't miss these tender, golden little S-shaped buns. Santa Lucia Buns, a traditional Swedish treat, keep well if you first wrap each one individually in plastic and then store them in plastic bags in the freezer.

Baking pan: two cookie sheets

1. Sprinkle the yeast over the warm water and stir with a warm spoon to dissolve the yeast; set aside for a few minutes.

2. Warm the milk in a small saucepan (do not boil), add the butter and stir to melt the butter. Transfer to a large bowl.

3. Add the sugar, saffron, salt, lemon rind, eggs and yeast mixture and stir well. Add three cups of the flour and beat at medium speed until smooth. Stir in the raisins.

4. Beat in by hand enough of the remaining flour, ½ cup at a time, to make a soft but not sticky dough. Turn the dough out onto a well-floured work surface and knead until smooth and elastic, about 15 minutes.

Put the dough in a buttered bowl and turn all around to coat with butter. Cover with a clean dish towel and place in a draft-free place (for example, the oven with no heat turned on) to rise until doubled in bulk, about 1½–1¾ hours.

5. Grease the cookie sheets.

Divide the dough into 24 equal pieces, shape each piece into a ball and let the balls rest for ten minutes. Roll each ball into a rope 11 inches long. Brush the opposite sides with egg glaze and roll up to form an S, as shown in the drawing. Transfer 12 buns to each greased cookie sheet, leaving two inches between buns.

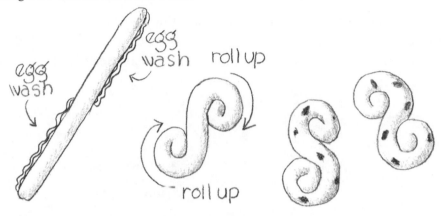

Brush the tops of the buns with melted butter, cover with dish towels and return to the draft-free place to rise a second time until doubled in bulk, about 50–60 minutes.

6. Preheat the oven to 350° F. Brush the tops of the buns with egg glaze and sprinkle with sugar. Bake for 20–23 minutes, or until golden brown. Immediately loosen the buns from the cookie sheet with a spatula and transfer to wire racks to cool.

Serve warm or cold.

OPTIONS: If you prefer, shape the buns differently, brushing egg glaze on the appropriate surfaces to "glue" the ropes in place.

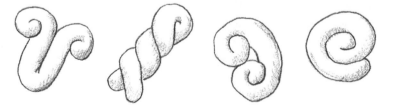

When the buns are baked and cool, you may decorate with Vanilla or Lemon Glaze (page 118) piped through a decorating bag fitted with a round tip or through a sturdy plastic bag with one corner snipped off.

COOK'S JOURNAL
Getting Organized for Baking

✳ Decide what you want to bake and read the recipes carefully. Check your pantry, refrigerator and freezer for staples and other ingredients you have on hand; make a list of ingredients you need.

✳ Make one trip to the store for everything. A last-minute dash for something you forgot is impossible when you're on a tight schedule.

✳ Clear off counters and kitchen table so you'll have plenty of space to spread out. Assemble baking pans, bowls, spoons, electric mixer and any other equipment you'll need.

✳ Do the prep work: Assemble and prepare all the ingredients required in the ingredients list. For instance, if the list calls for chopped nuts or grated lemon rind, prepare them now so they are ready when needed.

✳ Follow the recipe attentively. Don't forget to preheat the oven for at least 15 minutes.

✳ Allow time for breads, cakes and cookies to cool thoroughly before storing or freezing.

4 cups flour
½ teaspoon salt
½ cup sugar
2 packages (¼ ounce each) quick-
    rise dry yeast
½ cup dark raisins
½ cup finely chopped mixed
    candied peel
½ cup pine nuts
½ cup milk
¾ cup (1½ sticks) butter
1 teaspoon vanilla extract
3 eggs plus two egg yolks, beaten
Egg glaze (one egg beaten with
    one tablespoon water)

DECORATING MEMO
Christmas All Over the House

When you're decking the living room with boughs of holly, don't over-look the rest of the house—there are lots of spots for creative decorating ideas: front and back doors (inside and out); entryway or foyer; stairs; banis-ters, stair landing; doorframes and win-dowsills; mantel; open shelves—espe-cially hutches, sideboards and corner cabinets; kitchen; bedrooms, including the guest room.

SEE PHOTOGRAPH 6

Panettone di Natale

Makes four small loaves

Another traditional holiday bread, this one from Italy. The recipe makes four tempting little loaves, taller than they are wide, laced with bits of candied peel, raisins and the pine nuts characteristic of panettone.

Baking pans: four clean 28-ounce (one pound, 12 ounce) cans (for example, the kind that hold Italian-style peeled or crushed tomatoes)

1. In a large bowl, stir together three cups of the flour, the salt, sugar, yeast, raisins, chopped peel and pine nuts. Set aside.

2. In a saucepan, heat the milk and butter to a temperature of 125° to 130° F., measured with an instant-reading cooking thermometer. Remove from the heat and stir in the vanilla.

3. Add the hot milk mixture to the dry ingredients and stir well. Add the eggs and beat well to make a thick, sticky dough.

4. Add just enough of the remaining flour to make a dough that is soft and a little sticky. Scrape down the sides of the bowl and cover with a clean dish towel.

Turn the oven on for about 15 seconds—just long enough to take the chill off and warm it up—and turn it off again. Place the bowl of dough in the slightly warm oven and let it rise until doubled in bulk, about 1½ hours.

5. Grease the cans generously.

Punch down the dough in the bowl and put one fourth of it in each can, evening out the dough with your knuckles. Place the cans of dough on one shelf of the oven, cover the cans with the dish towel and let rise a second time until doubled in bulk, about 70 minutes.

Brush the dough with egg glaze.

6. Preheat the oven to 400° F. Bake for ten minutes at 400° F., then reduce the heat to 350° F. and continue baking for 30 minutes longer. (If the tops brown too quickly, cover loosely with foil.) Let the panettone cool in the cans on wire racks for five minutes, run a knife around each bread and then turn out to finish cooling right side up on the racks.

OPTIONS: Even though it isn't strictly traditional, you might like to drizzle the still-warm panettone with Vanilla Glaze or Lemon Glaze (page 118) and sprinkle with raisins and pine nuts, as shown in photograph 6. Serve glazed bread cold, unglazed bread warm or toasted.

QUICK TAKES
Holiday Brunch Menus

Any of the delicious buns, coffeecakes and loaves in this chapter will enhance your brunch menu, which might also include simple egg or meat dishes, fruit and coffee. Serve champagne, mulled cider or wine (page 162) or mixed drinks, and plenty of coffee, tea and hot chocolate.

Mustard-and-Maple-glazed Ham
(page 179)
Grits casserole with Cheddar cheese
Honey-Pecan Crescents (page 121)
Baking Powder Biscuits (page 153)
Butter, jam
Sliced oranges, grapefruit and
bananas, with toasted coconut

Apple fritters, *Spiced Hard Sauce*
(page 80)
Sausages or sausage patties
Corn muffins or corn bread
Butter, honey

Smoked salmon garnished with lemon
wedges and capers
Cream cheese with scallions
Cucumber Salad (page 148)
Toasted bagels and English muffins
Winter fruit compote (see page 103)

CHAPTER 6

Christmas Eve Menus and Recipes

Christmas Eve is a 24-hour flurry of excitement, the culmination of busy weeks of planning and cooking and wrapping and rushing around doing the dozens of wonderful things that make Christmas Christmas. By Christmas Eve you've done it all—the tree is trimmed, the house is decorated from top to bottom, the gifts are wrapped, the stockings are hung. Now it's time to slow down and enjoy all you have created.

Different families have different Christmas Eve traditions: Some attend church services and gather for a late supper afterward, others have a houseful of guests coming and going all day, still others snack from a simple buffet while opening the small gifts in their stockings or the large gifts under the tree. However you spend this special night, you'll want the Christmas Eve meal to be festive and delicious—and not too complicated. The menus and recipes in this chapter are simple and easily accomplished. Many of the dishes are made ahead, some make use of prepared foods and nothing requires elaborate cooking or presentation. Work Plan/ Checklists are here to help cut confusion—just follow the step-by-step schedule for the menu you choose.

Tips and Guidelines

❄ There are three complete menus in this chapter: *Festive Buffet Dinner, Super-Easy Smorgasbord for Christmas Eve Guests* and *Midnight Supper.*

❄ Each menu is followed by a Work Plan/Checklist, which will help you organize and serve the meal smoothly.

❄ Each Work Plan/Checklist is followed by the recipes that are listed in **boldface** in the menu.

In this chapter, one **boldface** recipe appears as a margin entry; several recipes mentioned in the menus are cross-referenced to other chapters in the book.

❄ Look for the items in the margins—you'll find lots of terrific ideas for holiday entertaining and decorating.

❄ If you live in an area where there is concern about the use of raw eggs, you may want to consider passing up any recipes calling for them.

Christmas Eggnog

Makes about 14 cups, 20 or more servings

6 egg yolks, room temperature
Note: To avoid harmful bacteria, be sure the eggs are not cracked before use.
1¼ cups superfine sugar
2½ cups milk
2 cups bourbon
½ cup dark rum
6 egg whites, refrigerated
2½ cups heavy cream
¼ teaspoon nutmeg

1. Beat yolks until well blended. Gradually add one cup of the sugar, beating continuously until yolks are thick and pale.

2. Add milk, bourbon and rum alternately, beating at low speed. Refrigerate the mixture for at least two hours.

3. Half an hour before serving eggnog, bring egg whites to room temperature. Beat whites until frothy, add the remaining ¼ cup of sugar and continue beating until the whites stand in firm peaks. In another bowl, whip the heavy cream.

4. Fold one cup of the yolk mixture into the whipped cream. Fold the egg whites and the whipped cream mixture into the remaining yolk mixture until partially blended. With a wire whisk, whisk the eggnog until smooth. Sprinkle with nutmeg and serve cold.

Festive Buffet Dinner

Serves eight

Christmas Eggnog
Shrimp Jambalaya with White Rice
Salad of Persimmon and Grapefruit Slices with Lime Dressing
Crisp baguettes, butter

Buttermilk-Pecan Fruitcakes (page 92)
Apple-Mince Tartlets (page 31)
Coffee, tea

Here's a perfect dinner to serve buffet-style, on the sideboard or dining room table, while family and friends finish trimming the tree, do last-minute gift-wrapping or just relax. And it's an especially appropriate menu if it is your custom to have seafood on Christmas Eve.

WORK PLAN/CHECKLIST

Two or more days before Christmas Eve
☐ Make fruitcakes and tartlet shells (do not fill yet); wrap well and freeze.

Two days before Christmas Eve
☐ Buy all liquor and food except fresh shrimp; wrap baguettes in foil and freeze.

One day before Christmas Eve

☐ Buy shrimp. If you like, make and refrigerate jambalaya (but not rice).

☐ Wash and dry watercress for salad; store in crisper. Make and refrigerate Lime Dressing.

☐ Make and refrigerate tartlet filling.

Morning and afternoon of Christmas Eve

☐ If you haven't made jambalaya, make it now.

☐ Make salad, cover with plastic and refrigerate.

☐ Take fruitcakes and tartlet shells out of freezer; fill shells and arrange on platter with fruitcakes.

☐ Set up buffet in dining room or living room; take out punch bowl, cups, serving utensils, etc.

☐ Make coffee and tea preparations.

Christmas Eve

☐ Assign eggnog-making and serving to another family member. (This delegation is important, since you will have many other things to do.)

☐ Take bread out of freezer and put right into 300° F. oven to warm; when breads are warm, remove foil and allow to crisp.

☐ Make rice for jambalaya; warm jambalaya and arrange as described in recipe.

☐ Dress salad but don't toss it.

☐ Take all food to buffet. Check menu to be sure you haven't forgotten anything.

Later in the evening

☐ Serve desserts, coffee and tea.

START WITH STORE-BOUGHT
Put-Together Parties

When you don't have time to cook, put together a simple spur-of-the-moment party from the food available at your local deli, supermarket or salad bar.

Delicatessen: Buy cold cuts and create your own overflowing platters of corned beef, roast beef, salami, tongue, ham and turkey; garnish with pickled tomatoes, olives, dill pickles. Add bowls of coleslaw and potato salad, crocks of mustard and stacks of rye and pumpernickel bread.

Supermarket: Pick up cans of creamy clam chowder, a selection of gourmet cheeses and crackers and whatever fancy fruit you like—kiwis, figs, clementine oranges, pineapple, pomegranates, Forelle pears. For dessert, choose two or three flavors of sherbet and a tin of imported butter cookies.

Salad bar: Buy the ingredients for a lettuce salad topped with interesting vegetables—for instance, snow pea pods, water chestnuts, baby corn, artichoke hearts and marinated mushrooms. Serve bottled blue cheese dressing (with additional crumbled blue cheese), cold pasta salads and crusty bread or rolls. Dessert comes from your local bakery.

SEE PHOTOGRAPH 11

Shrimp Jambalaya with White Rice

Makes eight or more servings

4 slices bacon, diced, *OR* two tablespoons vegetable oil
1 tablespoon vegetable oil
1 cup chopped onion
1 cup diced sweet green (bell) pepper
½ cup diced celery
2 cloves of garlic, minced
2 tablespoons flour
5 cups (most of two 28-ounce cans) canned tomatoes with liquid
¼ teaspoon cayenne pepper
½ teaspoon chili powder
½ teaspoon dried thyme
Fresh pepper
Tabasco sauce (optional)
48 (or more, up to 64) uncooked medium shrimp, shelled, deveined, rinsed and drained
½ cup chopped flat-leaf (Italian) parsley
Salt
6 cups cooked rice (two cups uncooked rice), hot

Jambalaya is often made and served as one big pot of food, with the rice and shrimp mixed together. In this version, the rice is made separately and arranged in a wreath around the shrimp, with the pretty red and green sauce spooned over it—a perfect Christmas presentation.

Tip: The recipe makes eight generous servings, but you may want to increase the number of shrimp by two per person and make a little more rice, to allow for second helpings.

Tip: If you're busy with other holiday activities, buy the shrimp already shelled, since shelling shrimp is a very time-consuming process.

1. In a large skillet or flameproof casserole, fry the bacon until crisp. Remove the bacon bits with a slotted spoon and drain on paper towels. Add the tablespoon of oil (or all three tablespoons of oil if you are not using bacon), the onion, green pepper and celery and sauté over medium-low heat until the onion is golden.

2. Add the garlic and stir well. Add the flour, stir again and cook for a minute or two.

3. Add the tomatoes, cayenne pepper, chili powder, thyme and a good grinding of fresh pepper. If you like peppery food, shake in a few drops (or more) of Tabasco sauce. Break the tomatoes into one-inch pieces and stir well. Simmer uncovered for 20 minutes over low heat; the flavors will blend and the sauce will thicken slightly.

4. Add the shrimp, parsley and bacon bits and bring to a simmer again. Cook until the shrimp are just done (pink all over), about three minutes. Do not overcook. Turn off the heat but continue stirring to release more heat. Add salt to taste.

At this point you may serve the hot shrimp mixture with rice or you may store it in the refrigerator overnight. (If it has been refrigerated, before serving bring it to room temperature and reheat it quickly—for just a few minutes—so the shrimp are not overcooked.)

When you serve Shrimp Jambalaya, choose a large platter with a lip or low sides to contain the sauce. First arrange a ring of hot rice around the platter, then use a slotted spoon to transfer the shrimp mixture to the center of the rice ring, mounding it neatly. Finally, spoon sauce over the rice and the mound of shrimp mixture. If there is extra sauce, serve it separately.

SEE PHOTOGRAPH 11

Salad of Persimmon and Grapefruit Slices with Lime Dressing

Makes eight servings

A refreshing and cooling accompaniment to the spicy jambalaya.

1. Pick over the watercress, discarding thick stems and yellowed leaves. Wash and drain the remaining leaves and tender sprigs and dry them on paper towels. Arrange in a layer on a serving platter. Set aside.

2 bunches watercress (or enough
   for eight servings)
4 *ripe* persimmons
4 seedless grapefruit, white or
   pink
Lime Dressing (recipe follows)

2. Cut the green stem end out of each persimmon and halve the persimmon from top to bottom. Cut each half in thin slices; each slice will be a half round.

Carefully cut the skin from each grapefruit, leaving no white pith, and halve it from top to bottom. Remove any tough white fiber from the center. Cut each half in thin slices; each slice will be a half round.

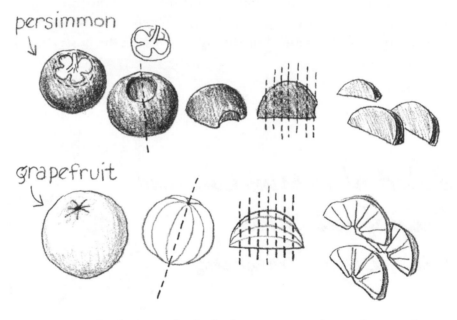

3. Arrange the fruit on the bed of watercress, alternating persimmon and grapefruit slices as shown. Serve Lime Dressing on the side.

Lime Dressing

Makes about 1½ cups

Whisk the ingredients together until sugar is dissolved and dressing is smooth and creamy.

1½ cups mayonnaise
   Note: Homemade mayonnaise is always nice to use, but commercial mayonnaise is perfectly acceptable here.
3 tablespoons fresh lime juice
1 tablespoon superfine sugar
3 pinches of cayenne pepper

Super-Easy Smorgasbord for Christmas Eve Guests

Serves 20

Mulled Wine (page 162), aquavit, beer
Gravlax with Condiments
Herring in cream sauce, herring in wine sauce
Beet Salad   **Cucumber Salad**
Holiday Potato Salad
Vegetable platter
Cheeses, assorted crackers and bread, butter
Strawberries
Brandied Prune Fruitcake (page 84)
with Spiced Hard Sauce (page 80)
Diana's Scandinavian Jam Tots (page 17)
Coffee

My sister-in law invented this party menu one year when she expected a Christmas Eve houseful of vegetarians and non-vegetarians of all ages. It's a lavish feast, super-easy to put together, since the menu is a balance of dishes made from scratch and dishes that make use of prepared foods.

At a smorgasbord, people generally eat small amounts of lots of different foods. It is not necessary to provide every guest with dinner-sized portions of every dish—not when there are so

ENTERTAINING NOTEBOOK
The Buffet Table

Aside from the actual food, here's what you need on your buffet table:

✳ Plates
✳ Forks, knives
✳ Napkins
✳ Glasses, wineglasses
✳ Pitcher of ice water
✳ Serving utensils (next to the appropriate platters)
✳ Salt and pepper shakers
✳ Butter, condiments (with serving utensils)
✳ Centerpiece, candles
✳ Warming trays (if needed)

At one end of the buffet table, or on a separate table or rolling cart, arrange everything required for dessert:

✳ Dessert plates
✳ Cake forks, spoons
✳ Cups and saucers (or mugs)
✳ Cream, milk, sugar
✳ Coffeepot, teapot

QUICK TAKES

Mix-and-Match Menus

More dinner suggestions, using recipes from *The Christmas Kitchen*, suitable for Christmas Eve or any other evening.

RED AND GREEN SUPPER

Spaghetti with *Savory Tomato-Eggplant Sauce (page 225)*

Christmas Chopped Salad (page 198)

French bread, butter

Ice cream with *Bittersweet Chocolate-Nut Sauce (page 231)*

DOWN-HOME DINNER

Red radishes with *Garlic and Herb Butter (page 240)*

Mustard-and-Maple glazed Ham (page 179)

Cucumber Salad (page 148)

Holiday Potato Salad (page 149)

Baking Powder Biscuits (page 153)

Fresh fruit, *Double Chocolate Bourbon Cookies (page 14)*

VEGETARIAN TREAT

Corn Pudding with Hot Peppers (page 182)

Black Bean Salad with Oranges, Avocado and Coriander (page 207)

Spinach and mushroom salad, *Lime Vinaigrette Sauce (page 176)*

White rice   Tortillas

Winter Salsa (page 237)

Pumpkin Pie with Walnut-Crumb Crust (page 54)

many good things to taste. Generally, the total amount of each dish should allow one small portion per person—and if a particular dish disappears quickly, there are always other things to eat.

Judging how much food to serve also depends on your particular group of guests; for instance, you may need two fruitcakes if they are dessert lovers. You must use common sense to alter the suggested amounts if you feel it is necessary. Roughly speaking, to feed 20 people generously at this smorgasbord, you will need the following:

❋ One recipe of Gravlax with Condiments

❋ Two large jars of herring in cream sauce

❋ Two large jars of herring in wine sauce

  Tip: When you put the herring in (separate) serving bowls, cut each piece of herring in half.

❋ One recipe of Beet Salad

❋ One recipe of Cucumber Salad

❋ Vegetable platter: 20 hot peppers; 20 small sour or dill pickles, halved lengthwise; 40–50 olives; six whole endives, ends trimmed, split lengthwise to make spears; 40 cherry tomatoes

❋ One recipe of Holiday Potato Salad

❋ Three or four pounds of cheese

  Tip: Choose three different cheeses—perhaps Muenster, Danish blue cheese and Gouda. Other possibilities are pepper cheese, caraway cheese, Havarti, Edam and Jarlsberg.

❋ Three or four boxes of crackers (crisp bread, rye crisp, flat bread, water biscuits, cream crackers, etc.)

❋ Three or four pounds of bread (cocktail rye rounds, Westphalian rye cut in squares, Russian pumpernickel cut in squares, Swedish limpa, etc.)

❋ ½ pound of butter

❋ 60 or more strawberries

❋ One fruitcake and four dozen or more cookies

WORK PLAN/CHECKLIST

Four or more days before the party

- ☐ Make fruitcake and cookies; wrap well and freeze.
- ☐ Make and refrigerate Spiced Hard Sauce.

Three days before the party

- ☐ Do all food shopping; buy wine, liquor and beer.
- ☐ Make and refrigerate gravlax and Honey Mustard Sauce.

One day before the party

- ☐ Make and refrigerate Beet Salad, Cucumber Salad and Holiday Potato Salad.
- ☐ Wash cherry tomatoes and prepare other vegetables; store in plastic bags in refrigerator.
- ☐ Prepare Mulled Wine; store in jars in a cool place or the refrigerator.

Morning of the party

- ☐ Take fruitcake and cookies out of freezer.
- ☐ Arrange vegetable platter and cover with plastic; refrigerate.
- ☐ Set up buffet table; get out serving platters and utensils.
- ☐ Refrigerate aquavit and beer.

Afternoon of the party

- ☐ Transfer herring from jars to serving bowls; cover and refrigerate.
- ☐ Put the three salads in serving bowls if you haven't already done so; cover and return to refrigerator.
- ☐ Scrape spices and dill off gravlax; place on serving platter or board, cover with plastic and return to refrigerator. Prepare lemon wedges and Wasabi Mayonnaise, if you are planning to serve them.
- ☐ Wash and drain strawberries; dry on paper towels; place in serving bowl; refrigerate.
- ☐ Make coffee preparations.

DECORATING MEMO

Scandinavian Style

❄ Cover the buffet table with a red cloth; wrap a white napkin around each set of utensils and tie with red yarn or red and white gingham ribbon. Put lots of red and white candles on the table and around the living and dining rooms.

❄ Collect and hang ornaments (such as snowflakes, stars and hearts) made of wood, paper, straw.

❄ Natural materials make perfect (simple) decorations: grapevine or straw wreaths; garlands of greenery; bowls of cranberries or shiny red and green apples; baskets of pinecones, nuts and seed pods.

Evening of the party
- ☐ Remove hard sauce from refrigerator; set aside to soften.
- ☐ Put cheeses on wooden board with knives.
- ☐ Put bread and crackers in baskets, butter in butter dish.
- ☐ Arrange platters and bowls of food on buffet. Check menu to be sure you haven't forgotten anything.

Last minute
- ☐ Heat Mulled Wine and either serve it from kitchen or put it in a punch bowl and serve at bar or buffet.

Later in the evening
- ☐ Serve desserts and coffee.

SEE PHOTOGRAPH 8

Gravlax with Condiments

Makes 20 or more servings

2 large bunches of fresh dill
¼ cup coarse salt
¼ cup sugar
2½ tablespoons coarsely ground black pepper
3 pounds center-cut raw salmon, halved lengthwise, all bones removed
Tip: Remove the small bones with needle-nose pliers.
Capers and chopped onions for garnish (optional)

Gravlax is a luxurious food, a fitting holiday treat. It's also somewhat adventurous—although once you've feasted on it, you'll want it again and again. The best news, however, for a busy cook, is the incredibly easy preparation.

Tip: Be sure the salmon you buy is perfectly fresh and firm. The better the salmon, the better the gravlax.

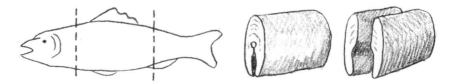

1. Pull the sprigs of dill from the main stems and discard the main stems. Divide the dill in thirds.

Stir together the salt, sugar and pepper and rub the mixture into the flesh (not the skin) of the salmon.

2. Spread one third of the dill in the center of a flat-bottomed glass or enamel baking dish or casserole with two-inch sides. Place one piece of salmon, skin side down, on the dill. Spread another third of the dill on the salmon and cover with the second piece of salmon, skin side up. Spread the remaining dill on top of the salmon and cover with two layers of plastic wrap placed directly on the salmon.

3. Place another flat-bottomed baking dish, platter, tray or board directly on top of the salmon and weight with a brick or several heavy cans. Refrigerate for 48 to 72 hours, turning over the salmon every 12 hours. Replace the top dish (or platter, tray or board) and the weight after each turn.

Before serving, scrape off the dill and other seasonings and pat the salmon dry. Transfer to a serving platter or board and slice thinly on the diagonal. If you like, garnish with capers and chopped onions, as shown in photograph 8. Surround the platter with lemon or lime wedges and small bowls of condiments (see the following OPTIONS).

OPTIONS: Serve gravlax with any or all of the following condiments.

❋ Lemon or lime wedges, placed around the platter

❋ Honey Mustard Sauce: Whisk together an eight-ounce jar of honey mustard (a prepared product made of sugar, mustard, vinegar, spices and other ingredients), an eight-ounce container of sour cream and salt to taste.

❋ Wasabi Mayonnaise: Whisk together one cup of mayonnaise, several teaspoons wasabi powder (a Japanese ingredient similar to horseradish) and salt to taste; let the flavor develop for an hour.

Christmas Touches

Mistletoe in the front and back hallways . . . at each dinner guest's place, a tiny bud vase holding one flower . . . bowls of goodies in the den, playroom, living room, kitchen—spiced nuts, sugarplums, ribbon candy . . . dozens of white votive candles in little glasses all over the house . . . a red and white patchwork quilt instead of a store-bought tree skirt . . . a folk art crèche.

SEE PHOTOGRAPH 8

Beet Salad

Makes 20 or more small servings

4 one-pound cans small whole
    beets
2 tart apples
¾ cup mayonnaise
¼ cup prepared horseradish
Salt
Fresh pepper

No smorgasbord would be complete without a beet salad and a cucumber salad (below) to round it out.

Tip: As shown in photograph 8, slices of Granny Smith apple make a handsome garnish for Beet Salad.

1. Drain the beets and cut them in ½-inch pieces. Peel the apples, cut in quarters and carefully remove the cores and seeds; cut in ½-inch pieces.

2. Mix the beets, apples, mayonnaise and horseradish together and add salt and pepper to taste. Refrigerate overnight, stirring the salad occasionally, for best flavor.

OPTIONS: To make the salad even crunchier, add 1½ cups coarsely chopped walnuts or a cup of drained cocktail onions.

SEE PHOTOGRAPH 8

Cucumber Salad

Makes 20 or more servings

9 medium cucumbers
2 medium red onions
Salt
¾ cup white wine vinegar or rice
    vinegar
3 tablespoons superfine sugar
¼ cup snipped fresh dill
Fresh pepper

1. If the cucumbers are waxed, peel them completely; if they are not waxed, peel partially, leaving alternating strips of green skin and white flesh. Cut off and discard a one-inch piece of each end of each cucumber; cut the cucumbers in thin slices. Peel the onions and cut in thin slices.

2. Put the cucumber and onion slices in a colander, sprinkle generously with salt and stir to distribute the salt evenly. Let stand 40 minutes, until limp. Rinse well to remove the salt; drain and pat dry on paper towels.

3. Stir the vinegar and sugar together in a large bowl. Add the cucumbers, onions, dill and a good grinding of fresh pepper and mix well. Cover and refrigerate until needed, stirring occasionally.

SEE PHOTOGRAPH 8

Holiday Potato Salad

Makes 20 or more servings

This is no ordinary potato salad. It's almost a meal in itself, enriched with eggs and crunchy vegetables, tossed with a generous amount of tangy mayonnaise dressing.

1. Make the dressing: Whisk together the mayonnaise, prepared mustard and vinegar; season with fresh pepper and salt to taste.

2. In a large bowl, toss all the ingredients except the dressing. Add the dressing and mix gently but thoroughly. Correct seasoning if necessary. Refrigerate, stirring occasionally, until serving time.

2 cups mayonnaise

½ cup Dijon or spicy prepared mustard

½ cup balsamic or red wine vinegar

Fresh pepper

Salt

25 small red potatoes (unpeeled), boiled, cooled completely and cut in ½-inch chunks

5 hard-cooked eggs, coarsely chopped

10 medium radishes, diced

½ cup chopped black olives
Note: Canned black olives, though bland, are convenient since they can be bought already pitted. If you prefer plump, salty Kalamata olives or any other loose-pack (not canned) black olives, remove pits before chopping.

½ cup finely chopped dill pickle

6 scallions, green parts only, sliced thin

QUICK AND EASY

Natural Ornaments

❄ Tie wheat stalks, grains, grasses and seed pods with red and gold cord.

❄ Wire tiny pinecones together, trim with holly and berries.

❄ Join broomstraws with green string or yarn to make stars, geometric shapes.

❄ Use silver cord to tie eucalyptus leaves and baby's breath in little bunches.

❄ String popcorn on heavy-duty thread and use as garland on Christmas tree.

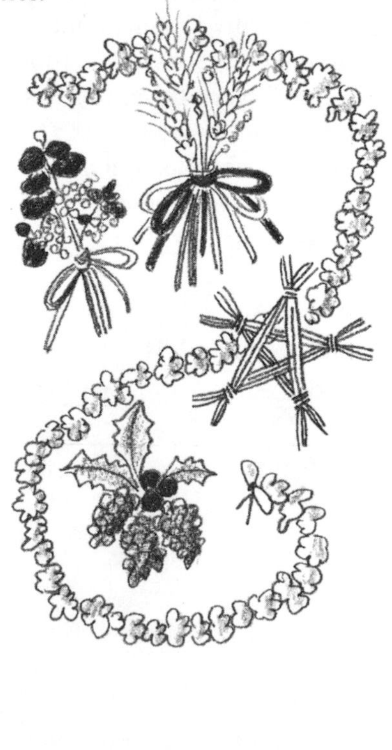

Midnight Supper

Serves eight

Creamy Carrot and Leek Soup

Cheese Biscuits, butter

Brandy-baked Apples with Nuts and Raisins

Buttery Gingerbread Santas, Chocolate Chip Shortbread or other Christmas cookies (Chapter 1)

Decaffeinated coffee

This is a cozy, comforting meal meant to bring Christmas Eve to a quiet finale, to soothe and calm the spirit before the whirl of Christmas Day activities begin. All the food is made ahead, so you'll have time, late at night, to relax and reminisce with friends and family.

WORK PLAN/CHECKLIST

Two or more days before Christmas Eve
☐ Make and freeze Christmas cookies and Cheese Biscuits.

Two days before Christmas Eve
☐ Do all food shopping.

Day before Christmas Eve
☐ Make and refrigerate soup and baked apples.

Afternoon of Christmas Eve
☐ Take cookies out of freezer and arrange on platter; cover with plastic.
☐ Set the table.
☐ Make coffee preparations.

Christmas Eve
☐ Put biscuits and baked apples in 325° F. oven to heat.
☐ Warm soup over low heat.
☐ Put hot biscuits in napkin-lined basket on the table, with butter.
☐ Serve soup from kitchen or transfer to tureen and serve at table.

Later in the evening
☐ Serve baked apples (with cream or ice cream, if you like), cookies and coffee.

COOK'S JOURNAL

Hearty Soups from Chicken Broth

With a simmering pot of hot chicken broth (canned or homemade) you can easily create a hearty soup using whatever other ingredients you happen to have.

❋ Add fresh or leftover vegetables (carrots, onions, celery, string beans, cabbage, whatever you have) and cook until tender; purée half the vegetables and stir them back into the soup. Add a little cream or milk if you like.

❋ Cook some diced potatoes, rice, barley, small pasta or canned beans (or any three of these) in the soup, with plenty of fresh, frozen or leftover vegetables.

❋ Mix one or two cans of another soup (minestrone, tomato rice, cream of chicken, split pea, etc.) into the broth and then enhance with extra vegetables, cooked pasta or rice, herbs or a dash of hot sauce. A little tomato paste helps if the flavor seems weak.

Garnish with any of these: sour cream; croutons; chopped parsley; chopped hard-cooked egg; diced tomato and avocado; sliced scallions; crumbled bacon; sliced cooked sausage; diced cooked chicken or turkey.

Serve with bread and cheese, and with fresh fruit and cookies for dessert.

5 tablespoons butter

1 pound carrots, peeled, trimmed, and sliced thin

6 leeks, white parts only, trimmed, split in half, washed carefully and sliced thin

1 medium onion, chopped

8 cups hot chicken broth

3 tablespoons flour

1½ cups light or heavy cream

Salt

2 pinches of ground nutmeg

CHRISTMAS MEMORIES FROM FRIENDS

Santa's Wing Tips

The big moment of Christmas for me, always, was when Santa Claus came to our house, bringing presents for my sister and me. He was so loud and jolly in his red suit and beard, and I believed in him completely. But one Christmas Eve, when I was about eight, and all the relatives were gathered around waiting for Santa, I suddenly noticed that only Mom was there. Where was Dad? Well, I forgot about Dad the moment Santa came into the room—until I happened to look down at Santa's feet and saw a familiar pair of wing-tipped shoes. I didn't say a word to anyone, but I guess I was getting ready to give up the idea of Santa Claus, because that's when it all began to come apart. The year after that, I stopped believing in Santa.

Creamy Carrot and Leek Soup

Makes eight or more servings

A rich, comforting soup. For the best flavor, make the soup one day ahead and reheat gently before serving.

1. Melt two tablespoons of the butter in a large heavy skillet. Add the carrots, leeks and chopped onion and sauté for a few minutes, stirring, until the onion is softened. Add two cups of the chicken broth, cover the skillet and cook over low heat for twelve minutes, or until the carrots are tender. Stir another cup of broth into the vegetables. Purée the vegetables with the broth, in a food processor or blender (in several batches, if necessary).

2. In a large heavy pot, melt the remaining three tablespoons of butter. Add the flour and cook for a minute or two. Add the remaining five cups of hot broth all at once and bring to a boil, stirring briskly with a wire whisk until the broth is smooth and slightly thickened.

3. Turn the heat down to low, add the puréed vegetables and cream and cook, stirring constantly, until well blended. Do not boil. Add salt to taste and two pinches of nutmeg.

Baking Powder Biscuits with Variations

Makes 24 biscuits

4 cups flour
1 teaspoon salt
5 teaspoons baking powder
6 tablespoons cold butter
6 tablespoons cold margarine
1⅓ cups milk or two five-ounce cans evaporated milk

The Cheese Biscuits listed in the Midnight Supper menu are a simple variation on this basic recipe for Baking Powder Biscuits (variations follow). I always allow three per person because everybody loves hot biscuits.

Tip: For fewer than eight people, you may want to cut the recipe in half—it will still work perfectly.

1. Preheat the oven to 425° F. In a large bowl or the bowl of a food processor, mix together the flour, salt and baking powder.

2. Cut the butter and margarine in small chunks and add them to the flour mixture: By hand, use a pastry blender to work the shortening into the flour until the mixture has the texture of coarse cornmeal; in a food processor, process with the chopping blade until the mixture has the texture of coarse cornmeal.

Note: If you are doing one of the variations, add the required ingredients now.

3. Add the milk a little at a time, stirring or processing just until the dough holds together in a ball. Do not add so much milk that the dough becomes sticky.

4. Turn the dough out onto a flour-dusted work surface and knead 25 strokes. Pat or roll the dough into an 8 × 11-inch rectangle about ½–¾ inch thick. Use a sharp knife to cut the dough into 28 squares, as shown. Place the biscuits on an ungreased cookie sheet, leaving ½ inch between biscuits.

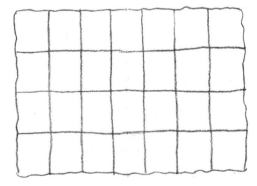

DECORATING MEMO

Christmas Centerpieces

❋ Fit florist's foam into a bright red fluted tube pan (or any attractive tube pan) and fill with sprigs of greenery or holly; add tall thin tapers to match your tablecloth; light the tapers just before dinner.

❋ For a buffet table: Buy a very small live evergreen in a pretty pot; decorate with tiny ornaments or candies, tiny candy canes, miniature toys and dollhouse furniture.

❋ For the children's table: Set up a wooden train and load the boxcars and flatcars with cookies, Christmas candy and small gifts.

5. Bake for 18–20 minutes, or until lightly browned and crisp on the outside, moist on the inside. Serve hot.

Note: Most people like their biscuits lightly browned outside and moist inside; when I have only myself to consider, I bake my biscuits for 20–25 minutes, which gives them a crisper, drier texture.

These biscuits may be frozen in a plastic bag and then defrosted as needed. Defrosted biscuits should be reheated in the oven at 325° F.

Variations

Cheese Biscuits: Add one cup grated mild or sharp Cheddar cheese to the dry ingredients and shortening before adding milk. Bake for 20–23 minutes.

Dill Biscuits: Add ¼ cup snipped fresh dill to the dry ingredients and shortening before adding milk.

Brandy-baked Apples with Nuts and Raisins

Makes eight servings

Baked apples make a nice, light finish for a simple meal. To make them fancier, pour a little heavy cream over each baked apple or top with a dollop of whipped cream or a small scoop of vanilla ice cream.

8 Rome Beauty apples
  Note: Jonathans or Cortlands
  may be used, too.
½ cup chopped walnuts or
  pecans
½ cup dark and/or light raisins
¼ teaspoon cinnamon
1 tablespoon (packed) light or
  dark brown sugar
1 cup sugar
1 cup brandy
1 cup water
2 tablespoons butter
Pinch of salt

1. Preheat the oven to 350° F.

Starting at the stem ends, peel the apples halfway down. (If the apples are waxed or otherwise coated, peel them all the way down.) Core each apple, making a hole about one inch wide and leaving a ½-inch base. Place the apples in a baking dish or baking pan.

2. Stir together the nuts, raisins, cinnamon and brown sugar. Pack about one eighth of the mixture into each apple.

3. In a small saucepan, heat the remaining ingredients and stir to dissolve the sugar and melt the butter. Simmer for ten minutes to make a thin syrup. Pour the syrup over the apples.

4. Bake uncovered for 45–60 minutes, basting often, until the apples are tender but still holding their shapes.

Refrigerate in the same pan until needed, then reheat in a 325° F. oven, basting a few times, and serve warm.

CHAPTER 7

Christmas Day Menus and Recipes

A Christmas memory: Christmas morning at last! Outside, the snow looks shadowy and blue in the faint light of this early hour. Inside our house, when my brother and I creep into the dim living room, the decorated tree looks almost as if it's waiting for us, so quiet and expectant is the scene. We do not rush wildly to open our pile of presents; rather, we approach incredulously, astonished as we are every year that this Christmas magic could happen overnight, while we slept. Then something—the furnace switching on, my parents getting up—rouses us from our trance, and Johnny and I pounce.

In my experience, most children are too excited to eat on Christmas morning and most adults are not. So, when the stockings have been turned upside down and shaken for the last time and the gifts have been exclaimed over, toast the holiday with champagne and serve a luxurious brunch to set the mood for the social events of the day.

Later on, perhaps you'll be welcoming friends and relatives to a lavish traditional Christmas dinner of roast turkey or crown roast of pork and all the fixings, right down to the plum pudding and hard sauce. Or maybe this is your year to have the whole neighborhood in for a Christmas open house—a feast of glazed ham, hearty baked beans, corn pudding and other good things to give your guests energy for caroling or sledding or just chatting companionably for the rest of Christmas Day.

Tips and Guidelines

❊ There are three complete menus in this chapter: *Christmas Morning Brunch*, *Christmas Dinner* and *Yuletide Open House*.

❊ Each menu is followed by a Work Plan/Checklist to help you organize and serve the meal efficiently and easily.

❊ Each Work Plan/Checklist is followed by the recipes that are **boldface** in the menu. In this chapter, three of the **boldface** recipes appear as margin entries; several recipes mentioned in the menus are cross-referenced to other chapters in the book.

❊ Other margin entries offer tips and suggestions for holiday entertaining and decorating.

DECORATING MEMO

More Christmas Centerpieces

❋ Fit florist's foam in a brightly printed Christmas cookie tin; fill the tin with baby's breath, dried flowers and sprigs of holly or greens.

❋ Loosely wrap an evergreen wreath with gold or silver ribbon; lay it flat and fill the center with chubby red candles of different heights. Alternative: Place a low bowl in the center and fill with gold or silver balls.

❋ Spray-paint a flat basket bright red; fill with little boxes wrapped in a variety of pretty gift wraps, tied with matching ribbon bows.

❋ Buy a cornucopia basket; fill with lady apples, small tangerines and nuts (in shells); nestle the basket in a bed of greenery, with fruit and nuts flowing out.

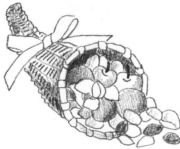

Christmas Morning Brunch

Serves eight

Champagne or other sparkling white wine

Sliced Oranges in Light Lemon Syrup

Oven-baked French Toast

Ham, bacon or sausage

Cranberry Spiral Bread, Honey-Pecan Crescents or other sweet breads or coffeecakes (Chapter 5)

Coffee, tea, milk

After expending so much energy opening your gifts on Christmas morning, a little nourishment is welcome. With this menu, the hearty eaters in the family can have a filling meal of fruit, French toast and ham (or bacon or sausage) while the light eaters enjoy warm coffeecake and hot coffee or tea.

WORK PLAN/CHECKLIST

Two or more days before Christmas
- [ ] Buy all food and wine.
- [ ] Slice and freeze bread for French toast.
- [ ] Make coffeecakes or sweet breads, wrap snugly in plastic and freeze.

Christmas Eve (morning or afternoon)
- [ ] Make, cover and refrigerate Sliced Oranges in Light Lemon Syrup.
- [ ] Cook sausage, bacon or ham; allow to cool, then wrap snugly in plastic and refrigerate.

Christmas Eve (evening)
- [ ] Take out frozen coffeecakes, sweet breads and sliced bread to defrost.
- [ ] Make coffee and tea preparations.
- [ ] Put champagne in refrigerator.

Christmas morning
- [ ] Prepare and bake Oven-baked French Toast.
- [ ] Put coffeecakes, sweet breads and foil-covered precooked meat in 325° F. oven to warm.
- [ ] Take prepared oranges out of refrigerator to come to room temperature, if you wish.
- [ ] Make coffee and tea.
- [ ] Transfer meat to serving platter; transfer warm coffeecakes to platters or napkin-lined baskets.
- [ ] Take all food to dining table. Check menu to be sure you haven't forgotten anything.
- [ ] Pop the champagne cork. Merry Christmas!

Christmas Touches

The chandelier decked lavishly with holly and red ribbons . . . red-and-white-checked napkins tied with green ribbon or green-and-white-checked napkins tied with red ribbon—or both . . . at every place setting, a small ribbon-tied basket filled with grapes, nuts, chocolates . . . evergreen wreaths trimmed in Victorian pink and gold, with satin bows and lacy ornaments . . . thin mints and glacé fruits after dinner.

SEE PHOTOGRAPH 9

Sliced Oranges in Light Lemon Syrup

9 navel oranges
Grated rind of two medium
lemons
Juice of one medium lemon
3 tablespoons sugar

Makes eight servings

Something magic happens to sliced oranges when they are infused with lemon flavor. This dish is one of my husband's favorites.

1. With a sharp knife, carefully peel eight oranges, removing all the white pith. Slice the oranges thinly, in cross sections.

2. Squeeze the juice of the remaining orange into a serving bowl. Add the lemon rind, lemon juice and sugar and stir to blend. Add the orange slices and mix gently with your hand, being careful not to break the slices. Cover and refrigerate all day or overnight, mixing two or three more times.

Serve chilled or at room temperature.

OPTIONS: Just before serving, add some sliced bananas, sliced strawberries and/or sliced kiwi fruit to the oranges. Sprinkle with coconut that you have toasted on an ungreased cookie sheet in a 350° F. oven for 5–10 minutes, until lightly browned and crisp.

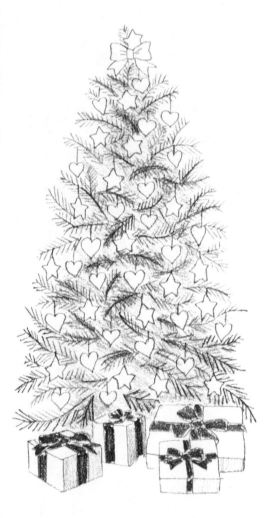

8. Clockwise from top right: **Holiday Potato Salad;** in the blue bowl, **Wasabi Mayonnaise;** in the pink bowl, **Honey Mustard Sauce; Gravlax; Cucumber Salad; Beet Salad**

9. On the left, **Oven-baked French Toast;** on the right, **Sliced Oranges in Light Lemon Syrup;** above, bowls of toppings, including **Old-fashioned Lemon Curd,** strawberry jam and fruit yogurt

10. Clockwise from the top: **Nora's Plum Pudding; Cranberry Ketchup; Wild Rice with Mushrooms and Onions; Crown Roast of Pork with Savory Fruit Stuffing,** surrounded by winter vegetables (**Individual Packets of Winter Vegetables**)

11. Clockwise from top right: **Buttermilk-Pecan Fruitcakes; Apple-Mince Tartlets; Lime Dressing; Salad of Persimmon and Grapefruit Slices; Shrimp Jambalaya with White Rice**

12. Clockwise from top left: **Hummus** with wedges of pita bread; **Couscous with Raisins and Walnuts**; **Cinnamon Stars**; **Spicy Yogurt Chicken with Vegetables**

13. In the jars on the plaid tin box, left to right: **Winter Salsa; Fresh Orange Relish; Apple-Onion Chutney; Cranberry Ketchup**

In the lightning jar, **Marinated Onion and Red Pepper Relish;** in the front bowl, **Fresh Orange Relish;** in the back bowl, **Winter Salsa;** in the brown crock, **Spiced Nuts**

Suggestions for creating the gift wraps seen here (and many other gift wraps) are found in the margins of Chapters 1, 3, 4, 5 and 10.

14. Clockwise from top right: **Individual Baked Pumpkin Puddings; Welsh Rabbit; Christmas Chopped Salad;** basket of toasted Italian bread

SEE PHOTOGRAPH 9

Oven-baked French Toast

Makes eight or more servings

If you like bread pudding, you'll love this French toast. It's amazingly easy to make, yet it's special enough for Christmas brunch.

Note: You will need a three-quart baking dish.

1. In a large bowl, beat the eggs and sugar for about a minute, until creamy and thick. Add the milk, butter, vanilla, nutmeg and salt and beat well. Stir in the currants.

2. Add the slices of bread a few at a time, pressing them down and turning them so they absorb the custard mixture. Let stand for 20 minutes, stirring carefully three or four times.

3. Preheat the oven to 350° F.; butter a shallow three-quart baking dish.

Carefully arrange the soaked bread slices in the dish, overlapping them as shown in the drawing. Pour the excess custard and currants evenly over the bread.

4. Bake for about 50 minutes, until custard is set and bread is pale gold. Serve warm. If you like, sprinkle with confectioners' sugar sifted through a fine strainer.

OPTIONS: For a more elaborate presentation, serve the French toast with small bowls of a variety of toppings—apple butter, Winter Pear Butter (page 233), all-fruit preserves, fruit yogurt, sour cream mixed with a little vanilla extract and sugar, Old-fashioned Lemon Curd (page 230).

4 eggs

½–¾ cup sugar
> *Note:* Use ½ cup sugar if you are serving syrup or preserves with the French toast (see OPTIONS at the end of the recipe); use ¾ cup sugar if you prefer a sweeter dish.

4 cups milk

¼ cup (½ stick) butter, melted and cooled

2 teaspoons vanilla extract

¼ teaspoon ground nutmeg

Pinch of salt

1 cup currants

16 slices French bread with crusts, each slice 2½ inches in diameter and about ½ inch thick

Confectioners' sugar (optional)

Mulled Wine or Mulled Cider

Makes about eleven cups, 15–20 servings

You may successfully double this recipe to make 30–40 servings, if necessary.

¾ cup water
¾ cup sugar
¾ cup dark raisins
4 sticks of cinnamon, each about 2½ inches long
8 whole cloves
8 whole allspice
Zest from one lemon and one orange, removed in long strips with a vegetable peeler
1 lemon, sliced thin, seeds removed
3 bottles (standard 750 ml) dry red wine *OR* 2½ quarts apple cider

Combine all ingredients except the wine or cider in a four-quart stainless-steel or enamel pot, bring to a boil and simmer, covered, for five minutes. Turn off the heat, add the wine or cider and stir well.

To serve immediately, heat gently (do not boil) and transfer to a punch bowl. To serve the next day, store overnight in a cool place or in the refrigerator. Before serving, heat gently and transfer to a punch bowl.

Christmas Dinner

Serves ten

Mulled Cider and Mulled Wine
Savory Toasts (page 166)
Crudités with **Browned Shallot Mayonnaise**

Roast Turkey, Sausage Stuffing and **Cream Gravy**
OR
Crown Roast of Pork with Savory Fruit Stuffing

Wild Rice with Mushrooms and Onions
Browned Brussels Sprouts (page 223)
Individual Packets of Winter Vegetables
Cranberry Ketchup (page 235)
Hot rolls and butter
Nora's Plum Pudding, Vanilla Hard Sauce (page 80)
Lady apples, clementines, grapes   Mixed nuts
Christmas cookies (Chapter 1)
Coffee, tea

Christmas dinner should be a real celebration, the fulfillment of all the anticipation leading up to it. The elaborate menu suggested here certainly fills the bill, but remember: Don't attempt it all alone. This menu depends on other people making some of the dishes or helping you in the kitchen. That's the spirit of traditional Christmas dinners!

The work plan that follows is based on the assumption that one guest will make the Mulled Cider and Mulled Wine, another will bring the crudités (washed, dried and cut in attractive pieces) and Browned Shallot Mayonnaise, a third will cook and bring the Individual Packets of Winter Vegetables (which you will warm before serving) and another will bake lots of Christmas cookies.

If you decide you must make Christmas dinner alone, simplify it! Eliminate the mulled wine and cider and just serve a good wine and plain apple cider. Serve one appetizer instead of two and drop one of the two vegetable dishes. The plum puddings can be made weeks ahead, but feel free to substitute something simpler, such as fruitcake (Chapter 3) or cookies which you can make ahead and freeze.

COOK'S JOURNAL
Crudités

Beautifully arranged raw and lightly cooked vegetables, accompanied by delicious dips, are wonderful appetizers. Design a platter of any of the following: spears of endive; leaves of radicchio; sliced fennel; slender green beans; snow pea pods; parboiled baby carrots; slices of zucchini; cornichons; Tuscan peppers; artichoke hearts; Niçoise and other fresh olives (not from jars or cans); sliced mushrooms; halved icicle radishes or water chestnuts; slices of peeled jicama or Jerusalem artichokes; baby beets; wedges of cooked sweet potato; tiny boiled red potatoes.

WORK PLAN/CHECKLIST

Two to four weeks before Christmas
- ☐ Make plum puddings.
- ☐ Check the guidelines in Entertaining Notebook, page 169.

One week before Christmas
- ☐ Make savory butters for Savory Toasts; shape in logs and freeze.
- ☐ Make and refrigerate Cranberry Ketchup.
- ☐ Make and refrigerate Vanilla Hard Sauce.
- ☐ Shop for nonperishable food; buy rolls and freeze.
- ☐ If you are planning to roast a frozen turkey, buy now and store in freezer until three days before Christmas.

Three days before Christmas
- ☐ Transfer frozen turkey from freezer to refrigerator to begin defrosting, following the guidelines given in the recipe on page 165.

Browned Shallot Mayonnaise

Makes about 1½ cups

Serve this tasty mayonnaise as a dip for crudités; use it instead of butter when you're making canapés on crackers and small rounds of bread; spread it generously on rolls for sandwiches.

½ cup minced shallots
3 tablespoons olive oil
1 teaspoon prepared Dijon mustard
½ teaspoon sugar
1 teaspoon balsamic vinegar
1¼ cups mayonnaise
Salt
Fresh pepper

1. Brown the shallots in the olive oil in a skillet over low heat. When the shallots are dark brown but not burned, turn off the heat and stir in the mustard, sugar and vinegar.

2. Put this mixture and the mayonnaise in a bowl and whisk until blended. Add salt to taste and a good grinding of pepper. Refrigerate overnight for best flavor.

Two days before Christmas
☐ Buy perishable food.
☐ Toast bread for Savory Toasts; freeze in plastic bag.

Christmas Eve (morning and afternoon)
☐ Prepare and refrigerate Cream Gravy.
☐ Prepare raw Brussels sprouts; refrigerate in plastic bag.
☐ Chop mushrooms and onions for wild rice; chop onions and celery for stuffing. Refrigerate in plastic bags.
☐ Wash, dry and arrange fruit in bowls; put mixed nuts in bowls.
☐ If possible, set the dining table.
☐ Take out serving platters, utensils, punch bowl, wine glasses, candles, etc.
☐ Make coffee and tea preparations.

Christmas Eve (evening)
☐ Take rolls, toasts and savory butters out of freezer; store butters in refrigerator.

Christmas morning
☐ Prepare turkey and put it in oven to roast; make Sausage Stuffing and refrigerate until last hour of turkey-roasting.
☐ Make Savory Fruit Stuffing while crown roast comes to room temperature. Stuff and roast according to recipe on page 169.

Two hours before dinner
☐ Make Wild Rice with Mushrooms and Onions.
☐ Steam plum puddings.
☐ Arrange platters of cookies and set aside.

One hour before dinner
☐ Serve appetizers, Mulled Wine and Mulled Cider.
☐ Make Browned Brussels Sprouts; keep warm.

Half an hour before dinner
- ☐ Take turkey or crown roast out of oven to rest; make pan gravy or heat Cream Gravy.
- ☐ Warm individual packets of vegetables.
- ☐ Warm rolls in oven.

Last minute
- ☐ Unmold plum puddings and set aside.
- ☐ Transfer cooked food to serving bowls and platters and take all food to table. Put rolls into napkin-lined baskets and take to table. Check menu to be sure you haven't forgotten anything.

Later in the afternoon or evening
- ☐ Serve desserts, coffee and tea.

Roast Turkey

Makes ten generous servings plus leftovers

If you've made roast turkey dozens of times, you know there are a few important do's and don'ts for preparing a beautiful and wholesome bird. Here are the basic guidelines:

❋ Fresh turkeys must be kept refrigerated at all times and cooked within one or two days of purchase.

❋ Never, never thaw a frozen turkey at room temperature. You *must* allow a couple of days for defrosting the bird in the refrigerator (24 hours per five pounds of turkey) or you must be prepared to dance attendance on a turkey defrosted by the cold water method: Leave turkey in original wrapping; place wrapped turkey in a large pot or in the sink; cover completely with cold water; change water every 30 minutes. Allow 30 minutes thawing time per pound of whole frozen turkey when you employ the cold water method.

❋ Never roast a turkey partially on one day and finish the roasting on the next day. Cook it all at once.

THE CHRISTMAS PANTRY CHECKLIST

Stocking the Bar

This is simply a reminder list of basics; use common sense and experience in deciding what you actually require.

❋ Scotch
❋ Rye
❋ Bourbon
❋ Vodka
❋ Gin
❋ Wines, champagne
❋ Beer, ale
❋ Sherry (dry, sweet)
❋ Rum (light, dark)
❋ Tequila
❋ Brandy, cognac
❋ Vermouth (dry, sweet)
❋ Liqueurs

❋ Olives, onions
❋ Lemons, limes
❋ Ice, ice bucket, tongs
❋ Water pitcher
❋ Seltzer, mineral water
❋ Tonic, ginger ale, cola
❋ Knife, corkscrew, bottle opener
❋ Assorted glasses
❋ Stirrers

COOK'S JOURNAL

Savory Toast

Keep two or three plastic-wrapped logs of different *Savory Butters (page 240)* in the freezer and you have almost instant hors d'oeuvres: Slice French or Italian bread at least ½-inch thick and toast to a light brown. Spread with any savory butter (and a sprinkling of grated Parmesan cheese, if you like) and bake in a 325° F. oven for 5–7 minutes, or until medium brown. Serve hot.

12-pound fresh turkey or
    defrosted frozen turkey,
    unstuffed
Butter or margarine for basting
    (optional)

❋ Cook your turkey at 325° F., or even 350° F., never lower. Use a meat thermometer, inserted in the meatiest part of the thigh (but not in contact with bone); the bird is done when the meat thermometer reads 180° F., the juices run clear and the drumsticks can be moved up and down freely.

❋ An unstuffed turkey cooks faster than a stuffed one. At 325° F., an unstuffed turkey weighing 8–12 pounds will take 3–4 hours to roast; the same bird stuffed will take 3½–4½ hours. An unstuffed turkey weighing 12–16 pounds will take 3½–4½ hours; a stuffed one, 4–5 hours. A 16–20-pound unstuffed turkey will take 4–5 hours, a stuffed one, 4½–5½ hours. These are estimates, so rely on your meat thermometer and the other indicators mentioned above to judge when the turkey is properly cooked.

❋ Leftovers and gravy should be refrigerated promptly.

Stuffing also requires special handling because of its potential for breeding bacteria. I prefer to avoid the problem completely by cooking my stuffing separately in a well-greased baking pan, during the last hour of turkey-roasting. However, if you feel differently, follow these rules:

❋ Prepare stuffing separately and keep it refrigerated.

❋ Stuff a turkey *just before* roasting and never freeze stuffing in a cooked or raw bird.

❋ As soon as the stuffed turkey is finished roasting, remove every bit of stuffing and serve separately.

❋ Leftover stuffing should be wrapped well and refrigerated promptly. Next day, reheat stuffing in a buttered baking pan.

Preheat the oven to 325° F. Remove neck, giblets and any fat from the cavity of the turkey. Wipe the turkey with a damp cloth. Place the turkey on a rack in a shallow roasting pan and insert a meat thermometer in the meatiest part of a thigh (be sure the thermometer is not touching bone). Roast for about 3½ hours, or until the thermometer reads 180° F., juices run clear and the drumsticks move easily. If you like, baste occasionally with melted butter or margarine.

If the turkey is very brown at the end of three hours, make a loose tent of foil to cover the breast and prevent it from browning further.

Sausage Stuffing

Makes ten servings plus leftovers

1. In a large skillet, brown the sausage meat over low heat, breaking it up into small pieces. Remove the sausage with a slotted spoon and drain on paper towels. Discard most of the fat.

2. Add the butter to the skillet and melt over low heat, stirring and scraping up the bits left from browning the sausage. Add the celery and onions and cook until the onions are soft. Stir in the herbs, pepper and parsley.

3. Transfer the onion mixture and the sausage and any optional ingredients you've chosen to a large bowl and mix well. Add the beaten eggs and mix again. Add the bread cubes and toss well.

4. Pack the stuffing lightly into one or two well-greased shallow casseroles and bake at 325° F. for an hour.

Note: You may bake the stuffing in the oven with the turkey, during the last hour of roasting.

1½ pounds sweet or spicy pork sausage meat (or a combination of both)
Note: If you must buy sausages instead of sausage meat, remove and discard the casings.
¾ cup (1½ sticks) butter
1½ cups diced celery
1½ cups diced onions
¾ teaspoon each dried thyme, sage and marjoram, and fresh pepper
6 tablespoons chopped flat-leaf (Italian) parsley
Choose one of the following combinations (optional):
❋ 3 cups coarsely chopped pecans; three cups raisins
❋ 2–2¼ pounds mushrooms, trimmed, sliced and sautéed until their liquid evaporates; three cups coarsely chopped water chestnuts
❋ 1½ pounds cooked chestnuts, coarsely chopped; three cups dried apricots, cut in pieces
3 eggs, beaten
12 cups crustless white bread cubes

Cream Gravy

Makes about four cups

½ cup (one stick) butter
½ teaspoon dried sage
¼ teaspoon dried thyme
½ cup flour
4 cups hot chicken or turkey
  broth
  Note: If you like, make rich
  broth by simmering the
  turkey giblets and neck in
  two cups chicken broth and
  two cups water for an hour.
  Keep the pot covered for all
  but the last 15 minutes.
  Strain and season well.
1 cup heavy cream or sour cream
Salt and pepper to taste

Gravy made with pan drippings is delicious—but frustrating to manage at the last minute, when the kitchen is full of people and pans and platters. Cream gravy is an alternative to pan gravy, made with turkey or chicken broth and no pan drippings at all. It can be made a day ahead and refrigerated until needed.

1. Melt the butter in a heavy saucepan. Powder the herbs between your palms or fingers, sprinkle over the butter and stir for a minute. Blend in the flour and cook, stirring, for another minute or two.

2. Add the hot broth all at once and stir briskly over moderate heat until thick and smooth. Turn off the heat and blend in the cream; add salt and pepper to taste. You may store this overnight in the refrigerator; reheat gently—do not boil.

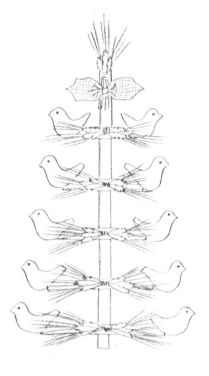

SEE PHOTOGRAPH 10

Crown Roast of Pork with Savory Fruit Stuffing

Makes ten or more servings

This roast provides two chops per person, although not everyone may be able to eat that much. When the butcher prepares the crown roast for you, be sure the ends of the ribs are properly stripped; have the butcher grind the rib trimmings for you to freeze and use at another time. Paper frills or kumquats are the traditional rib end decorations.

1. Let the roast stand out of the refrigerator for 1½ hours, to come to room temperature before cooking. Preheat the oven to 325° F. Place the roast in a shallow roasting pan (no rack) and insert a meat thermometer in the center of the meat between two ribs—don't let it touch a bone. Wrap each rib end with a piece of foil to keep it from charring and breaking off.

2. Roast uncovered for 2½ hours. Take the crown roast out of the oven, pack stuffing loosely into the center and cover the stuffing with foil. (Put remaining stuffing in a buttered baking dish, as described in the Savory Fruit Stuffing recipe.) Return the stuffed crown roast to the oven along with the extra dish of stuffing, and roast for another 30 minutes. Take the foil off the stuffing and the rib ends and continue roasting for 30 more minutes, or until the meat thermometer registers 170° F.

Leave the baking dish of stuffing in the oven for another 30 minutes (total cooking time 1½ hours). (It's a good idea to set your kitchen timer for this additional 30 minutes.)

Transfer the roast to a serving platter to rest for 30 minutes. Slip paper frills or kumquats over the rib ends, carve the roast and serve immediately with stuffing from the center. Serve second helpings with stuffing from the baking dish.

OPTIONS: The pan drippings make a delicious gravy, especially if the butcher has done a good job of removing the fat from the roast. To make the gravy, skim any fat from the pan and dilute the drippings with a little water. Heat the gravy before transferring it to a sauce boat.

1 crown roast of pork, 20 ribs (about 8–9 pounds)
Savory Fruit Stuffing (recipe follows)
Note: If you are not following the Work Plan on page 163, you might like to make the stuffing while the pork is roasting.

ENTERTAINING NOTEBOOK
Planning Christmas Dinner

❋ Assemble the guest list and work out a seating arrangement. Will you need one table or two? Do you have enough dining chairs? Enough china, flatware and glasses?

❋ Allow plenty of time before Christmas Day to take stock of your tablecloths (or place mats) and cloth napkins and to wash or iron them or borrow extras if necessary.

❋ Plan the menu, making sure you have all the pots, roasting pans, casseroles required in the recipes. Borrow any equipment you need.

❋ Look over your serving platters, serving bowls, trays, pitchers, punch bowl and cups, too. Double-check that you have the right ones for your menu and that they are clean and polished.

SEE PHOTOGRAPH 10

Savory Fruit Stuffing

Makes about ten cups

¼ cup vegetable oil
1 cup diced celery
1 cup chopped onions
4 medium-size sweet apples,
   peeled, cut in half, cored very
   carefully and chopped in
   ½-inch pieces
4 medium-size ripe pears, peeled,
   cut in half, cored very
   carefully and chopped in
   ½-inch pieces
¾ cup light raisins
½ cup chopped pecans
5 cups coarse bread crumbs made
   from two-day-old white
   bread
¼ cup prepared horseradish
1 cup applejack
½ cup (one stick) butter, melted
1 teaspoon dried sage
Salt
Fresh pepper

1. Heat the vegetable oil in a skillet over medium heat and sauté the celery and onions until the onions are golden. Transfer to a large bowl.

2. Add remaining ingredients (including salt and pepper to taste) and toss well.

3. Stuff about six cups of the mixture loosely into the crown roast of pork, as described on page 169. Pack the rest of the stuffing loosely in a well-buttered baking dish and bake uncovered for 1½ hours.

SEE PHOTOGRAPH 10

Wild Rice with Mushrooms and Onions

Makes ten or more servings

Wild rice is real party fare. Unfortunately, it's all too common to overcook wild rice and end up with mush. In order to prevent this, keep your eye on the rice while it's simmering and taste often—you want it to be just chewy, with a nutty flavor. The cooking times given for wild rice in this recipe are basic guidelines; you will have to be the final judge.

1. Melt the butter in a large heavy saucepan, add the onions and sauté until golden. Add the mushrooms and sauté just until softened.

2. Rinse the wild rice in a strainer under cold running water, stirring it around in the strainer for a minute or two. Add the rice, water, salt and a few grindings of pepper to the onions and mushrooms in the saucepan. Stir well, cover and bring to a boil over medium heat.

3. When the water boils, uncover the saucepan and lower the heat. Simmer 45–60 minutes, or until the rice is tender but chewy; keep a close watch on the rice to be sure it does not get mushy. Drain off any excess liquid. Fluff with a large fork and correct the seasoning if necessary.

For an even richer taste, add another two tablespoons of butter to the finished dish and stir to melt.

6 tablespoons (¾ stick) butter
1½ cups chopped onions
1 pound fresh mushrooms, trimmed, cleaned and sliced thin
2½ cups wild rice
6 cups water
2 teaspoons salt
Fresh pepper

CHRISTMAS MEMORIES FROM FRIENDS

The Best Gift

It wasn't a bicycle, a doll or a puppy. It was, in fact, a pair of presents, both homemade, and I received them on the same Christmas Day. The first was my heart's desire: a beautiful ballet costume with layers of crisp net skirt touched with silver glitter that sparkled as I twirled. My mother made it for me.

The second was a gift for my brother and me to share—a child-size "store" built of wood, with shelves full of small boxes and cans and packages to buy and sell. It was painted glossy white and across the top, hand-lettered in red and green, was a sign: LORRIE/STORE/JOHNNY. My father made it for us.

Now, *that* was a memorable Christmas.

SEE PHOTOGRAPH 10

Individual Packets of Winter Vegetables

Makes ten or more servings

Vegetables prepared this way come out moist and tasty, and it's fun to unwrap your own little Christmas package of carrots, parsnips, turnips and sweet potatoes. (Kids may even eat their vegetables.)

You can be inventive with this presentation, too, by tucking other things into each packet—some walnuts or cooked chestnuts, a few raisins, a short piece of scallion, half a small onion, and so on.

1. Preheat the oven to 350 °F.

Cut each slice of turnip in half to make a total of ten half-moons. Parboil the pieces of turnip: Bring a saucepan of water to a boil, add the turnips and boil for 5–7 minutes, or until a knife point pierces the turnip almost easily. Drain off the hot water and run the turnips under cold water for a minute or two. Set aside.

2. Cut the carrots on the diagonal, in ½-inch slices. Trim off and discard the narrow end of each parsnip; cut the remaining piece in half lengthwise. Cut each sweet potato in quarters, as shown in the drawing.

5 slices peeled yellow turnip (rutabaga)
Note: Peel one large yellow turnip and cut in ¾-inch slices. Use only the five center slices.

5 medium carrots, trimmed and peeled

5 medium parsnips, trimmed and peeled

2½ medium sweet potatoes, trimmed and peeled

6 tablespoons (¾ stick) butter, melted

Salt

Fresh pepper

⅔ cup finely chopped flat-leaf (Italian) parsley

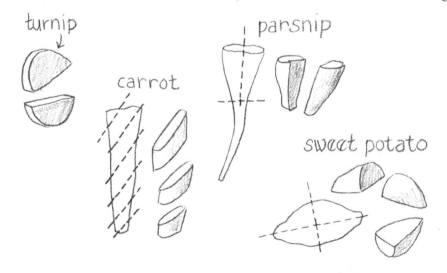

turnip

carrot

parsnip

sweet potato

3. To make each packet, tear off a 12 × 12-inch piece of heavy-duty aluminum foil. In the center of the foil arrange a half-moon of turnip, one sweet potato quarter and one piece of parsnip. Brush with melted butter and sprinkle with salt, pepper and parsley. Top with several slices of carrot, brush carrots with butter and sprinkle with salt, pepper and parsley. Add any extras now, too (see suggestions at the beginning of the recipe).

Bring the ends of the foil up and fold together several times to cover the vegetables; fold the sides twice and tuck them under to enclose the vegetables in a snug packet.

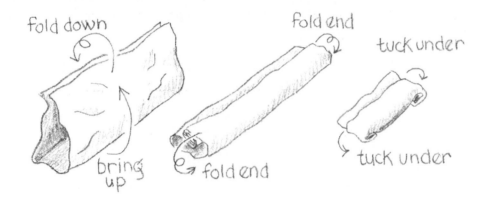

Repeat to make ten packets. (It's easiest to make several packets at a time, assembly-line fashion.)

4. Place the packets flat in a shallow pan, in one or two layers, and bake for 80 minutes, or until the vegetables are tender. You'll have to open one packet to check (watch out for the burst of steam); be sure to rewrap snugly if the vegetables need more cooking.

Serve one packet to each guest or, if you don't like the aluminum foil presentation, discard the foil and arrange the cooked vegetables on a serving platter or on the platter with the turkey or the crown roast, as shown in photograph 10.

DECORATING MEMO
More Decorations Using Candles

❋ Use bits of florist's or adhesive clay to secure slender four-inch candles to pretty little dishes; fill each dish with miniature Christmas balls.

❋ Put red or green candles in hurricane lamps and surround the bases of the lamps with holly.

❋ Core green-skinned apples, insert red or white tapers, tie with pretty ribbon or gold cord; group several apples on sideboard or mantel.

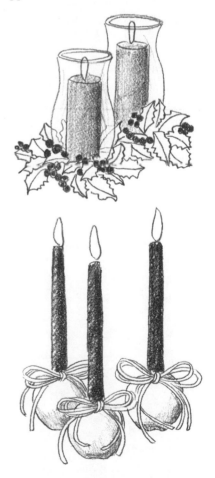

SEE PHOTOGRAPH 10

Nora's Plum Puddings

Makes two puddings, 12 servings each

1 cup cake flour

1 teaspoon salt

½ teaspoon cinnamon

½ teaspoon ground nutmeg

½ pound suet, shredded in food processor with metal chopping blade

½ pound white bread made into crumbs, about 3½ cups crumbs

Grated rind and juice of one lemon

1 medium carrot, peeled and grated (about ½ cup)

1¾ cups (packed) dark brown sugar

1½ cups (½ pound) dark raisins

1½ cups (½ pound) light raisins

2 cups (½ pound) currants

¾ cup (¼ pound) diced mixed peel

½ cup (¼ pound) pitted prunes, chopped

½ cup dark rum

3 eggs, beaten

2 tablespoons unsulfured molasses

½ pint Guinness stout

Hard sauce (see page 80)

I'm grateful to Nora Ephron for these marvelous plum puddings. The recipe yields two, so you'll have one for Christmas Day and one to give away or serve on another occasion. Make them well ahead of time.

Nora says, "Of course you can keep the puddings for months, but I do them a couple of weeks before Christmas. Depending on the anticipated mood of your guests, pour a little or a lot of brandy over the puddings as the weeks go by."

Note: You'll need two metal pudding molds (2½-quart capacity each) with tight-fitting metal lids and two big pots with tight-fitting lids, each pot large enough to hold one mold.

1. Sift the flour, salt and spices into a large bowl. Add the shredded suet, bread crumbs, lemon rind (but not the juice), grated carrot, sugar, dark and light raisins, currants, peel and prunes and stir well.

2. Stir together the lemon juice, rum and beaten eggs. Warm the molasses in a saucepan over low heat, add it to the egg mixture and blend well. Pour the egg mixture and the Guinness stout into the flour mixture and blend thoroughly. Cover with a dish towel and leave on the kitchen counter overnight to ripen (no need to refrigerate).

3. Boil a large kettle of water; butter the pudding molds.

Spoon half the pudding mixture into each mold. Cut a piece of waxed paper to fit snugly on the top of the pudding (be sure to cut a hole in the center of the waxed paper) and butter one side of the waxed paper. Press the waxed paper—butter side down—directly onto the pudding. Cover the mold with a clean napkin, square of clean cotton fabric or double-thick square of cheesecloth and tie the cloth tightly with string. Put the metal lids on the pudding molds.

Place each covered mold in a large pot and add boiling water to come one third of the way up the mold. Turn on the heat and steam the puddings for five hours, keeping the water simmering and adding more boiling water as needed to maintain the level.

4. Remove the molds from the pots and let the puddings cool in the molds. Store in the pantry until the day you want to serve the puddings. (As the weeks go by, you may occasionally remove the lids, cloth and waxed paper and pour a little brandy over each pudding. Replace the waxed paper, cloth and lids and return the puddings to the pantry.)

Before serving, replace the old buttered waxed paper with new, freshly buttered waxed paper, tie on the cloth again and cover with the metal lids. Steam (as described in step 3) for two hours.

Remove the lids, cloth and waxed paper and run a knife around each pudding to loosen it from the mold. Cover with an inverted serving platter and turn over to unmold the pudding. Serve warm with any of the hard sauces given on page 80.

Note: If you like, pipe rosettes of hard sauce on waxed paper and freeze until hard. Surround the warm pudding with frozen rosettes, as shown in photograph 10.

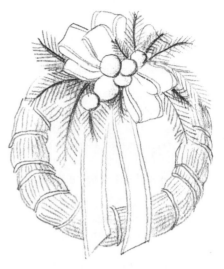

CHRISTMAS MEMORIES FROM FRIENDS

Mysterious Shapes

Every year I would wake up very early on Christmas morning and go downstairs to the living room entrance. In the dim light, the living room was filled with mysterious shapes that I knew were presents, and I would stand at the threshold and just stare at them. Then I would go back to bed and try to sleep until daylight, when my younger brother would wake me up and we could find out what the mysterious shapes were.

My parents never wrapped our gifts; instead, they placed the gifts all over the living room and each gift would have a little card near it, with my initial or my brother's initial written on it. My father would have assembled any toys or electric train accessories that needed it, and I loved that he did this because everything would be ready to play with—no waiting.

Basic Vinaigrette Sauce with Variations

Makes about one cup

Basic Vinaigrette Sauce (salad dressing), below, is the foundation for the variations that follow. This recipe differs from a classic vinaigrette sauce—it's lighter on oil and a bit heavier on vinegar. Make the sauce in your food processor.

⅓ cup balsamic vinegar *OR* ¼ cup wine vinegar plus one tablespoon water
¼ teaspoon salt (or more, to taste)
½ teaspoon dry mustard
Fresh pepper to taste
⅔ cup mild olive oil *OR* ⅓ cup olive oil and ⅓ cup safflower oil
1 clove garlic, split in half

Process all ingredients, except garlic, for about 30 seconds or until well blended. Adjust seasonings, pour into a jar with the garlic and store in the refrigerator.

Herb Vinaigrette Sauce: Add 1½–2 tablespoons of a chopped herb; choose fresh basil, chervil, tarragon, chives *or* dill, or choose any one of these herbs and combine it with chopped, fresh flat-leaf (Italian) parsley.

Shallot Vinaigrette Sauce: Omit garlic; add two tablespoons finely minced shallots.

Lime Vinaigrette Sauce: Substitute fresh lime juice for the vinegar.

Yuletide Open House

Serves 20

Christmas Eggnog (page 138)
Mustard-and-Maple-glazed Ham
Make-Ahead Boston Baked Beans
Corn Pudding with Hot Peppers
Homemade Chunky Applesauce
Green salad with **Herb Vinaigrette Sauce**
Baking Powder Biscuits (page 153), butter
Christmas Trifle (page 68)
Pumpkin Pies with Walnut-Crumb Crusts (page 54)
Seedless grapes
Coffee, tea

Almost everything on this menu can be prepared or cooked ahead of time; only the eggnog, the pumpkin pies and the final assembly of the Christmas Trifle must be done on the day of the party. You'll be very busy on Christmas Day, so enlist the aid of a couple of reliable friends or relatives who can do these at home and bring them to the party. Devote your own pre-party hours to a quick cleanup, the last-minute food preparation—and the pleasure of decking yourself out in your Christmas best.

WORK PLAN/CHECKLIST

One week before the party
- ☐ Make biscuits and freeze in plastic bags.

Two to three days before the party
- ☐ Buy all food and liquor.
- ☐ Make and refrigerate baked beans.
- ☐ Make and refrigerate applesauce.
- ☐ Glaze and bake the ham; cover with plastic wrap and refrigerate.
- ☐ Make two corn puddings; cover with plastic wrap and refrigerate.

One day before the party
- ☐ Call the cooks who are preparing the eggnog, pumpkin pies and trifle and make sure everything is going according to plan.
- ☐ Wash, dry and tear greens for salad; refrigerate in plastic bags.
- ☐ Make and refrigerate vinaigrette.
- ☐ Wash, drain and refrigerate grapes.
- ☐ Set up the buffet table; take out serving platters, utensils, punch bowl, etc.

Christmas morning
- ☐ Take ham and baked beans out of refrigerator to come to room temperature.

Christmas afternoon, before the party
- ☐ Take corn puddings out of refrigerator to come to room temperature.
- ☐ Make coffee preparations.
- ☐ Warm baked beans in 325° F. oven, adding water if necessary to prevent sticking.

ENTERTAINING NOTEBOOK
Breakfast in Bed

One of the nicest presents you can give your mate is breakfast in bed. Start by (gently) waking him or her in time to pull him- or herself together before you reappear with the breakfast tray. Make the tray appealing with a Christmas cloth and napkin, your prettiest dishes, a flower or two, the morning newspaper. The food should consist of easy-to-manage favorites—perhaps scrambled eggs, fresh muffins, sliced oranges and a small pot of hot coffee or tea. According to your mate's preference, stay for a cozy chat or leave your mate alone to enjoy peace and quiet.

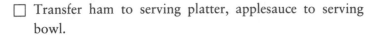

COOK'S JOURNAL

Simple Garnishes

Carrots: Peel and slice in thin rounds; cut with canapé cutters; sprinkle with a little paprika or finely chopped parsley.

Carrots: Peel and cut in half lengthwise; use peeler to cut long, paper-thin slices; loop each carrot slice with olives on a toothpick.

Cucumbers: Trim top and bottom; cut out long, narrow wedges from top to bottom; slice thin.

Lemons, limes: Cut in thin wedges; dip edge in paprika or finely chopped parsley.

Lemons, limes, oranges: Cut in thin slices; remove seeds; slit and twist.

Lemons, limes, oranges: Use vegetable peeler to peel zest; cut in slivers.

Radishes: Cut off stem and tip; make parallel cuts every 1/16 inch from tip almost to stem end; soak in salted water for ten minutes; rinse, squeeze out excess water and press into fans.

☐ Transfer ham to serving platter, applesauce to serving bowl.

☐ Dress and toss salad.

☐ Put all food (except corn puddings, biscuits and eggnog) on table. Check menu to be sure you haven't forgotten anything.

Half an hour before the party

☐ Put corn puddings and frozen biscuits in 325° F. oven for twenty minutes, or until warm.

☐ Carve at least a few slices of ham.

Last minute

☐ Put biscuits (in napkin-lined basket) and corn puddings on buffet table.

☐ In the kitchen, transfer eggnog to punch bowl; carry the punch bowl triumphantly to your waiting guests. Serve eggnog and toast the holiday.

Later in the evening

☐ Serve desserts and coffee.

carrots

cucumber

lemons
limes

lemons, limes, oranges

cut   fan
radish

Mustard-and-Maple-glazed Ham

Makes 20 or more servings

1 cup (packed) light brown sugar
¼ cup maple syrup
2 tablespoons dry mustard
10-pound (12-pound, if you want leftovers) fully cooked, semiboneless ham
Whole cloves (optional)

For a large, informal buffet like this, a big ham is always a good choice. This ham is baked ahead and served cold or at room temperature in order to keep the oven free for other dishes. Since the ham is fully cooked when you buy it, the purpose of baking is simply to make it even more delicious.

If there is time, a thoughtful host will carve about one third of the ham in thin slices and place the slices attractively around the serving platter. Guests will then continue to carve as needed.

1. Make the glaze by mixing together the brown sugar, maple syrup and mustard; set aside. Let the ham come to room temperature (1½–2 hours).

2. Preheat the oven to 325° F. Prepare the ham by cutting off the skin and most of the fat, leaving a ¼-inch layer of fat. Place the ham on a rack in a shallow roasting pan and insert a meat thermometer in the center, making sure the thermometer does not come in contact with bone. Bake the ham for 1½ hours.

3. When the ham has baked for 1½ hours, remove it from the oven and score the fat in a crisscross pattern of lines ¾ inch apart. Spread glaze over the entire ham and stud the ham with cloves, if you like.

Return the ham to the oven and bake for another half hour, or until the thermometer reads 130° F. (Remember: The ham was fully cooked to begin with, so there is no need to bake it excessively.) Baste the ham two or three times during this last half hour.

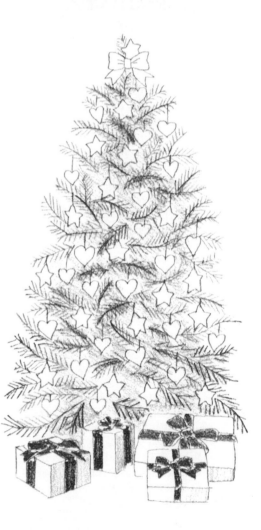

ENTERTAINING NOTEBOOK

Start a Family Tradition

❊ This year, take lots of photographs and put them in a special Family Christmas Album. Next year, add to the album—presto, a new tradition.

❊ Have each family member *make* one gift for another family member; pick names out of a hat.

❊ Make up a Christmas Grab Bag: Pick a theme—Puzzles and Games, Tasty Treats, Books—and tell everyone to spend no more than five dollars. Open the presents on Christmas Eve.

❊ Tell a story—in front of the fire, with popcorn and mulled cider close at hand. One person starts the story and stops at an exciting moment, the next person picks up the thread and continues. The story must end with the last person in the room.

❊ Hold a Christmas Treasure Hunt all over the house or neighborhood. The prize should be something really special, something everyone will enjoy—a Ping-Pong table, a VCR, tickets to a magic show.

❊ Take on a family project: Do something wonderful for another person or family so they have a merry Christmas, too.

Let the ham cool, then refrigerate either until serving time or until one hour before serving, if you want to bring it to room temperature. Transfer the ham to a large platter and carve at least a few slices so guests are not shy about cutting into your perfect ham.

OPTIONS: Baked ham is the perfect foil for all sorts of tasty condiments. Surround the ham with small bowls of rough-textured mustard (Tarragon Mustard, page 239, is a great choice), chutney (make Apple-Onion or Marnie's Dried Peach and Apricot Chutney, pages 234 and 236, or serve any good store-bought chutney), mustard fruits, sweet or sour pickles, cranberry sauce, pickled onions or pickled tomatoes.

Make-Ahead Boston Baked Beans

Makes 20 or more servings

This makes a lot of very tasty beans, so either you'll have terrific leftovers—or your guests will love them so much they'll be scraping the bottom of the bean pot.

1. Pick over the beans, discarding pebbles and shriveled beans. Rinse the beans and put them in a large pot with water to cover by two inches. Bring to a boil, cook for two minutes and turn off the heat. With the pot covered, let the beans soak for an hour.

2. Bring to a boil again. Turn the heat down, tilt the lid so steam can escape from the pot and simmer the beans for half an hour, or until the beans are partially cooked. (They must not be fully cooked or they will become too mushy during the long baking period.) Drain the beans, discarding the liquid.

3. Preheat the oven to 325° F.

Score the salt pork deeply with crisscross lines one inch apart. Cut the salt pork in four pieces and place one piece on the bottom of a large ovenproof casserole or bean pot. Add half the beans and place two more pieces of salt pork on the beans. Add the remaining beans and top with the last piece of salt pork.

4. In a medium bowl, stir together the mustard, brown sugar, molasses and salt. Add the warm water and stir again. Pour the mixture evenly over the beans and cover the casserole or bean pot.

5. Bake for 4–4½ hours, covered, checking often and adding water as needed to keep the beans from sticking to the bottom of the pot. At the end of this baking period, stir from the bottom up, to distribute the sauce.

Uncover the casserole and bake for one more hour. Stir again and serve immediately or refrigerate for up to three days.

5 cups navy beans, Great Northern beans or small white beans
¾ pound salt pork
3 tablespoons dry mustard
¾ cup (packed) dark brown sugar
¾ cup unsulfured molasses
2 teaspoons salt
3½ cups warm water

Corn Pudding with Hot Peppers

5 eggs, room temperature

2 cups milk, room temperature

¼ cup (½ stick) butter, melted and cooled

¾ cup yellow cornmeal

1½ teaspoons salt

2 tablespoons sugar

2 cups (one 16-ounce) can cream-style corn

1 package (10 ounces) frozen whole-kernel corn, defrosted, drained and patted dry on paper towels

2–3 tablespoons puréed or very finely minced pickled jalapeño peppers
Note: If you like a mild-hot pepper taste, use two tablespoons; for a hot-hot flavor, use three.

Butter or margarine for greasing the baking dish

Makes ten servings

Every cook has recipes that are unqualified hits. Corn Pudding with Hot Peppers is one of mine—people just love it and wolf it down and ask for the recipe every time I serve it. If there is any left over, which is unlikely, it's delicious served cold on the next day.

Note: To make 20 servings, make this ten-serving recipe twice (do *not* double the recipe), using two 2½-quart baking dishes.

1. Place the baking dish in the oven and set oven to 350° F.

In a large bowl, beat the eggs, milk and melted butter until smooth. Add the cornmeal, salt and sugar and beat again.

2. Stir in the cream-style corn, whole-kernel corn and puréed jalapeño peppers.

3. Remove the heated baking dish from the oven, add some butter or margarine and brush it around to coat the dish evenly. Briskly stir the corn mixture one more time (this is very important) and pour immediately into the dish. Bake for 65–80 minutes, or until the pudding is as firm as you prefer it. Some people like puddings that are a little soft, others like them thoroughly cooked (a tester inserted in the center comes out clean). Keep in mind that the pudding firms up as it cools, too.

When cool, cut the pudding in squares or rectangles. Refrigerate for up to three days; serve at room temperature.

Homemade Chunky Applesauce

Makes 20 or more servings

An applesauce far beyond the ordinary—more interesting, more delicious, but not much more complicated to make.

1. Peel the apples and cut in quarters, keeping the tart apples separate from the sweet ones. Carefully pare away all the seeds and hard matter from the center of each quarter. Cut each quarter in six pieces.

2. Put the pieces of tart apple in a large heavy pot with the brown sugar, cranberry juice, butter, salt and cinnamon. Cover the pot and cook over low heat, stirring occasionally, for two minutes. Add the pieces of sweet apple, stir and cover the pot again. Continue cooking for 40 minutes; there will be a lot of liquid in the pot.

3. Uncover the pot and reduce the heat as much as possible. Cook down the mixture until the sauce is thick but still partly chunky, about 1½ hours, stirring often to prevent burning. Help the sauce along by mashing with the back of a spoon to break down the pieces of apple.

Let the applesauce come to room temperature and then add fresh lemon juice to taste (optional). You may add a little more sugar if you prefer a sweeter sauce, but keep in mind that when the applesauce is cold it will taste sweeter than it does when warm or hot. Refrigerate the applesauce until needed.

8 Granny Smith apples (or other large tart apples)
8 large Red Delicious apples (or other sweet apples)
10 tablespoons (packed) dark brown sugar
1 cup cranberry juice cocktail
¼ cup (½ stick) butter
¼ teaspoon salt
½ teaspoon cinnamon
Fresh lemon juice (to taste; optional)

CHAPTER 8

Holiday Party Menus and Recipes

The holiday season is absolutely the best time of year to entertain, because everyone's already in a partygoing mood, ready to invite and be invited. So all you really have to do is telephone your friends (or send invitations—in either case, well in advance), set up a buffet table loaded with great food and drink and hang the welcoming Christmas wreath on the front door. The party will take care of itself.

In this chapter you'll find all the great food you need for your buffet table—menus, recipes and how-to tips for a caroling party complete with wassail bowl, a terrific Tex-Mex Christmas fiesta and an Italian-style celebration for a Saturday night (make this one a glittering dress-up affair).

Tips and Guidelines

❈ There are three complete menus in this chapter: *Saturday Night Gala, Caroling Party* and *Christmas Fiesta Buffet*.

❈ Each menu is followed by a Work Plan/ Checklist that will take you step by step through organizing and preparing the party food.

❈ Each Work Plan/Checklist is followed by the recipes that are **boldface** in the menu. In this chapter, two **boldface** recipes appear as margin entries; several recipes mentioned in the menus are cross-referenced to other chapters in the book.

❈ All through the chapter, in the margins, you'll find helpful hints for party-givers.

❈ If you live in an area where there is concern about the use of raw eggs, you may want to consider steering clear of recipes calling for them.

White Wine Punch

Makes about 14 cups; 20 or more servings

For a party, prepare several batches of basic punch mixture (store it in jars in the refrigerator) and serve one batch at a time, adding fresh fruit, soda and ice just before serving.

1 cup superfine sugar
1 cup fresh lemon juice
1 cup fresh orange juice
2 bottles (standard 750 ml) dry white wine, cold
½ cup orange liqueur (Triple Sec, Cointreau, Curaçao)
2 lemons, sliced in thin rounds, pits removed
1 navel orange, sliced in thin half-rounds
1 one-liter bottle club soda
Ice ring (see page 187)

1. Stir together the sugar, lemon juice and orange juice until the sugar is dissolved. Add the wine and liqueur and stir well. (At this point you may store the mixture in the refrigerator for later use.)

2. Pour into a punch bowl, add the sliced lemons and oranges, club soda and ice ring and stir well.

Saturday Night Gala

Serves 30

White Wine Punch
Tortellini on toothpicks, Parsley Pesto (page 241)
Italian cold cuts
Marinated Sun-dried Tomatoes, fingers of mozzarella cheese
Crunchy Vegetables with Crisp Garlic
Squares of **Mushroom and Roast Pepper Frittata**
Mascarpone, Bel Paese and Fontina cheeses
Anchovy Butter (page 240)
Italian bread, sesame breadsticks
Grapes, tangerines, seckel pears, lady apples
Christmas-Comes-But-Once-a-Year Chocolate Cakes (page 56)
Espresso with lemon peel

This menu, with its distinctively Italian flavor, is designed to please and impress a large party of about 30 merrymakers and at the same time keep your shopping, cooking and party preparations within reasonable limits. Of course, any party for so many people takes work—but this is a menu that looks far more elaborate than it really is, since some of the food is store-bought and all of the actual cooking is done ahead. (It's only fair to point out that the one major production necessary for this menu is making the Christmas-Comes-But-Once-a-Year Chocolate Cakes, although these are done ahead of time and kept frozen until party day.) Read the Work Plan/Checklist below to see just how manageable the menu is.

Nevertheless, only you can decide how much you can handle, and there is absolutely no need to give up your party plans just because you are short on time, energy or funds. There are two excellent ways to simplify the menu.

First, you can cut down on the number of different dishes. For instance, served chilled white wine instead of punch. Increase the amount of cold cuts. Eliminate the tortellini and the sun-dried tomatoes and offer only one or two cheeses. Instead of Christmas-Comes-But-Once-a-Year Chocolate Cakes, make (or buy) Christmas cookies, pound cake or fruitcake to serve with the fresh fruit.

The second way to simplify is to retain the menu as it is but give the party jointly with one or two friends and divide up the shopping, cooking and party preparations according to who does what best.

ENTERTAINING NOTEBOOK
Ice Rings

An ice ring will keep your punch cool for a long time because it melts slowly. For a plain ice ring, just fill a tube pan (fluted or plain) with tap water and freeze. (If you don't have a tube, use any pretty mold.) For a fancier ring, with fruit embedded in the ice, try this technique: Arrange pieces of fruit (see below) on the bottom of the mold; fill with just enough water to cover the fruit; freeze; repeat one or two more times. Unmold the ice ring by dipping the mold in warm water, inverting it carefully over the punch bowl and easing the ring into the punch.

Fruits suitable for ice rings: sliced lemons, limes or oranges; fresh strawberries (whole or sliced); frozen blueberries, raspberries and cherries; cranberries.

DECORATING MEMO

Finishing Touches

When you've got the basic party plans under control—clean house, good food and drink, holiday decorations, Christmas tree—consider the finishing touches that add polish to the party: candles, flowers and soft lighting; appropriate music in the background (or foreground, if it's that kind of party); comfortable seating, arranged attractively; holiday treats such as bowls of small candies, mints, nuts, glacé fruits.

WORK PLAN/CHECKLIST

One week before the party

☐ Buy all wine and nonperishable food, plus perishable ingredients needed for the pesto, Anchovy Butter, sun-dried tomatoes and chocolate cakes listed below.

☐ Make Parsley Pesto, Anchovy Butter and Marinated Sun-dried Tomatoes; cover and refrigerate.

☐ Make and freeze two Christmas-Comes-But-Once-a-Year Chocolate Cakes.

Three days before the party

☐ Buy all remaining perishable food. (Cold cuts and cheese must be wrapped snugly in plastic before refrigerating.)

☐ Wrap and freeze bread and breadsticks.

Two days before the party

☐ Prepare, cook and refrigerate carrots and cauliflower for Crunchy Vegetables with Crisp Garlic; cut up peppers and refrigerate in plastic bag.

☐ Cook tortellini, toss with a little oil, cover and refrigerate.

☐ Make ice ring for punch (see page 187).

One day before the party

☐ Make two Mushroom and Roast Pepper Frittatas; cut in squares and refrigerate.

☐ Finish making Crunchy Vegetables, but do not add crisp garlic until just before serving. Put vegetables in serving bowl; cover and refrigerate.

☐ Wash, dry and arrange fruit; store in a cool place.

☐ Cut mozzarella cheese in fingers and wrap well in plastic.

☐ Set up the buffet table; take out serving platters, punch bowl, serving utensils, etc.

☐ If other cooks are making things for the party, call them to be sure there are no problems.

Morning of the party
☐ Take bread and breadsticks out of freezer.
☐ Arrange cold cuts on platters, cover and refrigerate.
☐ Arrange frittata squares on platters, cover and refrigerate.

Afternoon of the party
☐ Make punch preparations, coffee preparations (including lemon peel).
☐ Arrange Marinated Sun-dried Tomatoes and mozzarella fingers on platters, cover and set aside.
☐ Put cheese on boards or platters, cover and set aside.
☐ Take chocolate cakes out of the freezer; transfer to the refrigerator when there is room.

Early evening before the party
☐ Transfer tortellini to serving platter; stick toothpicks in tortellini.
☐ Put Parsley Pesto in small serving bowl.
☐ Add crisp garlic to Crunchy Vegetables.
☐ Take all food to buffet table. Check menu to be sure you haven't forgotten anything.

Half an hour before the party
☐ Warm bread in oven; arrange bread and breadsticks in napkin-lined baskets and place on buffet table.
☐ Make punch; add ice ring.

Later in the evening
☐ Serve dessert and espresso.

ENTERTAINING NOTEBOOK
Cocktail Parties

Giving a cocktail party doesn't necessarily require you to serve cocktails. Offer your guests only the drinks they prefer—cocktails, red and white still wines, sparkling wine or champagne, sherry, punch, eggnog (spiked or not), even beer or soda. The menu can be as simple or elaborate as you can afford (in time or money), as long as it consists of finger food.

Marinated Sun-dried Tomatoes

Makes 30 or more servings

1 pound sun-dried tomatoes
2 cups olive oil
⅓ cup balsamic vinegar
3 large cloves of garlic, sliced
2 two-ounce jars capers, drained
1 teaspoon powdered dried basil
   Note: Powder some dried
   basil by crushing it between
   your fingers, then measure
   one teaspoon.

In winter, when fresh tomatoes are pretty disappointing, try these tangy, marinated sun-dried tomatoes arranged with fingers or slices of fresh mozzarella and sprinkled with coarsely chopped parsley. Make the marinated tomatoes at least two days before you want to serve them.

1. Put the sun-dried tomatoes in a saucepan with water to cover and simmer just until softened, about five minutes. Drain, rinse well in a strainer and drain again. (Rinsing the tomatoes washes away some of the excess salt.) Pat dry on paper towels.

2. Stir the remaining ingredients together in a large bowl. Add the softened tomatoes and stir again. Cover and refrigerate for at least two days, stirring occasionally. After two days, transfer the mixture to jars to make storage more convenient.

OPTIONS: One night when I had dinner guests and no appetizer prepared, I simply served squares of Russian pumpernickel bread topped with jalapeño mayonnaise (mayonnaise blended with finely minced jalapeño peppers to taste) and Marinated Sun-dried Tomatoes. Delicious. Keep Marinated Sun-dried Tomatoes in the refrigerator (they last for weeks) and you'll find many uses for them:

❊ Purée a few tomatoes with a little liquid (water, wine, tomato sauce) and add to plain tomato sauce to enrich the flavor spectacularly.

❊ Sliver or dice the tomatoes and add to salads, pasta or vegetables.

❊ Include marinated tomatoes in sandwiches—they're great with cold cuts, cheeses, chicken, avocado.

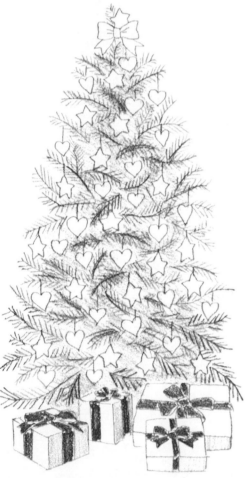

Mushroom and Roast Pepper Frittata

Makes 15 servings

To make 30 servings, you'll have to make this frittata twice—but you can ease the way by preparing four peppers and 1½ pounds of mushrooms at one time and then dividing them in half, ready to use for each frittata.

Note: You'll need a heavy, ovenproof 12-inch skillet.

1. Roast the peppers: Place the whole peppers under the broiler or impale each pepper on a kitchen fork and hold it directly over a gas flame, rotating until blackened all over. Immediately put the peppers in a plastic bag, close the bag tightly and leave for ten minutes. Peel the peppers under cold running water; the skins will slip off easily. Dry the peeled peppers on paper towels. Slit open, remove ribs and seeds and cut in ¼-inch-wide strips. Set aside.

2. Heat a little olive oil in a skillet and sauté the mushrooms until they are soft and their liquid has cooked away. Add a little more olive oil and the peppers and sauté for a minute or two.

3. Beat the eggs until frothy. Season with salt and fresh pepper. Pour the eggs over the peppers and mushrooms and sprinkle with the Parmesan cheese.

4. Cook over very low heat, stirring with a fork, until the frittata begins to set. Continue cooking very slowly until only the top is runny. (While the frittata cooks, turn on and preheat the broiler.) Put the skillet under the broiler for about 20 seconds—watch carefully—to set the top.

2 large sweet red (bell) peppers
Olive oil
¾ pound fresh mushrooms, trimmed, cleaned and chopped
15 eggs
1 teaspoon salt
Fresh pepper
½ cup grated Parmesan cheese

ENTERTAINING NOTEBOOK

Disposable Necessities

Using disposables for a big holiday party makes good sense—and saves wear and tear on the hosts. Here's what to buy: paper napkins (cocktail, luncheon or dinner size); plastic-coated paper plates (small, large); sturdy plastic forks, spoons (knives are not usually needed for a buffet); plastic glasses; paper or Styrofoam hot cups.

And don't forget paper towels, plastic wrap, waxed paper and aluminum foil for the kitchen; toilet paper, tissues and paper guest towels for the bathroom.

A word to the wise: Buy more than you think you'll need.

Loosen the frittata with a spatula and let it cool in the pan. Cut into about 30 squarish pieces (see drawing), wrap well and refrigerate until serving time.

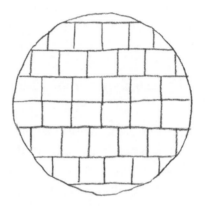

OPTIONS: Other ingredients may be added to—or substituted for—the peppers and mushrooms in the frittata. Try any of the following: artichoke hearts; diced American ham, Italian prosciutto or pancetta; slivered sun-dried tomatoes; sliced sweet onions; shredded Gruyère cheese; anchovies; slices of fresh sausage (cooked) or dried sausage; blanched zucchini or green beans; diced boiled potatoes.

Crunchy Vegetables with Crisp Garlic

Makes 30 servings

This is a chilled vegetable salad spiked with the bright taste of fresh lime juice. (Do not substitute lemon juice or—even worse—bottled lemon juice.) Thirty cloves may sound like a lot of garlic, but you'll find that the garlic is not at all overwhelming when sautéed to crispness.

1. Peel the garlic cloves and slice thinly. Heat ½ cup of the olive oil in a large heavy pot, add the sliced garlic and sauté over low heat, stirring, until medium brown but not burned, about four minutes. Remove the garlic with a slotted spoon and store at room temperature until serving time. Don't discard the leftover oil and don't wash the pot—you'll need both in step 3.

2. Bring a big pot of water to a boil. While it is heating, peel the carrots, trim the ends and cut in ½-inch dice. Cut or break the flowerets from the main stem of the cauliflower; rinse and drain flowerets well.

When the water is boiling, add the diced carrots, bring to a boil again and cook three minutes. Add the cauliflower and cook the two vegetables together for five more minutes, or until crisp-tender. Do not overcook. Drain in a colander and rinse with cold water to bring the temperature down quickly.

3. Wash, core and seed the peppers. Cut in ½-inch pieces.

Add the remaining ½ cup of olive oil to the olive oil left over from sautéing the garlic. Heat the oil and sauté the peppers until softened. Add the carrots and cauliflower and heat thoroughly, stirring well. Turn off the heat.

4. Add the lime juice and chopped parsley and mix well. Add salt and fresh pepper to taste. Transfer the mixture to a serving bowl and refrigerate until half an hour before serving. At that time, add the crisp garlic and mix well.

30 large cloves of garlic
1 cup olive oil
15 medium carrots
2 medium heads of cauliflower
15 green Italian frying peppers
1 cup fresh lime juice (juice of about four large limes)
1 cup chopped flat-leaf (Italian) parsley
Salt
Fresh pepper

Wassail Bowl

Makes about 15 cups; ten or more servings

2 cups sugar
¾ cup water
4 whole cloves, three whole allspice and three one-inch pieces of cinnamon, tied in a double-thick cheesecloth bag
½ teaspoon powdered ginger
½ teaspoon ground nutmeg
2 bottles (standard 750 ml) dry sherry
1 cup cognac
8 eggs, room temperature, separated into two large bowls
Note: Be sure to use eggs that are not cracked, to avoid harmful bacteria.

1. Combine the sugar and water in a large pot over low heat, stirring until the sugar is dissolved; do not boil. Add the bag of spices, the ginger and the nutmeg and simmer uncovered for ten minutes without stirring. Turn off the heat.

2. Add the sherry and cognac, stir well and let the mixture cool until it is just warm. (You must allow the mixture to cool because too-hot liquid may curdle the eggs.) Pour into a punch bowl.

3. Beat the egg whites until they hold firm, glossy, moist peaks. Without cleaning the beaters, beat the yolks until thick and pale. Fold the whites into the yolks. Pour the eggs slowly into the warm wine mixture, whisking continuously. Serve immediately.

Caroling Party

Serves ten

Wassail Bowl
Spiced Nuts (page 242)
Popcorn and Pretzel Snacks (page 241)
Welsh Rabbit on Toast
Christmas Chopped Salad
Individual Baked Pumpkin Puddings with Warm Custard Sauce
Coffee, tea

After an evening of caroling, bring your friends home to a simple, hearty supper—by the fire, if you are lucky enough to have a fireplace. Let your guests nibble the nuts and snacks and sample the wassail while you nip into the kitchen to put the finishing touches to the food you've prepared beforehand.

WORK PLAN/CHECKLIST

Two days before the party

- ☐ Buy all food and liquor.
- ☐ Make Spiced Nuts; store in tightly covered containers.
- ☐ Make, cover and refrigerate Warm Custard Sauce.
- ☐ Make candied cranberries (see step 2 of Apple Tart with Candied Cranberries and Caramel Sauce, page 60) if you want to garnish the pumpkin puddings.

One day before the party

- ☐ Wash, dry and cut vegetables for Christmas Chopped Salad; refrigerate in plastic bags.
- ☐ Make and refrigerate Lime Vinaigrette Sauce for chopped salad.
- ☐ Prepare Popcorn and Pretzel Snacks and store in tightly covered containers.
- ☐ Set up buffet table (including warming tray or chafing dish); take out punch bowl and cups.

Morning and afternoon of the party

- ☐ Make Individual Baked Pumpkin Puddings; follow recipe instructions for storage.
- ☐ Make Welsh Rabbit; cover and refrigerate in the saucepan.
- ☐ Make and set aside toast for Welsh Rabbit.
- ☐ Arrange Christmas Chopped Salad on a large serving platter, cover with plastic and refrigerate.
- ☐ Make Wassail Bowl through step 2, but leaving the sherry-cognac mixture in the pot so you can warm it later.

Before leaving for caroling

- ☐ Take pumpkin puddings and Welsh Rabbit out of the refrigerator to come to room temperature.
- ☐ Make tea and coffee preparations.

ENTERTAINING NOTEBOOK

How to Be a Good Holiday Party Host

❋ Be at the door to greet your guests.

❋ Have plenty of hangers in the coat closet—and room to stash hats and boots, too.

❋ Offer a bedroom or bathroom for freshening up. The guest bathroom should be well supplied with tissues, aspirin, guest towels.

❋ Accompany new arrivals into the party and make a few introductions. Introductions should include helpful clues—profession, hobby, hometown—so guests have a starting point for conversation.

❋ Be on the alert for guests in trouble—a spilled drink, a floundering conversation, a shouting match in the making. Go to the rescue.

❋ Serve plenty of good food and drink (some of the drink should be nonalcoholic). At the end of the evening, bring out a pot of coffee.

❋ Never let a guest drink and drive. Depute another guest to take him or her home, call a cab or take him yourself. It's your responsibility.

□ Transfer Spiced Nuts and Popcorn and Pretzel Snacks to small serving bowls and place on coffee table, end tables, etc.

When you arrive home after caroling

□ Warm the wassail mix, finish making the wassail and serve the Wassail Bowl.

□ Reheat Welsh Rabbit over low heat; warm the toast in the oven.

□ Uncover and dress salad (do not toss); place extra vinaigrette in a small serving bowl.

□ Transfer hot Welsh Rabbit to a heatproof bowl; place toast in a napkin-lined basket.

□ Take food to the table.

Later in the evening

□ Warm the puddings in the oven according to the recipe instructions; warm the custard sauce according to the recipe instructions.

□ Serve dessert, coffee and tea.

Christmas Touches

A guest book, for holiday visitors to write their names and Christmas greetings . . . the punch bowl set in a ring of greenery piled with holly and berries, shiny red apples, green pears and glossy lemons . . . pink lightbulbs to give everyone a rosy glow . . . gardenias floating in a glass bowl . . . slim candles on the plum pudding . . . red garnishes: radish roses, cherry tomatoes, diced red pepper, red grapes, spiced red crab apples . . . green garnishes: green beans, avocado slices, green onions, rings of green pepper, broccoli flowerets, Chinese pea pods, parsley.

SEE PHOTOGRAPH 14

Welsh Rabbit on Toast

Makes ten or more servings

Here's a traditional supper dish that fits right into your holiday entertaining. Feel free to alter the seasoning according to your taste—a little more Worcestershire, a dash more cayenne.

I prefer rounds of crusty French or Italian bread for the toast, but any good white or whole wheat bread will do.

1. Warm the oven, turn it off and put the toast in the oven until needed. Heat the milk in a small saucepan.

2. Melt the butter in a large heavy saucepan over low heat. Add the flour and cook, stirring, for a minute or two; do not let the flour brown. Add the mustard, cayenne pepper, paprika and Worcestershire sauce and stir again. Add the hot milk all at once and whisk until thickened and smooth.

3. Keeping the heat low, stir in the grated cheese a handful at a time, letting each handful melt. Turn off the heat.

4. Gradually stir one cup of the hot cheese mixture into the beaten egg yolks to warm them. Pour the egg mixture back into the saucepan of cheese mixture and stir to blend. Add the beer and stir again. Adjust the seasoning if necessary.

Keep the Welsh Rabbit warm in a chafing dish (or on a warming tray) and the toast warm in a napkin-lined basket or bowl. Let each guest place toast on a plate and ladle Welsh Rabbit over the toast.

20 or more pieces of toast
2 cups milk
¼ cup (½ stick) butter
¼ cup flour
2 teaspoons dry mustard
⅛ teaspoon cayenne pepper
⅛ teaspoon paprika
3 tablespoons Worcestershire sauce
1½ pounds sharp Cheddar cheese, grated
3 egg yolks, beaten
½ cup dark beer

SEE PHOTOGRAPH 14

Christmas Chopped Salad

20 cherry tomatoes
2 sweet red (bell) peppers
2 sweet green (bell) peppers
½ head red cabbage
2 medium cucumbers
3 cups broccoli flowerets
8 cups prepared lettuce (washed,
   dried and chopped in small
   pieces)
   Note: Choose two kinds of
   lettuce—romaine, Boston,
   Bibb, red or green leaf or
   chicory. Don't use iceberg
   lettuce.
Lime Vinaigrette Sauce
   (page 176)

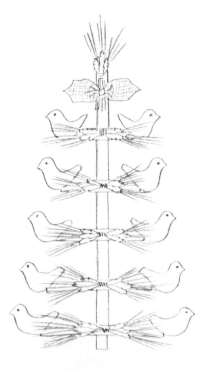

Makes 10 or more servings

Chopped salad is a California classic in which the salad ingredients are either cut in small dice or finely shredded, and arranged attractively on a plate or layered in a glass bowl. (In California, a chopped salad can be a whole meal, with meat or chicken and a blue cheese dressing, as well as fresh vegetables.)

Chopped salad lends itself perfectly to a Christmas menu—make it red and green and arrange the vegetables in a wreath or star shape.

1. Prepare the vegetables, keeping them in separate bowls or piles:
    ❋ Wash and dry the cherry tomatoes; cut in quarters.
    ❋ Wash and dry the red peppers; split open and remove stem, seeds and ribs; cut in ¼-inch pieces. Repeat with the green peppers (keep separate from the red).
    ❋ Remove and discard any wilted outer leaves of the red cabbage; finely shred the remainder of the cabbage.
    ❋ Cut off and discard the ends of the cucumbers; peel, cut in half lengthwise and remove the seeds; chop the flesh in ¼-inch pieces.
    ❋ Steam broccoli flowerets until crisp-tender; drain and plunge into a bowl of ice water; break into smaller flowerets and pat dry on paper towels.
2. On a large serving platter, make a bed of chopped lettuce. Arrange the prepared vegetables on the lettuce in alternating red and green concentric circles or in alternating red and green spokes, as shown in the drawings. Cover with plastic wrap until serving time.

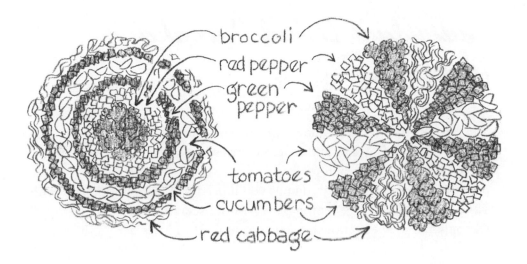

broccoli
red pepper
green
pepper
tomatoes
cucumbers
red cabbage

3. Just before serving, remove the plastic wrap and drizzle Lime Vinaigrette Sauce over the salad. *Do not toss.* Offer additional Lime Vinaigrette Sauce to your guests.

OPTIONS: Getting fresh, tasty salad ingredients in winter can be a tricky business, so you may be forced to make some changes in the ingredients for this pretty chopped salad. For instance, if the cherry tomatoes in your market are mealy and tasteless, don't ruin your salad by using them. Here are some possible alternatives; baby green peas; shredded or finely diced carrot; finely diced celery or jicama; sliced red radishes; diced or sliced mushrooms; olives; cubes of red-skinned apple; kidney beans; alfalfa or mung bean sprouts; shredded Chinese cabbage; diced cooked or raw beets.

QUICK TAKES
Food for Cocktail Parties

A cocktail party menu might include several of the following:

❋ Selection of canapés (small sandwiches, open-faced or closed)

❋ Two or three cheeses with plain crackers

❋ Small fresh fruits (strawberries, grapes, tangerines)

❋ Crudités (see page 163) with dips

❋ Cheese straws, nuts, pretzels, chips and dips

❋ Patés to spread on slices of French bread

❋ Tartlets with savory fillings, miniature quiches

❋ Deviled eggs

❋ Caviar with all the trimmings (chopped onions, chopped egg, capers, lemon wedges, black bread)

❋ Smoked salmon, salmon mousse

❋ Shrimp on toothpicks, with a spicy sauce

❋ Broiled cubes of chicken breast on skewers, tasty chicken wings

❋ Stuffed mushrooms

❋ *Hummus (page 213)*, pita wedges, stuffed grape leaves

SEE PHOTOGRAPH 14

Individual Baked Pumpkin Puddings

Butter for greasing the muffin
    pans
1¾ cups cake flour
2 teaspoons baking powder
1¼ teaspoons cinnamon
¾ teaspoon powdered ginger
¾ teaspoon ground allspice
½ teaspoon ground nutmeg
½ teaspoon salt
3 tablespoons milk
1⅓ cups canned pumpkin purée
½ cup (one stick) butter, room
    temperature
1 cup (packed) light brown sugar
3 eggs
Warm Custard Sauce (recipe
    follows)
Candied cranberries (optional; see
    step 2 of Apple Tart with
    Candied Cranberries and
    Caramel Sauce, page 60)

Makes ten small puddings

Make individual puddings, arrange on a pretty platter and top with Warm Custard Sauce. Candied cranberries make an attractive garnish. Serve one pudding per guest.

Note: To make ten puddings you'll need one large muffin pan with 12 sections or two large muffin pans with six sections each (though you'll use only ten of the sections); each section is 3¼ inches across the top.

1. Preheat the oven to 325° F.; bring a kettle of water to a boil.

Generously grease the muffin pan. Tear off a piece of aluminum foil four inches longer than the muffin pan (two pieces if you are using two pans) and brush butter on one side; set aside.

Sift together the flour, baking powder, spices and salt; set aside.

Whisk together the milk and pumpkin purée; set aside.

2. In a large bowl, cream the butter and sugar until light. Add the eggs one at a time, beating well after each addition. Continue beating until the mixture is pale and thick.

3. Add the pumpkin mixture and the dry ingredients alternately, in four parts each, blending well *by hand*. Divide the mixture equally among *ten* sections of the greased muffin pan or pans.

4. Cover the muffin pan or pans with the buttered foil, butter side down, crimping the foil tightly around the edges so no steam will escape. Put the muffin pan or pans in a larger pan (for example, a jelly roll pan or roasting pan) and place both on a shelf a third of the way down from the ceiling of the oven. Carefully pour boiling water into the larger pan to a depth of ½ inch.

Bake for 30 minutes, or until a toothpick stuck through the foil comes out with moist crumbs (not liquid) clinging to it. Do not overbake. Remove the foil and let the puddings cool for ten minutes in the muffin pan(s) on a wire rack.

Run a knife around each pudding. Pick up the pan(s) and tap firmly on each edge to loosen the puddings. Cover with an inverted cookie sheet and turn the puddings out. With a spatula, arrange the puddings on an ovenproof serving platter, cover with plastic wrap and refrigerate until 45 minutes before serving time.

Let the puddings come to room temperature (about half an hour). Remove the plastic wrap, cover lightly with foil and warm in a 300° F. oven for 15 minutes. Meanwhile, warm the custard sauce in the top of a double boiler over simmering water.

Drizzle each pudding with Warm Custard Sauce and top with several candied cranberries (optional). Offer additional Warm Custard Sauce to your guests.

OPTIONS: Instead of candied cranberries, garnish each custard-sauced pudding with a dab of red currant jelly, a few chopped walnuts or pecans, a spoonful of maple syrup or a dollop of vanilla whipped cream.

Warm Custard Sauce

Makes about two cups

4 egg yolks
2 cups milk
½ cup sugar
Pinch of salt
1 teaspoon vanilla extract

1. Beat the yolks until thick and pale.

2. In a saucepan over medium heat, bring the milk, sugar and salt almost to a boil, stirring until the sugar dissolves.

3. Stir a little of the hot milk mixture into the egg yolks to warm the yolks; repeat. Now pour the yolk mixture and the milk mixture into the top of a double boiler over simmering water and cook, stirring, for about 35 minutes, or until the sauce has thickened. Do not let the sauce boil. The sauce should coat a spoon and have no taste of raw egg.

4. Take the pan off the simmering water and stir in the vanilla. Strain the sauce into a bowl, set the bowl of sauce in a bowl of cold water and stir briskly to bring down the temperature. Refrigerate until needed, up to three days.

To serve, warm the sauce in the top of a double boiler over simmering water.

THE CHRISTMAS PANTRY CHECKLIST

Cheese

The choices are many; here are some widely available favorites for serving at parties, with good bread and unseasoned crackers.

❈ Mozzarella, smoked mozzarella
❈ Feta
❈ Mascarpone
❈ Port du Salut
❈ Bel Paese
❈ Muenster
❈ Tilsit
❈ Havarti
❈ Edam
❈ Gouda
❈ Jarlsberg
❈ Emmentaler
❈ Fontina
❈ Gruyère
❈ Provolone
❈ Monterey Jack
❈ Mild or sharp Cheddar
❈ Cheshire
❈ Colby
❈ Stilton
❈ Danish blue
❈ Bleu de Bresse
❈ Roquefort
❈ Gorgonzola
❈ Brie
❈ Camembert
❈ Chèvre
❈ Boursin

Christmas Fiesta Buffet

Serves 12

Mexican beer
Chicken or Cheese Enchilada Stacks
Calabacitas con Elote (Zucchini with Corn)
Black Bean Salad with Oranges, Avocado and Coriander
Winter Salsa (page 237)
Flour tortillas, corn tortillas
No-fail Flan
Christmas cookies (Chapter 1)
Coffee with cinnamon sticks

Tex-Mex food, with its lively flavors, makes a marvelous party. Even if you've never cooked this kind of food before, you'll find it's quite easy to prepare and serve.

The bright colors of Mexico—pink, red, turquoise, yellow—are often chosen for a fiesta table and centerpiece, but you might prefer to use tablecloth and napkins in soft desert colors, earthenware dishes and handsome baskets to enhance the beautiful look of this southwestern menu.

WORK PLAN/CHECKLIST

One week before the party

☐ Buy beer and nonperishable food, plus perishable food for making Christmas cookies and Winter Salsa.

☐ Make and freeze Christmas cookies.

☐ Make and refrigerate Winter Salsa.

Two days before the party

☐ Buy all remaining perishable food.

☐ Put beans to soak for Black Bean Salad, if you like.

☐ Poach and shred chicken for Chicken Enchilada Stacks; store in plastic bags in refrigerator.

☐ Shred cheese for Cheese Enchilada Stacks and refrigerate in plastic containers.

☐ Make and refrigerate Green Sauce for Enchilada Stacks.

One day before the party

☐ Prepare Calabacitas, following recipe instructions for making it ahead.

☐ Cook beans and complete the Black Bean Salad, but do not add avocado.

☐ Make and refrigerate No-fail Flan; do not unmold.

Morning of the party

☐ Take Christmas cookies out of freezer and arrange on platters; set aside.

☐ Chill the beer.

☐ Set up the buffet table; take out serving platters, baskets, utensils, etc.

☐ Make coffee preparations.

Afternoon of the party

☐ Transfer Winter Salsa to serving bowls.

☐ Assemble Enchilada Stacks.

CHRISTMAS MEMORIES FROM FRIENDS

Presents

We always got four kinds of Christmas gifts: gifts in our stockings, gifts from Mom and Dad, gifts from Santa and gifts that were hung on our Christmas tree like ornaments. The only presents we could catch sight of before Christmas Day were the ones hanging on the tree, so my brother and I would spend hours lying on our backs under the eight-foot tree, peering up into the branches, trying to read the tags on the gifts to see who was getting what. Now each Christmas I see my nephews doing the same thing and I realize how funny it must have looked to any passing adult—four little legs sticking out from under a fully decorated tree, each leg with its own floppy sock and half-tied sneaker, each little boy completely intent on the branches above.

ENTERTAINING NOTEBOOK

How to Be a Good Holiday Party Guest

❋ Arrive as close as possible to the time indicated in the invitation; don't be early or more than 15 minutes late.

❋ Bring a small gift (see page 112) and deliver it graciously; don't expect your host to open it right away.

❋ Join the party with a friendly attitude. Introduce yourself to other guests, shake hands, initiate conversation.

❋ Be considerate of your hosts—they have lots of things to do, including spending some time with each guest, so don't monopolize them.

❋ If you're a close friend, offer to help with food or drinks and then do what's asked of you. If your host declines your offer, don't press the issue.

❋ Don't leave early unless you absolutely must—for instance, if you have a sick child at home—and then be sure you have explained the situation to your host. It is terribly rude to the host (who has, after all, made a great effort) when guests leave too soon, especially if the guests imply they are going on to someplace more interesting or important.

❋ Stay as late as seems expected, but don't overstay your welcome. Make your goodbyes warmly and quickly.

❋ Call your hosts on the day following the party to tell them how much you enjoyed yourself.

Evening of the party

☐ Add avocados to Black Bean Salad and transfer to serving bowl.

☐ Bake Enchilada Stacks and, in the same oven, heat additional corn and/or flour tortillas (wrapped in aluminum foil); when hot, transfer Enchilada Stacks to serving platters and tortillas to napkin-lined baskets.

☐ Finish cooking Calabacitas and transfer to serving bowl.

☐ Take all food to buffet table. Check menu to be sure you haven't forgotten anything.

Later in the evening

☐ Unmold flan.

☐ Serve flan, cookies and coffee.

Chicken or Cheese Enchilada Stacks

Makes four stacks (each stack makes six wedges)

Each stack is a layering of tortillas, Green Sauce and *either* shredded chicken *or* grated Monterey Jack cheese. The recipe makes two stacks of each flavor. This may sound like a lot of food, but every guest will want one wedge of chicken and one wedge of cheese—so you'll need all 24 wedges.

1. Preheat the oven to 350° F.

Heat ⅛ inch of oil in a skillet. With tongs, hold one tortilla in the oil for five seconds, or until soft on one side. Turn the tortilla over and hold it in the oil for five more seconds. Place on paper towels to drain. Repeat with all the tortillas, adding a little more oil if needed.

2. Make two Chicken Enchilada Stacks: Lightly oil a sturdy cookie sheet. Divide the Green Sauce in half and set aside one half for the cheese stacks. Divide the shredded chicken in half; you will use one half for each chicken stack.

Put two tortillas side by side on the cookie sheet with an inch between them. Spread three tablespoons of Green Sauce on each tortilla and top each with an even layer of about three tablespoons of shredded chicken. Cover each with another tortilla. Repeat the sequence with more Green Sauce, chicken and tortillas until you have built two stacks of seven tortillas each. Top with more Green Sauce and the last of the chicken. Set aside while you make the Cheese Enchilada Stacks.

3. Make two Cheese Enchilada Stacks: Lightly oil another cookie sheet. Divide the cheese in half; you will use one half for each cheese stack. Have ready the remaining Green Sauce.

Put two tortillas side by side on the cookie sheet with an inch between them. Spread three tablespoons of Green Sauce on each tortilla and top each with an even layer of about three tablespoons of grated

Vegetable oil for softening the tortillas
28 seven-inch-diameter corn tortillas
Green Sauce (recipe follows)
2½ cups shredded cooked chicken
   Note: The meat from a 3½-pound poached chicken will yield about the right amount.
2½ cups shredded Monterey Jack cheese (about ¾ pound)

cheese. Cover each with another tortilla. Repeat the sequence until you have built two stacks of seven tortillas each. Top with more Green Sauce and the last of the cheese.

4. Bake the stacks for 20 minutes. Transfer to serving platters and use a sharp knife to cut each stack in six wedges. Serve hot.

OPTIONS: Keep the basic foundation—tortillas and Green Sauce—but add or substitute other ingredients to make new kinds of enchilada stacks. Chopped black olives, refried beans, lightly steamed green vegetables, cooked corn, spicy ground meat (cooked, of course), shredded turkey and chopped hard-cooked eggs all make fine replacements for or additions to the chicken or cheese in the recipe.

Green Sauce

Makes about six cups

6 tablespoons vegetable oil
3 cups chopped onions
2 large cloves of garlic, minced
3 pickled jalapeño peppers, stemmed, seeded and cut in chunks
4 cans (13 ounces each) tomatillos
   Note: Put the tomatillos in a strainer to drain off the canning liquid. Pierce each tomatillo and press lightly to drain the interior juices, too.
50 coriander (cilantro) leaves
2 cups sour cream

1. Heat the oil in a skillet and sauté the onions until golden. Add the garlic and cook for a minute or two.

2. Put the onions, garlic, jalapeños, drained tomatillos and coriander leaves in a food processor or blender and process until fairly smooth but not completely puréed. Transfer to a bowl and stir in the sour cream.

Black Bean Salad with Oranges, Avocado and Coriander

Makes 12 or more servings

Instead of refried beans or another hot bean dish, make this fresh-tasting cold bean salad for your fiesta. Be vigilant when cooking the beans, because you want them to be fully cooked but not at all mushy.

1. Pick over the beans and discard pebbles and shriveled beans; rinse the beans.

If you have time, soak the beans overnight, then drain and put the beans in a large pot with fresh water to cover by two inches; proceed to step 2.

If you forget or have less time, put the beans in a large pot with water to cover by two inches. Bring to a boil, cook for two minutes and turn off the heat. With the pot covered, let the beans soak for an hour.

2. Keeping the pot covered, bring the water to a boil. Turn the heat down and simmer the beans for one hour if they have soaked overnight, 30 minutes if they have boiled and soaked. The beans should be firm, not mushy.

Drain the beans in a colander and rinse with plenty of cold water to bring the temperature down quickly. Spread beans on paper towels to dry.

3. In a large bowl, whisk together the olive oil, lime juice, salt, coriander and the clove of garlic pulped in a garlic press.

With a sharp knife, peel the oranges, removing the skin and all the white pith; cut in ½-inch pieces. Stir the pieces into the olive oil dressing, along with any orange juice puddled on the cutting board.

4. Add the beans and stir gently but thoroughly. Taste and add more salt if necessary. At this point you may cover and refrigerate the salad until needed.

5. Just before serving, peel the avocados, cut in half, discard the pits and chop the flesh in ½-inch pieces. Add the pieces to the beans and stir gently until thoroughly combined.

Serve chilled or at room temperature.

3 cups dried black beans
½ cup olive oil
6 tablespoons fresh lime juice
1 teaspoon salt
3 tablespoons finely chopped coriander (cilantro)
1 large clove of garlic
3 navel oranges
2 ripe but firm black-skinned (Hass) avocados

Calabacitas con Elote (Zucchini with Corn)

5 medium zucchini, trimmed and
    sliced thin
Salt for the zucchini
1 ten-ounce package frozen
    whole-kernel corn, defrosted
    and drained
1 can (28 ounces) peeled Italian
    plum tomatoes, plus one
    14½-ounce can peeled
    tomatoes to use if needed
¼ cup vegetable oil
1 cup chopped onions
2 cloves of garlic, minced
1 teaspoon oregano, powdered
    Note: Measure one teaspoon
    of dried oregano leaves, then
    powder them by crushing
    between your fingers or
    palms.
1 four-ounce can peeled,
    chopped, mild green chiles
Salt
Fresh pepper

Makes 12 or more servings

A vegetable medley of Latin-American favorites, richly flavored but not peppery-hot.

1. Put the zucchini in a colander in the sink and sprinkle generously with salt, stirring to coat evenly; leave it there to "sweat" and drain for half an hour. This removes any bitterness from the zucchini.

Pat the defrosted corn dry on paper towels.

Empty the 28-ounce can of tomatoes into a strainer and cut each tomato in half. The tomatoes used in this dish must be firm, not mushy, so remove (and use for another purpose) any tomatoes that fall apart when you halve them. After draining, cut the tomatoes in ½-inch pieces to make about 1¾ cups. Depending on how many unusable tomatoes you removed, you may have to dip into the 14½-ounce can.

2. In a large skillet or saucepan, heat the oil and sauté the onions until golden. Add the garlic and oregano and sauté for another minute or two.

3. Rinse the zucchini very well and drain it in the colander, shaking out excess water. Put the zucchini and corn in the skillet and cook over low heat, stirring, for five minutes, or until the zucchini is just tender. Add the tomatoes and chopped chiles and cook for two minutes to heat thoroughly. Season with salt and fresh pepper to taste. Serve hot.

Note: If you are making this dish one day ahead, cook the zucchini and corn in the skillet for only three minutes; the zucchini will be undercooked. Complete the dish with the undercooked zucchini and stir the finished dish for a minute or two to release heat; refrigerate until needed. To serve, let the dish come to room temperature, then reheat quickly in a skillet just long enough to finish cooking the zucchini and make the vegetables good and hot.

No-fail Flan

Makes six or more servings

This version of an especially luscious flan is adapted from a recipe in the collection of Señora Irma de Anchondo.

Note: For 12 or more servings, make this recipe twice, one recipe at a time (do not double it), using two one-quart baking dishes. Prepare the flans the day before you want to serve them.

½ cup sugar
2 tablespoons Triple Sec liqueur
3 eggs
2 cups whole milk
1 can (14 ounces) sweetened
    condensed milk
1 tablespoon vanilla extract

1. Preheat the oven to 375° F.; have ready a one-quart baking dish and a kettle of boiling water.

Cook the sugar in a small, heavy pan over medium heat for several minutes, stirring constantly, until all the sugar melts and turns golden brown. Be very careful not to let it burn. Remove from the heat and let cool for several minutes. Stand back from the pan and add the liqueur, stirring with a long-handled spoon. The caramelized sugar may get lumpy and sticky; put the pan back on medium heat and stir until smooth again.

Immediately pour the caramelized sugar into the baking dish and tilt the dish so the syrup coats all of the bottom and a bit of the sides. Set aside for now.

2. In a large bowl, beat the remaining ingredients until well blended. Pour the mixture into the baking dish, right onto the caramelized sugar.

3. Place the baking dish in a larger pan (for instance, a roasting pan) on the middle rack of the oven. Pull the rack out just far enough to fill the larger pan with an inch of boiling water. Slowly and carefully push the rack back in. Bake for 70 minutes, or until a knife inserted in the center of the custard (not as far down as the caramelized sugar) comes out clean.

Let the flan cool for an hour, then cover with plastic wrap and refrigerate overnight. Before serving, run a knife around the edge of the flan to loosen it from the baking dish. Cover tightly with an inverted serving platter and turn over to unmold.

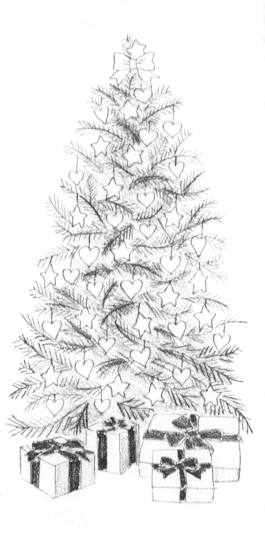

CHAPTER 9

Head-Start Dinners for Busy Days

Here's an immutable holiday fact: Along with relaxed days of get-togethers and cookie-baking and tree-trimming, there are bound to be hectic days when you've scheduled holiday activities from morning to evening—and you arrive at suppertime with nothing to put on the table. And then there are bound to be weekends when company's coming but you've also promised to take the kids Christmas shopping—and you won't have time to cook a company dinner.

Help is on the way in the form of Head-Start Dinners, a system for preparing delicious make-ahead main dishes you can tuck away to use on the busiest days of the holiday season. The system revolves around recipes for basic poached chicken and basic braised beef, which you convert into ready-to-eat frozen entrées, plus two pasta sauces—one to freeze and one to make on the spur of the moment. With a few main courses and plenty of sauce stashed in the freezer, you'll be ready for anything.

And to give you even more of a head start, meal planning is simplified because I've included a suggested menu for each main dish. Check the margins, too, for additional menus you might like to try, ways to dress up your favorite pasta and lots of other tips.

Tips and Guidelines

Here's how to get the most out of Head-Start Dinners: First read the chapter and see which menus and recipes you can use for your family and your style of entertaining. Then spend one day in the beginning of December, (A) making enough basic poached chicken breasts or basic braised beef cubes for several meals, and (B) turning them into the main courses you have chosen. Pack into containers (as described at the end of each recipe), label and date the containers and pop them right into the freezer, ready for defrosting at a later date. Do this as many times as you wish, to make as many frozen meals as you wish.

On a different day, make enough Savory Tomato-Eggplant Sauce for several meals. Freeze the sauce as instructed in the recipe.

❋ Don't try to do everything at once unless you have help.

❋ When you're really frazzled and don't have time to prepare much of anything for dinner, rely on Creamy Spinach and Herb Sauce tossed with a big pot of spaghetti. Add a salad and you're set to eat.

❋ The recipes serve from four to twelve people, so you can adjust them to suit your needs: a family meal for four, a dinner for eight on a day's notice, a supper party for twelve.

❋ There are six complete menus with recipes in this chapter, as well as ideas for augmenting or jazzing up these dinners. The menus and recipes are so good that you can use them for any holiday entertaining—and you don't *have* to make them ahead and freeze them!

Basic Recipe 1: Poached Chicken Breasts

6 whole chicken breasts with
  bones, split (12 half breasts)
2 tablespoons butter
1 can (13¾ ounces) chicken
  broth

Christmas Touches

Red-and-green-plaid fabric for tablecloth, napkins, tree skirt . . . red and green napkins tucked into the (unfilled) water goblets at lunch or dinner . . . brass bowl filled with greens and piled with lemon and orange pomanders . . . in the children's room, a small tree decorated with strings of popcorn, shiny paper chains and little gingerbread girls and boys . . . a late-night snack of sherry, apples and toasted walnuts.

Makes 12 servings (six cups boneless, cubed cooked chicken)

This is the basic recipe for the poached chicken used in preparing Spicy Yogurt Chicken with Vegetables (page 214) and Chicken with Mushrooms in Sherried Cream Sauce (page 218).

The basic method is to poach six whole breasts at a time, cube the poached chicken and then prepare either or both of the recipes, using the amount of cubed chicken appropriate for your needs. Each recipe yields four servings but may be doubled or tripled; thus, you might make one recipe (four servings) of Chicken with Mushrooms in Sherried Cream Sauce to freeze for your own family and a double recipe (eight servings) of Spicy Yogurt Chicken with Vegetables to freeze for weekend guests.

Here's a tip: If you're pressed for time, make one recipe of cubed poached chicken and freeze it in three packages, each package containing four servings (two cups). Defrost as needed, using the cubes to make the recipes in this chapter or to make any other favorite chicken recipe.

Just to keep things clear: One whole chicken breast looks like the drawing on the left; half a chicken breast looks like the drawing on the right. The recipes allow half a breast per serving.

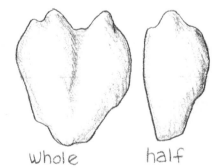

whole   half

Note: You will need two large skillets (or sauté pans) with lids.

1. Pull off and discard as much skin and fat as you can from the chicken breasts. Rinse them well.

2. Put a tablespoon of butter and half a can of chicken broth in each skillet. Bring the broth to a simmer and place six pieces of chicken, flesh side up, in each skillet. Cover the skillets, tilting the lids slightly so a little steam can escape during cooking.

3. Cook the chicken for 15 minutes, keeping the broth at a simmer (not a boil) over low heat. Then turn off the heat and leave the chicken in the skillets for 15 more minutes.

Cut open one piece of chicken in each skillet to see if the meat is cooked: If the meat is pink, turn the heat on and simmer five more minutes.

4. Remove the chicken from the hot broth and rinse in cool water; refrigerate until cool. Strain the broth into a jar and refrigerate for future use.

At this point, if you're pressed for time, you may cover the chicken, leave it in the refrigerator overnight and deal with it tomorrow (but no later than tomorrow). Otherwise, proceed to step 5.

5. Separate the chicken meat from the bones, discarding the bones as well as any bits of fat and gristle. Cut the boned chicken into ¾-inch cubes and use it in one of the following recipes or divide it in three equal amounts and freeze it in plastic bags or freezer containers.

Tip: For more menus using cubed poached chicken, see QUICK TAKES on page 217.

SEE PHOTOGRAPH 12

Hummus

Makes about 1¾ cups

1 can (19 ounces) chick-peas, drained and rinsed
¼ cup fresh lemon juice
1 large clove garlic, cut in four pieces
½ teaspoon salt
Handful of curly or flat parsley leaves
⅓ cup plain (unflavored) yogurt
¼ cup tahini (sesame seed paste)
   Note: Stir the tahini before measuring it.
Olive oil
3 thin slices of lemon, each cut in half, for garnish
Chopped parsley for garnish

1. Put the first four ingredients in a food processor or blender and process until smooth. Add parsley and process just until the parsley is coarsely chopped.

2. Add yogurt and tahini and blend just until the mixture is a good consistency for dipping. Transfer hummus to a bowl, smooth the top and pour a thin layer of olive oil over it; garnish by arranging the lemon slices on top like the petals of a flower and sprinkle with a bit of chopped parsley.

If you prefer, serve in a hollowed-out red cabbage as shown in photograph 12.

COOK'S JOURNAL
Fruit Garnishes

Frosted grapes: Dip small clusters of red or green grapes into slightly beaten egg white; roll in sugar; place on waxed paper to dry.

Skewered fruit: Thread short wooden skewers with cranberries, grapes, small pieces of pineapple, etc.

Strawberry flowers: Slice each strawberry in quarters from point to stem end, without cutting through the stem end. Press a grape or cranberry into the center to open the petals.

Chicken Menu 1

Spicy Yogurt Chicken with Vegetables
Couscous with Raisins and Walnuts
Oven-crisped wedges of pita bread
Ripe pears
Cinnamon Stars (page 25) or other Christmas cookies

To extend the meal or jazz it up a little, start with an appetizer of Hummus (page 213) with more pita wedges, plus stuffed grape leaves (from a can) and spiced or oil-cured olives. Serve Apple-Onion Chutney (page 234) as a condiment.

SEE PHOTOGRAPH 12

Spicy Yogurt Chicken with Vegetables

2 medium zucchini, washed, trimmed and cut in ½-inch dice
Salt for the zucchini
1 tablespoon vegetable oil
1 large or two medium yellow onions, chopped (about 1¼ cups chopped)

Makes four servings

Double the ingredients to make eight servings; triple the ingredients to make 12 servings.

Almost a one-pot meal, since the zucchini and carrots are combined with the cubed chicken in a gently spiced yogurt sauce. If you don't have couscous, rice is good with this dish, too.

Note: To make four servings, use a large skillet with a tight-fitting lid. To make eight or twelve servings, use a large pot or flameproof casserole with a lid.

1. "Sweat" the zucchini to remove any bitter liquid and to help it cook faster: Put the diced zucchini in a colander in the sink and sprinkle generously with salt, tossing to coat evenly. Leave it there to drain for half an hour.

2. Put the vegetable oil in a large skillet over low heat, add the chopped onions and sauté until lightly browned. Add the garlic and diced carrots and stir well. Add the water; cover and cook over low heat for ten minutes.

3. Meanwhile, make a light sauce: In a saucepan over low heat, melt the butter, add the flour and cook for two or three minutes, stirring constantly; don't let the mixture burn. Add the hot broth all at once, stirring briskly. Bring to a boil, lower the heat and stir until the sauce is thickened and smooth; set aside.

4. Rinse the zucchini well and shake off excess water. Add the zucchini to the carrots and cook, uncovered, for five minutes, stirring often. Add the ½ teaspoon salt, the spices and a few grindings of fresh pepper, stir well and cook for another minute or two. The zucchini should be tender but still slightly undercooked. Remove from the heat.

5. Add the chicken cubes, sauce and yogurt and stir gently but thoroughly. Serve hot. If you are freezing it, let the mixture cool for 30 minutes; pack in freezer containers (labeled and dated) and freeze for up to two months.

To defrost, leave frozen Spicy Yogurt Chicken with Vegetables in the refrigerator overnight, then warm it briefly but thoroughly in a saucepan over low heat. If the sauce seems too thin, remove the chicken and vegetables with a slotted spoon and gently cook down the sauce a bit.

1 large clove of garlic, minced (about 1½ teaspoons minced)
4 medium carrots, peeled, trimmed and cut in ¼-inch dice
¼ cup water
1½ tablespoons butter
1½ tablespoons flour
¾ cup hot chicken broth
½ teaspoon salt
½ teaspoon ground cumin
½ teaspoon red pepper flakes
Fresh pepper
2 slightly heaping cups poached, cubed boneless chicken (two whole chicken breasts, split, poached and cubed as described in *Poached Chicken Breasts, page 212*)
1 cup plain (unflavored) yogurt

SEE PHOTOGRAPH 12

Couscous with Raisins and Walnuts

2 tablespoons butter
¾ cup chicken broth
½ cup water
⅓ cup dark raisins
1 cup couscous
Salt
Fresh pepper
¼ cup chopped walnuts

Makes four servings

Double the ingredients to make eight servings; triple the ingredients to make 12 servings.

Couscous—pastina-like granules made of semolina wheat—is the perfect Middle Eastern accompaniment for Spicy Yogurt Chicken. Be sure to read the OPTIONS at the end of the recipe for variations on couscous.

Note: You'll need a large skillet, heavy pot or flameproof casserole with a tight-fitting lid.

1. Melt the butter in a large skillet. Add the broth and water and bring to a simmer. Add the raisins, cover the skillet and let the raisins simmer for three minutes (longer if the raisins are hard), until softened and plumped.

2. Bring the broth to a boil and stir in the couscous, making sure there are no lumps. Turn off the heat, cover securely and let stand three or four minutes. All the liquid should be absorbed and the couscous should be soft and cooked all the way through. If there is still liquid in the skillet, cover and let stand for a few more minutes. If all the liquid is absorbed and the grains of couscous are still slightly hard, add half a cup more boiling water or broth, stir well, cover the skillet and let stand for a few more minutes.

Fluff the couscous with two forks, add salt (if needed) and a good grinding of fresh pepper. Transfer the couscous to a serving platter and sprinkle with the chopped nuts, or garnish as shown in photograph 12.

OPTIONS: There are many other ways to dress up couscous if you don't care for raisins and nuts. Browned onions and diced cooked carrots, as well as cooked cubed zucchini, are delicious additions, if you are not serving Spicy Yogurt Chicken with Vegetables. Or add one or two of the following: diced roasted red peppers; chick-peas; chopped tomatoes; baby green peas; cubes of steamed acorn squash; minced parsley.

Chicken Menu 2

Chicken with Mushrooms in Sherried Cream Sauce
White and wild rice *OR* buttered egg noodles
Broccoli purée seasoned with grated Parmesan cheese
Tangerines and Christmas cookies (Chapter 1)

To make the meal more festive, add a simple appetizer of whole cooked artichokes served hot with melted butter or cold with Shallot Vinaigrette Sauce (page 176), or thin slices of smoked salmon on buttered toast with a squeeze of lemon and a grinding of fresh pepper.

To augment the meal, precede or follow it with a green salad garnished either with chopped walnuts and diced (canned) beets or with chick-peas and red onion rings.

QUICK TAKES
More Menus Using Poached Chicken Breasts

Chicken pot pie made with carrots, peas and potatoes
Baked acorn squash
Sautéed apples
Chocolate-Marzipan-Mocha Layered Bars (page 28)

Chicken stir-fry with pea pods, sweet red pepper, water chestnuts, minced ginger and garlic, seasoned with teriyaki sauce
Japanese noodles or white rice
Fresh fruit, assorted Christmas cookies (Chapter 1)

Spanish-style chicken made with chopped sautéed onions, chopped pimientos, strips of ham, well-seasoned tomato sauce
White rice
Green salad with *Shallot Vinaigrette Sauce (page 176)*
No-fail Flan (page 209)

Chicken salad made with chopped apples, chopped mushrooms, cubed avocado, dressed with mayonnaise and Dijon mustard, served on lettuce leaves
Dill Biscuits (pages 153–154)
Chocolate-Cherry Fruitcake (page 82)

Chicken with Mushrooms in Sherried Cream Sauce

2 cups chicken broth
5 tablespoons butter
2 tablespoons minced shallots
½ pound fresh mushrooms, cleaned, trimmed and sliced thin
¼ cup flour
½ cup heavy cream
½ cup dry sherry
¼ cup chopped flat-leaf (Italian) parsley
Salt
2 slightly heaping cups poached, cubed boneless chicken (two whole chicken breasts, split, poached and cubed as described in *Poached Chicken Breasts, page 212*)

Makes four servings

Double the ingredients to make eight servings; triple the ingredients to make 12 servings.

A smooth, elegant dish—but not so elegant that you must save it for company!

1. On a back burner, heat the chicken broth.
   Meanwhile, melt one tablespoon of the butter in a large skillet over moderate heat. Add the shallots and mushrooms and cook, stirring, until the shallots are soft and the mushrooms have given up some of their liquid. Remove the shallots and mushrooms with a slotted spoon; set aside.

2. Simmer the liquid in the skillet until it is reduced to about one tablespoon. Add the remaining four tablespoons butter to the skillet and let it melt. Add the flour and cook for a minute or two, stirring constantly; do not let the mixture burn. Pour in the hot broth all at once, stirring briskly. Bring to a boil, lower the heat and stir until the sauce is smooth and thick.

3. Reduce the heat to very low and stir in the cream, sherry, parsley, shallots and mushrooms and a little salt. Continue cooking and stirring for three minutes; add more salt if necessary.

4. Add the chicken and stir well. Serve hot. If you are freezing it, let the mixture cool for 30 minutes; pack in freezer containers (labeled and dated) and freeze for up to two months.
   To defrost, leave frozen Chicken with Mushrooms in Sherried Cream Sauce in the refrigerator overnight, then reheat briefly but thoroughly in a saucepan over low heat. The sauce looks grainy when defrosted, but smooths out when reheated. If the sauce seems too thin, remove the chicken and vegetables with a slotted spoon and gently cook down the sauce a bit.

Basic Recipe 2: Braised Beef Cubes

Makes 12 servings (allowing ½ pound uncooked beef per serving)

6 pounds boneless beef chuck, bottom round or rump roast, cut in ¾-inch cubes
2 large yellow onions, chopped (about three cups chopped)
1 can (13¾ ounces) beef broth
Salt
Fresh pepper

This is the astonishingly easy basic recipe for the braised beef cubes used in preparing Jenny's Beer Stew (page 221) and Beef Stroganoff (page 222).

The basic method is to braise six pounds of beef cubes at one time and then prepare either or both of the recipes, using the amount of braised beef cubes appropriate to your meal or entertainment plans. Each recipe makes four servings but may be doubled or tripled; for instance, you might make one recipe (four servings) of Beef Stroganoff to freeze for a family dinner and a double recipe (eight servings) of Jenny's Beer Stew to freeze for a dinner party.

Tip: If you have time to do only one thing, make braised beef cubes according to the recipe and freeze in three packages, each package containing four servings (about 2¾ cups). Defrost as needed, using the beef cubes to make the recipes here or any other favorite beef recipe.

Note: You will need a large, heavy ovenproof pot with a tight-fitting lid.

1. Preheat the oven to 325° F. Put all the ingredients (including a small amount of salt and a generous grinding of fresh pepper) in the heavy pot and stir well. Bring to a simmer over medium heat, stirring often to heat evenly. (If meat was cold to start with, this will take about 15–20 minutes.) The meat will lose most of its pink exterior color.

2. Cover the pot with a tight-fitting lid and place in the oven. Leave in the oven for 1½ hours, until the meat is tender.

3. Use a slotted spoon to remove the beef cubes from the pot; strain the broth into a jar and refrigerate for another use. At this point, if necessary, you may either cover and refrigerate the beef until tomorrow or divide it into three equal amounts and freeze until needed. Otherwise, proceed to one of the following recipes.

Tip: For more menus using braised beef cubes, see QUICK TAKES on page 220.

QUICK TAKES

More Menus Using
Braised Beef Cubes

Italian-style beef casserole made with
fried peppers and hearty tomato
sauce, seasoned with red wine
Gnocchi with Parmesan cheese or
other pasta
Zucchini sautéed with garlic
Lemon Cookies (page 000),
fresh fruit

Shepherd's pie made with diced
carrots, celery and yellow turnip,
topped with well-seasoned mashed
potatoes
Cucumber Salad (page 148) and
pickled onions
Lightly Spiced Dark Fruitcake
(page 86)

Chili con carne, with side dishes of
sour cream, chopped onions and
beans
Green salad with *Lime Vinaigrette*
Sauce (page 176)
Brown rice
Apple Tart with Candied Cranberries
and Caramel Sauce (page 60)

Stir-fried beef with broccoli, bean
sprouts and mushrooms, seasoned
with soy sauce
White rice
Brandy-baked Apples (page 155),
Christmas cookies (Chapter 1)

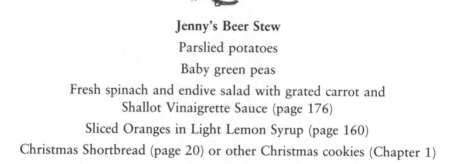

Beef Menu 1

Jenny's Beer Stew
Parslied potatoes
Baby green peas
Fresh spinach and endive salad with grated carrot and
Shallot Vinaigrette Sauce (page 176)
Sliced Oranges in Light Lemon Syrup (page 160)
Christmas Shortbread (page 20) or other Christmas cookies (Chapter 1)

To expand this hearty meal just a bit, serve the spinach salad first, with crusty bread, and add Homemade Chunky Applesauce (page 183) to the main menu.

A note about parslied potatoes: Use three or four small white or red potatoes per person. Don't peel them—just wash well, cut in half or in quarters and boil in water to cover. When the potatoes are tender, drain off the water. Return the hot potatoes to the saucepan and shake briskly over medium heat to evaporate any moisture left on the potatoes. Turn off the heat, add a lump of butter, a handful (or two) of finely chopped parsley, a little salt and a good grinding of fresh pepper. Mix well to melt the butter and dress the potatoes. Keep warm until serving time.

Jenny's Beer Stew

Makes four servings

Double the ingredients to make eight servings; triple the ingredients to make 12 servings.

Beer stew is a felicitous marriage of simple ingredients, simply combined. Many thanks to Jenny Snider for this version.

Note: You will need a large skillet, heavy pot or flameproof casserole.

1. Melt the butter in the large skillet. Add the onions, stir well and sauté uncovered over low heat until browned, about 15–20 minutes.

2. Add the herbs and sugar, stir well and sauté for a minute. Add beer and beef and stir again. Bring to a boil and simmer uncovered over low heat for 20 minutes. Add salt to taste and a good grinding of pepper.

3. Remove the beef cubes with a slotted spoon. Simmer the gravy until it is reduced by one third, about five minutes. Return the beef to the skillet and stir.

Serve hot. If you are freezing it, let the stew cool for 30 minutes; pack in freezer containers (labeled and dated) and freeze for up to two months. Defrost in the refrigerator overnight, then reheat on top of the stove or in the oven.

2 tablespoons butter
2 cups thinly sliced onions
Scant ½ teaspoon dried herb mixture: one pinch marjoram, one pinch oregano, two pinches thyme, one pinch savory
½ teaspoon sugar
2 cups dark beer
2¾ cups braised beef cubes (two pounds beef, cubed and braised, as described in *Braised Beef Cubes, page 219*)
Salt
Fresh pepper

Beef Menu 2

Beef Stroganoff
Buttered bow tie pasta
Browned Brussels Sprouts
Brandied Prune Fruitcake (page 84) *OR* other fruitcake (Chapter 3)
Red and green seedless grapes

For a refreshing first course, serve Cucumber Salad (page 148) on a bed of crisp chicory and romaine lettuce. To stretch the meal further, mix cooked kasha and a few good grindings of fresh pepper into the bow tie pasta.

Beef Stroganoff

2½ tablespoons butter
1 pound fresh mushrooms, cleaned, trimmed and sliced thin
2¾ cups braised beef cubes (two pounds beef, cubed and braised, as described in *Braised Beef Cubes, page 219*)
Salt
Fresh pepper
½ cup dry red wine
1 cup sour cream

Makes four servings

Double the ingredients to make eight servings; triple the ingredients to make 12 servings.

This is not a true Beef Stroganoff, which would include mustard but very little sour cream and no mushrooms. Rather, it is what we've come to think of popularly as Beef Stroganoff, with no mustard and lots of mushrooms and sour cream. I can't explain how this switch happened, but it does taste delicious.

1. Melt the butter in a large skillet or heavy pot. Add the mushrooms and sauté over low heat until the mushrooms begin to soften. Turn off the heat.

2. Add the beef, a little salt and pepper to taste and stir well. This will cool the mushrooms and warm the beef.

3. Add the wine and sour cream and stir well. Very slowly bring to a simmer and cook gently for 20 minutes, until the ingredients are heated through and the sauce is reduced slightly. Correct seasoning if necessary.

Serve hot. If you are freezing it, let the Beef Stroganoff cool for 30 minutes; pack in freezer containers (labeled and dated) and freeze for up to two months. Defrost in the refrigerator overnight, then warm thoroughly in a saucepan over low heat.

Browned Brussels Sprouts

Makes four servings

Double the ingredients to make eight servings; triple the ingredients to make 12 servings.

1 pound Brussels sprouts
3 tablespoons butter
Salt
Fresh pepper

Even people who don't usually like Brussels sprouts will like them prepared this way, and people who like them will love them.

1. Prepare the Brussels sprouts: Trim off the stem ends and discard any wilted or yellowed leaves. Cut in ⅛-inch slices, from top to stem end. (If you like, slice the sprouts in a food processor and don't worry about the direction of the slices.) Rinse well in a colander and shake out excess liquid.

2. Put the sliced sprouts in a large skillet, cover tightly and steam over low heat for a few minutes, just until slightly wilted. (The amount of water clinging to the rinsed sliced sprouts is sufficient for steaming.) Uncover and turn off heat.

3. Add the butter and stir well to melt. Cook over medium heat, stirring often, until well browned but not burned. Scrape browned bits from pan. Add salt and a good grinding of pepper and stir again. Serve hot.

START WITH STORE-BOUGHT

Pasta

Hot pasta can be dressed quickly with any number of handy ingredients. Here are some basic ideas; add your favorite seasonings—fresh pepper, basil, oregano, and so on.

❋ Minced garlic sautéed in butter and/or olive oil; freshly grated Parmesan cheese on top

❋ Slivers of dried sausage, chopped roasted red pepper, capers, all sautéed in olive oil

❋ *Parsley Pesto (page 241)*

❋ Mixed steamed vegetables, sautéed garlic, Parmesan cheese, butter

❋ Cubed ham, green peas, cheese sauce

❋ Butter, cream, thin-sliced sautéed mushrooms, chopped scallions

❋ Strips of smoked turkey, artichoke hearts, chopped parsley, cream sauce; Parmesan cheese on top

❋ Caponata, chopped peeled tomatoes, chopped garlic; pine nuts for topping

❋ Flaked oil-packed tuna, chopped peeled tomatoes, chopped black olives, capers

❋ Chopped cooked shrimp, chopped green pepper, chopped cherry tomatoes, hot red pepper

Two Sauces for Pasta

One savory sauce to freeze in four-serving portions; one creamy sauce to make when you need a fast, flavorful main course. With these meatless sauces you can vary the chicken and beef menus with pasta menus—and keep your favorite vegetarians happy, too.

Pasta Menu 1

Linguine or spaghetti with **Savory Tomato-Eggplant Sauce**

Grated Parmesan cheese

Swiss chard sautéed with olive oil and garlic *OR*
salad of arugula, endive and radicchio
with Lime Vinaigrette Sauce (page 176)

Crusty Italian bread or breadsticks

Rich Holiday Pound Cake (page 66) with raspberry sorbet *OR*
fruit and Christmas cookies (Chapter 1)

To make the meal even more substantial, begin with an antipasto that includes three or more of the following: sliced mozzarella cheese; olives; marinated artichoke hearts (from a jar; drained of excess oil and tossed with a little balsamic vinegar); roasted peppers (from a jar; drained, patted dry); anchovies; caponata (from a can); wedges of hard-cooked egg.

Savory Tomato-Eggplant Sauce

Makes four or more servings

Double the ingredients to make eight or more servings; triple the ingredients to make 12 or more servings.

This is a thick, intensely flavored sauce that you may want to dilute slightly with water, according to your family's taste.

1. Put the eggplant cubes in a colander in the sink and sprinkle generously with salt, tossing to coat evenly. Leave in the sink for an hour. Meanwhile, put the sun-dried tomatoes in a small saucepan with water to cover and simmer just until softened, about five minutes. Drain, rinse well in a small strainer and drain again. (In addition to being leathery, sun-dried tomatoes are usually very salty. Simmering and rinsing them counteracts both of these conditions.) Put the softened sun-dried tomatoes in a food processor or blender with a cup of tomato purée and process until almost smooth; set aside. Reserve the remaining tomato purée.

2. In a large heavy pot or casserole, heat the olive oil and add the chopped onions. Cook over low heat until the onions are golden. Add the garlic and cook just until the garlic is soft.

3. Rinse the eggplant very well to wash off the salt. Squeeze it, one handful at a time, to release bitter liquid. Add the eggplant to the onions and garlic. Cook over low heat, stirring often, until it is very soft. It will become somewhat sticky and brown bits will cling to the pot; this is fine—keep scraping them off the pot with a wooden spoon.

4. Add the sun-dried tomato mixture, the reserved tomato purée and all the remaining ingredients (including a few grindings of fresh pepper and the red pepper flakes, if desired) and mix well. Cook over low heat, stirring occasionally, for 30 minutes. Correct the seasoning, if necessary. Serve hot. If you are freezing the sauce, let it cool for 30 minutes; pack the sauce in freezer containers (labeled and dated) and freeze for up to two months.

1 medium eggplant (about one pound), peeled and cut in ½-inch cubes
Salt for preparing the eggplant
15 sun-dried tomatoes
1 can (29 ounces) tomato purée
3 tablespoons olive oil
1 large yellow onion, chopped (about 1½ cups chopped)
2 large cloves garlic, minced
1 six-ounce can tomato paste
2 tablespoons balsamic or red wine vinegar
1 tablespoon sugar
Fresh pepper
½ teaspoon red pepper flakes (optional; use only if you like a spicier sauce)
Salt to taste

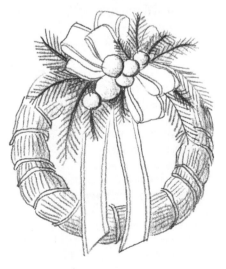

THE CHRISTMAS PANTRY CHECKLIST

Appetizers and Hors d'Oeuvres

Keep unexpected guests happy with appetizers you pull from a well-stocked pantry and refrigerator.

❋ *Popcorn and Pretzel Snacks (page 241)*
❋ *Spiced Nuts (page 242)*
❋ Mixed nuts
❋ Trail mixes
❋ Mixed dried fruit
❋ Glacé fruits
❋ Assorted cheeses
❋ Assorted pickles
❋ Assorted olives
❋ Assorted crackers
❋ Canned pâté
❋ *Savory Butters (page 240)*
❋ Smoked salmon
❋ Anchovies
❋ Smoked oysters
❋ Canned shrimp
❋ Sardines
❋ Herring in cream sauce or wine sauce
❋ Marinated artichoke hearts
❋ Canned caponata
❋ Roasted red peppers
❋ Pickled peppers
❋ Italian pickled vegetables
❋ Dried sausage
❋ Cocktail sausages
❋ *Hummus (page 213),* pita
❋ Stuffed grape leaves
❋ Taramasalata
❋ Frozen egg rolls
❋ Tortilla chips, refried beans (canned), Monterey Jack cheese

Defrost overnight in the refrigerator or pop the frozen sauce out of the container and heat it gently in a heavy saucepan or pot. The sauce is quite concentrated, so gradually add water (not too much) until it reaches the consistency you prefer.

OPTIONS: After defrosting the sauce (or when it is ready, if you're not freezing it), add cooked meatballs, chunks of cooked fresh sausage, slices of dried sausage, shredded chicken or kidney beans. Simmer gently until all ingredients are hot.

Linguine or spaghetti with **Creamy Spinach and Herb Sauce**

Marinated Sun-dried Tomatoes (page 190)
and sliced mozzarella cheese

Crusty French or Italian bread

Ice cream with Bittersweet Chocolate-Nut Sauce (page 231)
OR fruit and Christmas cookies (Chapter 1)

To stretch the meal or make it a bit fancier, serve scallops for starters: For four people, cook 16–20 (or more) medium scallops in ½ cup water, ¼ cup white wine, one garlic clove and a dash of salt, for three minutes. Drain and dry the scallops and marinate them for an hour in a mixture of ¼ cup olive oil and the juice of one lemon. Grind fresh pepper over them and serve with toothpicks for spearing and fresh bread for dipping into the marinade.

Creamy Spinach and Herb Sauce

Makes four servings

Double the ingredients to make eight servings; triple the ingredients to make 12 servings.

This sauce is amazingly easy to make and absolutely delectable. It's not a sauce to freeze—it's a sauce to make when you've forgotten to defrost something for dinner. Prepare it whenever you have a free minute during the day or right before dinner.

Tip: Powder the herbs a little at a time between your fingers. This helps release the flavor and aroma.

Cook the spinach in water, breaking it up as it thaws. When it's heated all the way through, drain well and press out the excess water. Purée all the ingredients in a food processor or blender. Stir the mixture in a saucepan over low heat until hot. Correct the seasoning if necessary; the sauce must be adequately salted. Refrigerate until needed, then reheat gently and stir into hot pasta.

Note: The sauce can sometimes get rather sticky; you may need to add a little more half-and-half when you stir it into the pasta.

1 package frozen chopped spinach
1 teaspoon dried oregano, powdered
1 teaspoon dried basil, powdered
1½ cups half-and-half
1½ cups (one 15-ounce container) whole-milk ricotta cheese
Salt
Fresh pepper

CHAPTER 10

Gifts from Your Kitchen

Nothing warms the hearts (and delights the tastebuds) of friends and relatives more than receiving a delicious, beautifully wrapped gift of homemade food from your own Christmas kitchen. In this chapter you'll find an irresistible variety of savory and sweet condiments, sauces, butters and other goodies—something to satisfy each and every person on your gift list.

And here's a Christmas present for you, too: You won't be spending hours over a hot stove. These homemade treats can be made in double-quick time because they are not canned—you don't need sterilized jars and all the other paraphernalia of water-bath canning. Instead, most of the easy-to-make gifts in this chapter are cooked briefly (or not at all) and then stored in pantry, refrigerator or freezer. (There are a few important things you should know and remember about preparing these homemade gifts, so please read the tips and guidelines below.)

Tips and Guidelines

❉ Use glass jars with screw-top lids or ceramic crocks with well-fitting tops. I prefer standard half-pint and pint canning jars (also called jelly jars) with screw-top lids, but you may certainly use recycled jars without chips or cracks, with matching lids. Or you might like to try lightning jars made of thick glass with glass tops, rubber rings and clamp closures—they make very attractive gifts. Avoid plastic containers, except for packaging nuts and snacks.

❉ Scrub the containers and lids with hot, soapy water and rinse very well. If the recipe calls for hot jars, leave the clean jars in a pot of very hot water until they are needed. At that time, lift them out and invert on a rack to drain for a minute or two. (The jars are kept heated so the glass won't break when you fill them with simmering-hot condiments.)

❉ Refrigerator condiments have a much shorter life than canned (water-bath-processed) condiments. Therefore, it is imperative that you label or tag each jar with the name of the recipe and the date by which it should be eaten. (The refrigerator life is stated in each recipe.)

❉ Once you have made your food gifts, you'll want to wrap them to look as pretty as possible. To help you accomplish this, you'll find gift wrap ideas in this chapter and in photograph 13. Use the drawings and photograph as guides or to give you inspiration for your own gift wrap designs.

SEE PHOTOGRAPH 9

Old-fashioned Lemon Curd

⅔ cup (1 stick plus
    2⅔ tablespoons) butter
2 cups sugar
⅔ cup fresh lemon juice
3 tablespoons grated lemon rind
¼ teaspoon salt
5 eggs

COOK'S JOURNAL

Labeling

Every gift of food should be identified and dated, either with a lick-and-stick label pressed right onto the container or, if the container won't hold a label, with a gift tag tied on or a three-by-five card tucked inside.

Jars must be labeled with the name of the food and the date by which it should be eaten. If there are special instructions on preparation (such as "heat in a double boiler") or storage, include those, too. You may also wish to list the ingredients (if there is any question of food restrictions or allergies) or to suggest what foods go well with this gift.

Photograph 13 will give you some ideas for making labels and tags.

Makes about three cups

Lemon curd is a thick, smooth spread with a tangy-sweet lemon flavor. It makes a delightful filling for tarts, cakes and cake rolls. Great on muffins, biscuits and tea breads, too.

1. Melt the butter in the top of a double boiler over barely simmering water. Add the sugar, lemon juice, grated lemon rind and salt and stir until the sugar dissolves. Turn off the heat.

2. In a large bowl, beat the eggs until frothy. Slowly add one cup of the lemon mixture to the eggs, stirring well. Return the egg mixture to the top of the double boiler, stir well and continue cooking for 25–30 minutes over low heat, stirring occasionally, until the lemon curd is thick.

3. Remove the top of the double boiler and continue stirring for a few minutes to release more heat. Strain the lemon curd into another bowl and then spoon it into clean, hot jars. Wipe the rim of each jar, cover and allow to come to room temperature. Label the jars and refrigerate for up to a month.

(Remember: The label should include the name of the recipe and the date by which it should be eaten. Be sure the recipient stores the lemon curd in the refrigerator.)

Bittersweet Chocolate-Nut Sauce

Makes about 5½ cups

A luscious, chunky sauce to spoon over ice cream, pound cake, poached pears, sautéed bananas or anything else you like. Chocolate lovers have been known to eat the sauce straight from the jar.

½ cup (one stick) butter
8 squares (eight ounces) unsweetened chocolate, chopped
1½ cups boiling water
1½ cups sugar
1 cup light corn syrup
2 teaspoons vanilla extract
1½ cups chopped pecans or blanched almonds, toasted
Note: See *How to Toast Nuts* on page 40.

1. In a heavy saucepan, melt and stir the butter and chocolate over the lowest possible heat. Add the water, sugar and corn syrup and blend well. Raise the heat just enough to produce a simmer and cook the mixture for 15 minutes. Do not stir while simmering.

2. Remove the chocolate sauce from the stove and stir for a minute or two to release heat. Add the vanilla and chopped nuts and blend well.

3. Pour the hot sauce into clean, hot jars and wipe the rim of each jar. Allow the sauce to come to room temperature. Cover, label and refrigerate for up to three months.

To serve, heat the sauce in the top of a double boiler and pour over plain cake, cream puffs, ice cream, pudding, poached pears, etc.

(Remember: The label or gift tag should include the name of the recipe, the date by which it should be eaten, and instructions for heating. Be sure the recipient stores the sauce in the refrigerator.)

CHRISTMAS MEMORIES FROM FRIENDS

The Aprons

Many years ago my young aunt and uncle, with not much money for Christmas presents, sewed and appliquéd a beautiful felt apron for each family member. The many-colored appliqués depicted the favorite subject or hobby of each recipient. My mother's was decorated with vegetables and fruits, a salad bowl, salt and pepper shakers. Mine had an enchanting ballerina dancing off into a handsome arched stage set. What impressed me, then and now, was the way my aunt and uncle implicitly honored each person, from the youngest to the oldest, by noticing and celebrating something special about him or her—*that* was the real gift.

GIFTS FROM YOUR KITCHEN

SEE PHOTOGRAPH 13

Fresh Orange Relish

6 medium navel oranges
1½ cups water
2 cups light raisins
¼ cup chopped crystallized ginger
¼ teaspoon powdered ginger
1 cup sugar
½ cup honey
1½ cups coarsely chopped
    walnuts

QUICK AND EASY
Do-It-Yourself Gift Assortments

Salad Lover's Gift: balsamic vinegar, garlic, shallots, pepper grinder, dry mustard, olive oil and the recipe for *Shallot Vinaigrette Sauce (page 176)*, packed in a wooden salad bowl tied with gingham ribbon and wooden salad utensils

Morning Coffee Gift: *Christmas Stollen (page 117)*, or other holiday bread from Chapter 5, wrapped in cellophane and tied neatly to a paddle breadboard; add a little packet of fresh coffee beans or ground coffee

Teatime Gift: jar of *Winter Pear Butter (page 233)*, cut-glass condiment jar with lid and a pretty condiment spoon, packaged in a small basket lined with a lace-edged napkin

Cocktail Snack Pack: *Popcorn and Pretzel Snacks* and *Spiced Nuts (pages 241 and 242)* in screw-top plastic containers, plus ribbon-tied cocktail napkins

Makes about 7½ cups

This relish is brightly flavored, juicy and crunchy, a great side dish for roast duck or Cornish hens, pork roasts and—surprise—for cheese omelets. Also spectacular with vanilla yogurt, ricotta cheese or cottage cheese.

1. Use a vegetable peeler to remove long, thin pieces of orange zest from two oranges. Cut the zest in long ⅛-inch-wide strips.

Working on a plate (to catch the juice), use a sharp knife to cut the peel from the oranges, making sure to remove all the bitter white pith; cut the oranges in ½-inch chunks, discarding the white fiber in the center. Reserve the juice; set the orange chunks aside.

2. In a large saucepan, bring the water to a boil, add the strips of zest and the raisins and simmer, covered, for ten minutes.

3. Add the crystallized and powdered ginger, the sugar, honey and reserved orange juice and simmer, uncovered, for 15 minutes. Add the oranges and chopped nuts and stir well. Let the relish cool.

4. Spoon relish and liquid into clean jars; there will be a lot of liquid. Wipe the rim of each jar. Cover, label and refrigerate for up to two weeks.

(Remember: The label should include the name of the recipe and the date by which it should be eaten. Be sure the recipient stores the relish in the refrigerator.)

Winter Pear Butter

Makes about four cups

Smooth, delicate pear butter is delicious on toast, popovers, biscuits and other light breads. Try it on waffles and pancakes, too.

1. Peel, quarter and core the pears; chop in ½-inch pieces.
Put all the ingredients in a large heavy pot and bring to a boil. Reduce the heat and cook, stirring often, for 15 minutes, or until the pears are soft.

2. Purée the mixture in a food processor or blender and then return the purée to the pot. Cook uncovered over very low heat, stirring often, for 1–1½ hours, or until the pear butter is very thick. Be careful not to let it scorch. Remove from the heat.

3. Stir the hot pear butter for a minute or two to release more heat and then spoon into clean, hot jars, leaving ¼ inch of space at the top of each jar. Wipe the rim of each jar. Cover and allow to come to room temperature. (You'll notice that the pear butter is a rather gray-green color; this is the correct color.) Label the jars and refrigerate for up to three weeks.

(Remember: The label should include the name of the recipe and the date by which it should be eaten. Be sure the recipient stores the pear butter in the refrigerator.)

8 large ripe pears (about
  4½ pounds)
1 cup sugar
⅓ cup brandy
⅓ cup water

Gift Wraps for Jars

Take your choice of several gift wraps that make jars look their Christmas best. (Remember: Every jar must have an identifying label before you gift-wrap it.)

❋ Tie something pretty around or just below the lid—grosgrain ribbon, lace, several strands of yarn or rickrack, gold or silver cord. Under the tie, tuck a bit of evergreen, some dried or fabric flowers or a small ornament.

❋ Top the jar with a pinked circle of fabric (try calico or Christmas prints, stripes, dots), secure with a rubber band and tie with narrow ribbon, macramé cord or yarn (over the rubber band).

❋ Use something unusual: Top the lid with a round or square paper doily and tie carefully with narrow satin ribbon. Or cover the lid with a small crisp hanky and tie with a matching ribbon.

❋ Wrap the entire jar (not just the lid): Slip jar into a shiny bottle bag, cut the top of the bag down to size and tie with ribbon or cord. Stash two or more jars in a small shiny paper bag and tie with ribbon and a gift tag. Center the jar in a square of cellophane, two sheets of tissue paper or a circle of pinked fabric; bring the wrapping up and twist it closed; secure and tie with pretty cord.

SEE PHOTOGRAPH 13

Apple-Onion Chutney

Makes about four cups

1 tablespoon mixed pickling
    spices
1 three-inch cinnamon stick,
    broken in pieces
3 cups (packed) light brown sugar
1½ cups dark raisins
1 teaspoon salt
1½ cups chopped onions
1 clove of garlic, sliced
2 tablespoons minced fresh ginger
2 cups cider vinegar
3 large Rome Beauty apples (or
    other baking apples)

A spicy, savory chutney that goes perfectly with any curry, with roast chicken and turkey or with pork. Terrific with sausage patties, too.

1. Tie the pickling spices and broken cinnamon stick in a double layer of cheesecloth and put the bag of spices in a large enameled or stainless steel pot. Add all the remaining ingredients except the apples and stir well. Bring to a boil, lower the heat and simmer for one hour, stirring often.

2. Meanwhile, peel the apples, cut in quarters and carefully remove the cores, seeds and other hard matter. Chop the apples into ¼-inch pieces. When the spice mixture has simmered for an hour, add the apples and simmer for 30 minutes more, or until the chutney is very thick.

3. Spoon the hot chutney into clean, hot jars, leaving ¼ inch of room at the top of each jar. Wipe the rim of each jar. Cover and let the chutney come to room temperature. Label the jars and refrigerate for up to four weeks.

(Remember: The label should include the name of the recipe and the date by which it should be eaten. Be sure the recipient stores the chutney in the refrigerator.)

SEE PHOTOGRAPHS 10 AND 13

Cranberry Ketchup

Makes about six cups

Tart and refreshing—great with Christmas roast turkey or on a turkey sandwich.

1. Combine all the ingredients in an enameled or stainless steel saucepan. Bring slowly to a boil, stirring occasionally, to dissolve the sugar. Lower heat and simmer, uncovered, for ten minutes, or until ketchup is thick.

2. Let the ketchup cool slightly and then spoon into clean, hot jars, leaving ¼ inch of room at the top of each jar. Wipe the rim of each jar. Cover and let cool to room temperature. Label the jars and refrigerate for up to three weeks.

(Remember: The label should include the name of the recipe and the date by which it should be eaten. Be sure the recipient stores the cranberry ketchup in the refrigerator.)

2 bags (16 ounces each) fresh cranberries, chopped fine
Note: Chop the cranberries in a food processor.
3 cups sugar
1 cup cider vinegar
1½ teaspoons cinnamon
1 teaspoon ground cloves
1 teaspoon ground allspice
½ teaspoon salt
½ teaspoon fresh pepper

QUICK AND EASY
Sampler Gifts

Tea Sampler: Put a selection of five-bag tea packets in a china teapot; cover with a tea cozy and tie with ribbon that matches the cozy.

Candy Sampler for Kids: Pack candy canes, small bags of candy and chocolate Santas into a toy dump truck or child-size suitcase; wrap with cellophane and lots of curled ribbons.

Herb and Spice Sampler: Choose a dozen boxes of herbs and spices; gather a bright bandanna around them to make a hobo bag and tie it up with a long-handled wooden spoon.

Dried Fruit Sampler: Layer peaches, pears, apricots, pineapple, raisins in a wide-mouthed glass canning jar or apothecary-style jar, tie with gold cord and tuck in a sprig of baby's breath.

Marnie's Dried Peach and Apricot Chutney

Makes about six cups

5 Granny Smith apples
¾ cup dried peaches, cut in sixths
¾ cup dried apricots, cut in quarters
½ cup light raisins
6 cloves of garlic, mashed
2 tablespoons finely minced fresh ginger
1¾ cups red wine vinegar
2½ cups sugar
1 teaspoon salt
¼–½ teaspoon red pepper flakes (optional)

Many thanks to writer Marnie Mueller for this sweet, rich chutney. It's delicious with roast chicken or turkey, of course, but it enhances roast lamb or baked ham just as well. Try it on cheese sandwiches, too.

1. Peel the apples, cut in quarters and carefully remove the cores, seeds and other hard matter. Chop in ½-inch chunks.

2. Put all the ingredients in an enameled or stainless steel saucepan, stir well and bring to a boil. Lower the heat and simmer for 50 minutes, stirring occasionally. At the end of the cooking time the mixture should have the consistency of thick jam.

3. Spoon the chutney into clean, hot jars, leaving ¼ inch of room at the top of each jar. Wipe the rim of each jar. Cover and allow to come to room temperature. Label the jars and refrigerate for up to three months.

(Remember: The label should include the name of the recipe and the date by which it should be eaten. Be sure the recipient stores the chutney in the refrigerator.)

Christmas Touches

A favorite china bowl filled with little ribbon-tied bundles of cinnamon sticks . . . strings of lights in the kitchen, for the cooks to enjoy . . . a grapevine wreath decorated with dried chiles of different sizes and colors . . . jars of red and green jelly beans or gumdrops . . . your child's old red wagon piled with gaily wrapped gifts, parked near the Christmas tree . . . a basketful of pinecones and shiny Christmas balls

SEE PHOTOGRAPH 13

Winter Salsa

Makes about seven cups

Many salsas are made with fresh tomatoes, a real problem in winter when fresh tomatoes are usually mealy and tasteless. Winter Salsa is made with canned tomatoes—and you will be amazed at how crisp and fresh-tasting it is. Guaranteed to perk up winter appetites and winter meals.

1. Set a large strainer over a large bowl and empty the tomatoes into the strainer to drain. Split each tomato in half so the inner juices can drain, too. In another large bowl, stir together all the remaining ingredients.

2. When the tomatoes are well drained, chop them in ¾-inch pieces, add the pieces to the other ingredients and stir well. Correct the seasoning if necessary, keeping in mind that the flavor of the hot peppers will develop; salsa that may not seem very hot the day you make it will be hotter in a day or so.

3. Spoon the salsa into clean jars and wipe the rim of each jar. Label the jars and refrigerate for up to three weeks.

(Remember: The label should include the name of the recipe and the date by which it should be eaten. Be sure the recipient stores the salsa in the refrigerator.)

Tomatoes from two cans (28 ounces each) Italian-style peeled tomatoes, plus ½ cup liquid from one of the cans
1¼ cups chopped onions
1 cup grated carrot (about two medium carrots)
1 four-ounce can peeled, chopped, mild green chiles
3 pickled jalapeño peppers (stems removed) puréed with ¼ cup pickling liquid from the jar
¼ cup wine vinegar

Simple Wraps for Gift Assortments

❄ Nestle homemade foods in a straw or slatted wood basket (or a mushroom basket from the supermarket) padded with packing straw or crumpled tissue paper; trim with ribbon, ornaments, holly or other decorations.

❄ Several jars of homemade goodies will fit in a small shopping bag, with a piece of stiff cardboard on the bottom. Decorate the bag with Christmas stickers; first tie the handle with string to keep it closed and then overtie with metallic garland bows.

❄ Lay three tightly closed half-pint jars of condiments in a clear plastic shoebox padded with packing straw or tissue paper. Instead of wrapping the box with paper, just tie it up with wide plaid ribbon.

SEE PHOTOGRAPH 13

Marinated Onion and Red Pepper Relish

Makes about nine cups

2 tablespoons olive oil
2 sweet red (bell) peppers, seeded and cut in ¼-inch pieces
3 cups red wine vinegar
1 cup water
½ teaspoon salt
2 bay leaves
2 teaspoons dried oregano
Fresh pepper
6 medium red onions, peeled and sliced in thin rings

Best with beef—hamburgers, meat loaf and even roasts—but also terrific with tacos and other Mexican food, with cold cuts or on hero sandwiches.

1. Heat the olive oil in a large enameled or stainless steel saucepan. Add the peppers and sauté over medium heat until slightly softened.

2. Add the remaining ingredients, except the onions, and simmer uncovered for five minutes. Turn off the heat, add the onion slices and stir well. Cover and allow the onions to sit in the marinade for four hours at room temperature.

3. Use tongs to put the onions into clean jars; fill with peppers and marinade. Wipe the rim of each jar. Cover, label and refrigerate for up to four weeks.

(Remember: The label should include the name of the recipe and the date by which it should be eaten. Be sure the recipient stores the relish in the refrigerator.)

Tarragon Mustard

Makes about 1¾ cups

Crunchy mustard seeds and a distinct flavor of tarragon make this mustard a marvelous accompaniment to pâtés and other charcuterie.

1. Put all the ingredients in an enameled or stainless steel saucepan and stir until blended. Bring to a boil, lower the heat and simmer uncovered, stirring occasionally, for three minutes. Cover and refrigerate for eight hours or overnight.

2. Bring to a boil again, stirring constantly and adding a little water as needed to keep the mustard from scorching. Cook for a minute or two, until thickened. Let the mustard cool and then spoon it into clean crocks or jars. Wipe the rim of each jar. Cover, label and store in the refrigerator for up to one month.

(Remember: The label should include the name of the recipe and the date by which it should be eaten. Be sure the recipient stores the mustard in the refrigerator.)

½ cup mustard seeds
½ cup dry mustard
   Note: Do not use Chinese or other oriental powdered mustards.
1 tablespoon prepared horseradish
¾ cup cider vinegar
¾ cup dark beer
2 teaspoons finely minced garlic
2 teaspoons dried tarragon leaves
1 teaspoon salt
2 tablespoons dark brown sugar

More Gift Ideas from the Christmas Kitchen

❋ Christmas cookies from Chapter 1 (gift wrap suggestions on page 44)

❋ Fruitcakes from Chapter 3 (gift wrap suggestions on page 83)

❋ Candies from Chapter 4 (gift wrap suggestions on page 109)

❋ *Christmas Stollen (page 117)*

❋ *Cranberry Spiral Bread with Vanilla Glaze (page 123)*

❋ *Panettone di Natale (page 134)*

❋ *Ginger-Nut Loaves (page 127)*

❋ *Mexican Three Kings Bread (page 130)*

❋ *Date and Honey Loaves (page 125)*

❋ *Nora's Plum Puddings (page 174)*

❋ *Marinated Sun-dried Tomatoes (page 190)*

Gifts for the Chef

Stocking Stuffers

❋ Kitchen timer
❋ Poultry shears
❋ Wooden spoons
❋ Set of canapé cutters
❋ Small wire whisk
❋ Pastry cutting wheel
❋ Pepper mill
❋ Corkscrew
❋ Candy thermometer
❋ Frosting spatula
❋ Tartlet tins
❋ Paper doilies

Moderately Priced Gifts

❋ Set of handsome kitchen utensils (slotted spoon, metal spatula, etc.) to hang from a matching rack
❋ Wok (with metal ring), wok utensils, Chinese cookbook
❋ Electric coffee grinder
❋ Ceramic baking stone, pizza pan, pizza cutter
❋ Cake-decorating set, including a selection of tips
❋ Fancy-shaped molds (for gelatin salads, aspics, ice cream bombes, etc.)
❋ Earthenware casserole or terrine

Extravagant Gifts

❋ Full-size or compact food processor
❋ Toaster oven
❋ Tin- or stainless steel–lined copper bowls, pots or skillets
❋ Electric waffle iron
❋ Portable barbecue
❋ Electric ice cream maker
❋ Heavy-duty standing mixer

Savory Butters

Use these butters for sautéing or basting, to make savory toast, for dressing steamed vegetables or cooked pasta or as a foundation for canapés.

To make each savory butter, you will need two cups (four sticks) of sweet butter, at room temperature but not oily. The method is simple: In a food processor, blend the sweet butter with the ingredients listed for any one of the savory butters listed below. When the mixture is smooth, pack into clean jars or crocks. Label and refrigerate for up to two weeks. If you prefer to freeze the butters, either pack into plastic containers or place chilled butter on kitchen parchment or plastic wrap, shape into logs and roll snugly; frozen butters will last for months.

(Remember: The labels should include the names of the recipes and the dates by which they should be eaten. Be sure the recipients store the butters in the refrigerator or freezer.)

Garlic and Herb Butter (makes about two cups): four large cloves of garlic, cut in pieces; ½ cup flat-leaf (Italian) parsley leaves; one teaspoon dried oregano, crushed; 1½ teaspoons dried basil, crushed; ½ teaspoon freshly ground pepper; ¼ teaspoon salt; ¾ teaspoon fresh lemon juice

Blue Cheese Parsley Butter (makes about 2¾ cups): one cup crumbled blue cheese; one cup flat-leaf (Italian) parsley leaves

Anchovy Butter (makes about two cups): 14 anchovy fillets, drained; two teaspoons lemon juice; two dashes of Tabasco sauce

Chili Butter (makes about 2¾ cups): two four-ounce cans chopped mild green chiles, drained; 1¼ teaspoons chili powder; ¼ teaspoon salt; two dashes Tabasco sauce

Parsley Pesto

Makes about two cups

Any variety of cooked pasta becomes a special treat when dressed with Parsley Pesto—a winter version of the familiar basil pesto we make in the summer.

Put all the ingredients except the fresh pepper in a food processor and process until puréed. Add freshly ground pepper to taste. Divide the pesto between two clean jars and wipe the rims of the jars. Cover, label and refrigerate. Parsley Pesto will last, covered and refrigerated, for up to three weeks.

(Remember: The label should include the name of the recipe and the date by which it should be eaten. Be sure the recipient stores the pesto in the refrigerator.)

4 cups firmly packed flat leaf
  (Italian) parsley leaves
1 cup pine nuts
3 cloves of garlic, cut in pieces
⅔ cup freshly grated Parmesan
  cheese
1 cup extra-virgin olive oil
½ teaspoon salt
Fresh pepper

Popcorn and Pretzel Snacks

Makes about 15 cups

For maximum freshness, make this treat a very short time before eating or giving it away.

Preheat the oven to 325° F. In a large bowl or pot, mix the popcorn and pretzel sticks. Stir the chili powder and grated cheese into the melted butter or margarine and pour over the popcorn and pretzel sticks. Toss well, spread on cookie sheets and place in the oven for 15 minutes. Let cool, then transfer to large clean jars or other containers. Label the containers and store at room temperature. Eat as soon as possible.

(Remember: The label should include the name of the recipe and a recommendation to eat the snacks as soon as possible.)

10 cups fresh popcorn (about
  ½ cup unpopped corn)
5 cups pretzel sticks
2 teaspoons chili powder
⅓ cup freshly grated Parmesan
  and/or Romano cheese
½ cup (one stick) butter or
  margarine, melted and cooled

SEE PHOTOGRAPH 13

Spiced Nuts

Makes four cups

Take your choice of two spice combinations that flavor the nuts delicately, without overpowering them.

1. Preheat oven to 325° F. Put the nuts in a large bowl, pour the butter over them and toss well. Spread the nuts on a jelly roll pan and bake, stirring occasionally, for half an hour, or until the nuts look browned and smell toasty.

2. In a small bowl, stir together the ingredients of Spice Mixture 1 or 2. Sprinkle the spice mixture on the toasted nuts and stir well. Return the pan to the oven for five more minutes.

3. Spread the nuts on paper towels to drain. Sprinkle with salt to taste and let the nuts cool. Pack in clean containers, label and store at room temperature, or store in the refrigerator or freezer for longer life.

(Remember: The label should include the name of the recipe and instructions for storing the nuts.)

4 cups (about one pound) unsalted mixed nuts
¼ cup (½ stick) butter, melted
Spice Mixture 1: two teaspoons cinnamon, one teaspoon powdered ginger, one teaspoon ground cloves; *OR*
Spice Mixture 2: two teaspoons chili powder, two teaspoons curry powder
Salt

Gift Wraps for Nuts and Snacks

Containers for nuts and snacks must be clean (scrubbed and dried) or lined completely with something clean (fresh tissue paper, waxed paper, plastic wrap) or you must put the food in a plastic bag before packing it in the container. Choose a simple or even whimsical container—like the ones below—and trim it festively.

❉ Small bucket (metal, plastic, cardboard)
❉ Printed or metallic cardboard gift box
❉ Glass jar with cork stopper
❉ Plastic jar with brightly colored lid
❉ Paper shopping bag or gift bag, decorated and trimmed
❉ New (clean) take-out food container
❉ Christmas stocking
❉ Square of pretty fabric with pinked edges, secured with ribbon or cord

Index

Almonds
  Almond Chocolate Mousse, 59
  Almond-layered Fruitcakes,
    79–80, **photo 3**
  Almond Spritz Cookies, 18–19
  Brown Sugar Butter Crunch with
    Toasted Almonds, 104–5,
    photo 7
  Chocolate-dipped Almonds, 59
  Orange-Almond Filling, 128
Anchondo, Irma de, 209
Anchovy Butter, 240
Appetizers
  checklist for, 226
  Crudités, 163
Apples
  Apple-Mince Tartlets, 31–32,
    photo 11
  Apple-Onion Chutney, 234,
    photo 13
  Apple Tart with Candied
    Cranberries and Caramel
    Sauce, 60–62, **photo 4**
  Brandy-baked Apples with Nuts
    and Raisins, 155
Applesauce, Homemade Chunky, 183
Apricots
  Apricot Brandy Filling, 23

Chocolate-dipped Apricots and
    Pears, 110–11
  Fluffy Apricot Sauce, 91
  Marnie's Dried Peach and
    Apricot Chutney, 236
  Prune-Apricot Custard Tart with
    Sweet Lemon Crust, 70–72,
    photo 4
Avocados
  Black Bean Salad with Oranges,
    Avocado and Coriander, 207

Baking Powder Biscuits with
    Variations, 153–54
Bar, checklist for the, 165
Basic Vinaigrette Sauce with
    Variations, 176
Beans
  Black Bean Salad with Oranges,
    Avocado and Coriander, 207
  Make-Ahead Boston Baked
    Beans, 181
Beef
  Beef Stroganoff, 222–23
  Braised Beef Cubes, 219
  Jenny's Beer Stew, 220, 221
Beer
  Jenny's Beer Stew, 220, 221

Beet Salad, 148, **photo 8**
Beverages
  Christmas Eggnog, 138
  Mulled Cider, 162
  Mulled Wine, 162
  Wassail Bowl, 194
  White Wine Punch, 186
Biscuits
  Baking Powder Biscuits, 153–54
  Cheese Biscuits, 154
  Dill Biscuits, 154
  Sugar Biscuits with Currants, 25
Bittersweet Chocolate Glaze, 83
Bittersweet Chocolate-Nut Sauce, 231
Black Bean Salad with Oranges,
    Avocado and Coriander, 207
Blue Cheese Parsley Butter, 240
Boston Baked Beans, Make-Ahead,
    181
Bourbon
  Double Chocolate Bourbon
    Cookies, 14, **photo 2**
Braised Beef Cubes, 219
Brandy
  Apricot Brandy Filling, 23
  Brandied Prune Fruitcakes, 84
  Brandy-baked Apples with Nuts
    and Raisins, 155

Breads, 114
   baking equipment checklist, 129
   Christmas Stollen, 117–18
   Cranberry Spiral Bread with
      Vanilla Glaze, 123–24,
      photo 5
   Date and Honey Loaves, 125
   gift wraps for, 120
   Ginger-Nut Loaves, 127
   Honey-Pecan Crescents, 121–22,
      photo 5
   Mexican Three Kings Bread,
      130–31, **photo 6**
   Panettone di Natale, 134–35,
      photo 6
   Santa Lucia Buns, 132–33,
      photo 5
   tips and guidelines for baking,
      115–16
   yeast breads, 116
   See also Coffeecakes
Breakfast fruits, 127
Breakfast in bed, 177
Brown Butter Frosting, 64
Browned Brussels Sprouts, 223
Browned Shallot Mayonnaise, 164
Brown Sugar Butter Crunch with
   Toasted Almonds, 104–5,
   photo 7
Brunch, Christmas Morning,
   158–61
Brunch menus, 135
Brussels sprouts
   Browned Brussels Sprouts, 223
Bûche de Noël (Yule Log), 50–54,
   photo 4
Buffets
   buffet table, items needed for,
      143

Christmas Fiesta Buffet, 202–9
   Festive Buffet Dinner, 138–42
Butter
   Brown Butter Frosting, 64
   Brown Sugar Butter Crunch with
      Toasted Almonds, 104–5,
      photo 7
   Buttery Gingerbread Santas,
      15–16, **photo 2**
   Savory Butters, 166, 240
   Winter Pear Butter, 233
Buttercream
   Chestnut Buttercream Filling, 53
   Mint Buttercream Filling, 30
   Rum Buttercream Frosting, 58
Buttermilk
   Buttermilk-Pecan Fruitcakes,
      92–93, **photos 3 and 11**
   Buttermilk-Spice Cupcakes with
      Brown Butter Frosting, 63–65,
      photo 4

Cakes, 48
   Bûche de Noël (Yule Log),
      50–54, **photo 4**
   Buttermilk-Spice Cupcakes with
      Brown Butter Frosting, 63–65,
      photo 4
   Christmas-Comes-But-Once-a-
      Year Chocolate Cake, 56–59,
      photo 4
   Christmas Trifle, 68–69, **photo 4**
   decorations for, 67
   Old-fashioned Burnt-Sugar
      Gingerbread with Double
      Cream Topping, 73–75
   pound cake desserts, 66
   Rich Holiday Pound Cake,
      66–67

rolled cakes, 61
   Simple Sponge Cake, 69
   storage of, 71
   supplies checklist, 52
   tips and guidelines for baking,
      49
   See also Fillings; Frostings;
      Fruitcakes; Gingerbread;
      Glazes; Icing
Calabacitas con Elote (Zucchini
   with Corn), 208
Calta, Diana, 17
Candied Cranberries, 60
Candies, 94
   Brown Sugar Butter Crunch with
      Toasted Almonds, 104–5,
      photo 7
   Caramel Popcorn Balls, 103
   Chocolate-dipped Apricots and
      Pears, 110–11
   Chocolate-dipped Meringue
      Kisses, 106–7, **photo 7**
   Christmas Sugarplums, 102,
      photo 7
   Colorful Marzipan Fruits,
      100–1, **photo 7**
   Dark Chocolate Raisin-Peanut
      Clusters, 96
   decorating with, 96
   gift wraps for, 109
   Kids' Christmas Crispies, 105
   Old-fashioned Chocolate Pecan
      Fudge, 108–9, **photo 7**
   Pastel Peppermint Patties,
      112–13, **photo 7**
   Rum-Walnut Balls, 107
   tips and guidelines for making,
      95
   Truffles, 98–99, **photo 7**

Candies (*continued*)
White Chocolate Coconut-Pecan Clusters, 97
Candles, decorating with, 84, 93, 173
Candy Cane Cookies, 26–27, **photo 1**
Candy Sampler for Kids (gift idea), 235
Caramel
Caramel Popcorn Balls, 103
Caramel Sauce, 62
Caroling Party menu, 194–201
Carrots
Carrot-Pineapple Fruitcakes, 81
Creamy Carrot and Leek Soup, 152
Crunchy Vegetables with Crisp Garlic, 193
garnishes, 178
Individual Packets of Winter Vegetables, 172–73, **photo 10**
Spicy Yogurt Chicken with Vegetables, 214–15, **photo 12**
Cauliflower
Crunchy Vegetables with Crisp Garlic, 193
Centerpieces, 154, 158
Cheese
Blue Cheese Parsley Butter, 240
checklist for, 202
Cheese Biscuits, 154
Chicken or Cheese Enchilada Stacks, 205–6
Welsh Rabbit on Toast, 197, **photo 14**
Chef, gifts for, 240
Cherries
Chocolate-Cherry Fruitcake with

Bittersweet Chocolate Glaze, 82–83, **photo 3**
Spiced Pear and Cherry Kuchen, 119–20, **photo 5**
Chestnut Buttercream Filling, 53
Chicken
Chicken or Cheese Enchilada Stacks, 205–6
Chicken with Mushrooms in Sherried Cream Sauce, 217, 218
Poached Chicken Breasts, 212–13
Spicy Yogurt Chicken with Vegetables, 214–15, **photo 12**
Chicken broth, soups from, 151
Chili Butter, 240
Chocolate
Almond Chocolate Mousse, 59
Bittersweet Chocolate Glaze, 83
Bittersweet Chocolate-Nut Sauce, 231
Chocolate-Cherry Fruitcake with Bittersweet Chocolate Glaze, 82–83, **photo 3**
Chocolate Chip Shortbread, 21
Chocolate-dipped Almonds, 59
Chocolate-dipped Apricots and Pears, 110–11
Chocolate-dipped Meringue Kisses, 106–7, **photo 7**
Chocolate Liqueur Coating, 23
Chocolate-Marzipan-Mocha Layered Bars, 28–29
Chocolate Sandwiches with Mint Buttercream Filling, 29–30
Chocolate Truffles, 98
Christmas-Comes-But-Once-a-Year Chocolate Cake, 56–59, **photo 4**

cookie decorations, 39
Dark Chocolate Raisin-Peanut Clusters, 96
Double Chocolate Bourbon Cookies, 14, **photo 2**
Old-fashioned Chocolate Pecan Fudge, 108–9, **photo 7**
Orange-Chocolate Chip Shortbread, 21
tips on working with, 95
White Chocolate Coconut-Pecan Clusters, 97
Christmas Chopped Salad, 198–99, **photo 14**
Christmas-Comes-But-Once-a-Year Chocolate Cake, 56–59, **photo 4**
Christmas Day menus, 156
Christmas Dinner, 162–75
Christmas Morning Brunch, 158–61
tips and guidelines for preparing, 157
Yuletide Open House, 176–83
Christmas Dinner menu, 162–75
Christmas Eggnog, 138
Christmas Eve menus, 136
Festive Buffet Dinner, 138–42
Midnight Supper, 150–55
Super-Easy Smorgasbord, 143–49
tips and guidelines for preparing, 137
Christmas Fiesta Buffet menu, 202–9
Christmas Memories from Friends
The Aprons, 231
The Best Gift, 171
Christmas at Home in Barbados, 51

Christmas Memories (*continued*)
 Christmas in Bavaria, 27
 The Crèche, 62
 A Doctor's Christmas, 85
 Maple Sugar Candy, 102
 Mysterious Shapes, 175
 Presents, 203
 Santa's Wing Tips, 152
Christmas Morning Brunch menu,
 158–61
Christmas Shortbread, 20–21,
 photo 2
Christmas Stollen, 117–18
Christmas Sugarplums, 102,
 photo 7
Christmas Touches, 34, 75, 91, 99,
 125, 147, 159, 196, 212, 236
Christmas Trifle, 68–69, **photo 4**
Chutney
 Apple-Onion Chutney, 234,
  photo 13
 Marnie's Dried Peach and
  Apricot Chutney, 236
Cider
 Mulled Cider, 162
Cinnamon
 Cinnamon Glaze, 118
 Cinnamon Stars, 25, **photo 12**
 Marbled Cinnamon Coffeecake
  with Streusel Topping, 126
Coatings, for cookies
 Chocolate Liqueur Coating, 23
Cocktail parties, 189
 food for, 199
Cocktail Snack Pack, 232
Coconut
 White Chocolate Coconut-Pecan
  Clusters, 97
Coffeecakes, 114

baking equipment checklist, 129
gift wraps for, 120
glazes for, 118
Lattice Coffeecake with Orange-
 Almond Filling, 128–29,
 photo 6
Marbled Cinnamon Coffeecake
 with Streusel Topping, 126
Spiced Pear and Cherry Kuchen,
 119–20, **photo 5**
tips and guidelines for baking,
 115
Coffee Hard Sauce, 80
Colorful Marzipan Fruits, 100–1,
 photo 7
Compote
 Winter Fruit Compote, 103
Cookie decorations
 for baked cookies, 25
 chocolate, 39
 icing, recipe for, 16
 piping methods, 19, 46
 for unbaked cookies, 32
Cookie Houses, Miniature, 33–37,
 photo 2
Cookie ornaments, 15–16, 21,
 24–25
Cookies, 12
 Almond Spritz Cookies, 18–19
 Apple-Mince Tartlets, 31–32,
  photo 11
 Buttery Gingerbread Santas,
  15–16, **photo 2**
 Candy Cane Cookies, 26–27,
  photo 1
 Chocolate Chip Shortbread, 21
 Chocolate-Marzipan-Mocha
  Layered Bars, 28–29
 Chocolate Sandwiches with Mint

 Buttercream Filling, 29–30
 Christmas Shortbread, 20–21,
  photo 2
 Cinnamon Stars, 25, **photo 12**
 Cranberry-Orange Tartlets,
  31–32, **photo 2**
 Diana's Scandinavian Jam Tots,
  17
 Double Chocolate Bourbon
  Cookies, 14, **photo 2**
 gift wraps for, 44
 Gingerbread Cottage, 38–47,
  photo 1
 Lemon Cookies, 26
 Lemon Shortbread, 21
 Liz's Hazelnut Crescents and
  Hazelnut Sandwiches, 22–23,
  photo 2
 Miniature Cookie Houses,
  33–37, **photo 2**
 Nut Shortbread, 21
 Orange-Chocolate Chip
  Shortbread, 21
 Rolled Sugar Cookies, 24–26,
  photos 1 and 2
 Spice Cookies, 26
 storage of, 45
 Sugar Biscuits with Currants, 25
 supplies checklist, 42
 tips and guidelines for baking,
  13
 See also Fillings; Frostings;
  Glazes; Icing; Shortbreads
Cook's Journal
 Cake Storage, 71
 Cookie Storage, 45
 Crudités, 163
 Decorating Your Cookies with
  Simple Piping: Method #1, 19

Cook's Journal (*continued*)
  Decorating Your Cookies with
    Simple Piping: Method #2, 46
  Decorations for Fruitcakes, 78–
    81, 89
  Fruit for Breakfast, 127
  Fruit Garnishes, 214
  Getting Organized for Baking,
    133
  Hearty Soups from Chicken
    Broth, 151
  How to Toast Nuts, 40
  Labeling, 229, 230
  Plump Fruit, 81
  Rolled Cakes, 61
  Savory Toast, 166
  Simple Garnishes, 178
  Winter Fruit Compote, 103
Cook's Tree, 74
Coriander
  Black Bean Salad with Oranges,
    Avocado and Coriander, 207
Corn
  Calabacitas con Elote (Zucchini
    with Corn), 208
  Corn Pudding with Hot Peppers,
    182
Couscous with Raisins and
    Walnuts, 216, **photo 12**
Cranberries
  Candied Cranberries, 60
  Cranberry Filling, 124
  Cranberry Ketchup, 235,
    photos 10 and 13
  Cranberry-Orange Tartlets,
    31–32, **photo 2**
  Cranberry Spiral Bread with
    Vanilla Glaze, 123–24,
    photo 5

Cream
  Double Cream Topping, 75
  Cream Gravy, 168
  Sherried Cream Sauce, 218
Creamy Carrot and Leek Soup,
    152
Creamy Spinach and Herb Sauce,
    227
Crown Roast of Pork with Savory
    Fruit Stuffing, 169–70,
    photo 10
Crudités (vegetable appetizers),
    163
Crunchy Vegetables with Crisp
    Garlic, 193
Cucumbers
  Cucumber Salad, 148, **photo 8**
  garnishes, 178
Cupcakes
  Buttermilk-Spice Cupcakes with
    Brown Butter Frosting, 63–65,
    photo 4
  Decorations for, 65
Currants
  Sugar Biscuits with Currants, 25
Custard
  Prune-Apricot Custard Tart with
    Sweet Lemon Crust, 70–72,
    photo 4
  Vanilla Custard, 69
  Warm Custard Sauce, 201

Dark Chocolate Raisin-Peanut
    Clusters, 96
Date and Honey Loaves, 125
Decorating Icing, 16, 113
Decorating Memo
  Christmas All Over the House,
    134

Christmas Centerpieces, 154,
    158
Cookie Ornaments, 15–16, 21,
    24–25
A Cook's Tree, 74
Decorations Using Candles, 84,
    93
Finishing Touches, 188
Herb and Spice Ornaments for
    the Christmas Tree, 101
More Christmas Centerpieces,
    158
More Decorations Using
    Candles, 173
Natural Ornaments, 150
Party Favors, 96
Scandinavian Style, 145
Dessert party, tips for, 72
Desserts. *See* Cakes; Custard; Pies;
    Plum puddings; Tarts
Diana's Scandinavian Jam Tots, 17
Dill Biscuits, 154
Disposable necessities, 192
Double Chocolate Bourbon
    Cookies, 14, **photo 2**
Double Cream Topping, 75
Down-Home Dinner menu, 144
Dressings
  Lime Dressing, 142
  for pasta, 224
Dried Fruit Sampler (gift idea), 235

Eggnog, 138
Eggplant
  Savory Tomato-Eggplant Sauce,
    225–26
Enchiladas
  Chicken or Cheese Enchilada
    Stacks, 205–6

Entertaining Notebook
  Breakfast in Bed, 177
  The Buffet Table, 143
  Candles, 84, 93, 173
  Cocktail Parties, 189, 199
  Dessert Party, 72
  Disposable Necessities, 192
  Host and Hostess Gifts, 112
  How to Be a Good Holiday
    Party Guest, 204
  How to Be a Good Holiday
    Party Host, 195
  Ice Rings, 187
  Planning Ahead, 169
  Start a Family Tradition, 180
  Stocking Stuffers for Kids, 110
Ephron, Nora, 174

Festive Buffet Dinner menu,
  138–42
Fillings
  Apple-Mince Filling, 31, 32
  Apricot Brandy Filling, 23
  Chestnut Buttercream Filling, 53
  Cranberry Filling, 124
  Cranberry-Orange Filling, 31–32
  Honey-Pecan Filling, 122
  Mint Buttercream Filling, 30
  Orange-Almond Filling, 128
  for rolled cakes, 61
Flan, 209
Fluffy Apricot Sauce, 91
Four Delicious Hard Sauces, 80
French Toast, Oven-baked, 161,
  photo 9
Fresh Orange Relish, 232, photo 13
Frittata
  Mushroom and Roast Pepper
    Frittata, 191–92

Frosted Grapes, 214
Frostings
  Brown Butter Frosting, 64
  Mocha Frosting, 29
  Mocha Silk Frosting, 54
  for rolled cakes, 61
  Rum Buttercream Frosting, 58
Fruit
  for breakfast, 127
  checklist for, 87
  garnishes, 214
  plump fruit, method for, 81
  Savory Fruit Stuffing, 170,
    photo 10
  Winter Fruit Compote, 103
  See also specific fruits
Fruitcakes, 76
  Almond-layered Fruitcakes,
    79–80, photo 3
  Brandied Prune Fruitcakes, 84
  Buttermilk-Pecan Fruitcakes,
    92–93, photos 3 and 11
  Carrot-Pineapple Fruitcakes,
    81
  Chocolate-Cherry Fruitcake with
    Bittersweet Chocolate Glaze,
    82–83, photo 3
  decorations for, 78, 89
  gift wraps for, 83
  Lightly Spiced Dark Fruitcakes,
    86–87
  Orange-Hazelnut Cake, 85
  Sherry Fruitcakes with Fluffy
    Apricot Sauce, 90–91,
    photo 3
  tips and guidelines for baking,
    77–78
  Tipsy Dark Fruitcakes, 88–89,
    photo 3

Fudge
  Old-fashioned Chocolate Pecan
    Fudge, 108–9, photo 7

Garlic
  Crunchy Vegetables with Crisp
    Garlic, 193
  Garlic and Herb Butter, 240
Garnishes, 178, 214
Gifts, homemade, 228
  Apple-Onion Chutney, 234,
    photo 13
  Bittersweet Chocolate-Nut
    Sauce, 231
  Cranberry Ketchup, 235,
    photos 10 and 13
  Fresh Orange Relish, 232,
    photo 13
  gift assortments, 232, 237
  labels for, 230
  Marinated Onion and Red
    Pepper Relish, 238, photo 13
  Marnie's Dried Peach and
    Apricot Chutney, 236
  Old-fashioned Lemon Curd,
    230, photo 9
  Parsley Pesto, 241
  Popcorn and Pretzel Snacks,
    241
  sampler gifts, 235
  Savory Butters, 240
  Spiced Nuts, 242, photo 13
  Tarragon Mustard, 239
  tips and guidelines, for
    preparing, 229
  Winter Pear Butter, 233
  Winter Salsa, 237, photo 13
Gifts for the Chef, 240
Gift wraps, photo 13

Gift wraps (*continued*)
  for candies, 109
  for coffeecakes, 120
  for cookies, 44
  for fruitcakes, 83
  for gift assortments, 237
  for jars, 233
  for loaves and rings, 120
  for nuts and snacks, 242
Ginger-Nut Loaves, 127
Gingerbread
  Buttery Gingerbread Santas,
    15–16, **photo 2**
  Gingerbread Cottage, 38–47,
    photo 1
  Old-fashioned Burnt-Sugar
    Gingerbread with Double
    Cream Topping, 73–75
Glazes
  Bittersweet Chocolate Glaze,
    83
  Cinnamon Glaze, 118
  for coffeecakes, 118
  Lemon Glaze, 118
  Orange Glaze, 118
  for rolled cakes, 61
  Thick Vanilla Glaze, 131
  Vanilla Glaze, 118
Grapefruit
  Salad of Persimmon and
    Grapefruit Slices with Lime
    Dressing, 141–42, **photo 11**
Grapes
  Frosted Grapes, 214
Gravy
  Cream Gravy, 168
  from pan drippings, 169
Gravlax with Condiments,
  146–47, **photo 8**

Green Sauce, 206
Guests, tips for, 204

Ham
  Mustard-and-Maple-glazed
    Ham, 179–80
Hard sauces, 80
Hazelnuts
  Hazelnut Truffles, 99
  Liz's Hazelnut Crescents and
    Hazelnut Sandwiches, 22–23,
    photo 2
  Orange-Hazelnut Cake, 85
  toasting, method for, 77
Head-Start Dinners, 210
  basic braised beef, 219
  basic poached chicken, 212–13
  beef menus, 220–23
  chicken menus, 214–18
  pasta menus, 224–27
  tips and guidelines for preparing,
    211
Herb and Spice Ornaments, 101
Herb and Spice Sampler, 235
Herbs
  Creamy Spinach and Herb
    Sauce, 227
  Garlic and Herb Butter, 240
  Herb Vinaigrette Sauce, 176
Holiday Potato Salad, 149,
  photo 8
Homemade Chunky Applesauce,
  183
Honey
  Date and Honey Loaves, 125
  Honey Mustard Sauce, 147,
    photo 8
  Honey-Pecan Crescents, 121–22,
    photo 5

Honey-Pecan Filling, 122
Hors d'Oeuvres, 226
Host and Hostess Gifts, 112
Hosting a party, tips on, 195
Hummus, 213, **photo 12**

Ice cream, toppings for, 57
Ice rings for punch, 187
Icing
  decorating with, 19, 25, 46
  recipes for, 16, 113
Individual Baked Pumpkin
    Puddings, 200–1, **photo 14**
Individual Packets of Winter
    Vegetables, 172–73, **photo 10**

Jalapeño Mayonnaise, 190
Jam
  Diana's Scandinavian Jam Tots,
    17
Jambalaya
  Shrimp Jambalaya with White
    Rice, 140–41, **photo 11**
Jenny's Beer Stew, 220, 221

Ketchup
  Cranberry Ketchup, 235,
    photos 10 and 13
Kids' Christmas Crispies, 105
Kuchen
  Spiced Pear and Cherry Kuchen,
    119–20, **photo 5**

Lattice Coffeecake with Orange-
    Almond Filling, 128–29,
    photo 6
Leeks
  Creamy Carrot and Leek Soup,
    152

Lemons
    garnishes, 178
    Lemon Cookies, 26
    Lemon Glaze, 118
    Lemon Hard Sauce, 80
    Lemon Shortbread, 21
    Old-fashioned Lemon Curd,
        230, **photo 9**
    Prune-Apricot Custard Tart with
        Sweet Lemon Crust, 70–72,
        photo 4
    Sliced Oranges in Light Lemon
        Syrup, 160, **photo 9**
Lightly Spiced Dark Fruitcakes,
    86–87
Limes
    garnishes, 178
    Lime Dressing, 142
    Lime Vinaigrette Sauce, 176
Liz's Hazelnut Crescents and
    Hazelnut Sandwiches, 22–23,
    photo 2

Make-Ahead Boston Baked Beans,
    181
Maple syrup
    Mustard-and-Maple-glazed
        Ham, 179–80
Marbled Cinnamon Coffeecake
    with Streusel Topping, 126
Marinated Onion and Red Pepper
    Relish, 238, **photo 13**
Marinated Sun-dried Tomatoes, 190
Marnie's Dried Peach and Apricot
    Chutney, 236
Marzipan
    Basic Marzipan, 100
    Chocolate-Marzipan-Mocha
        Layered Bars, 28–29

Colorful Marzipan Fruits,
    100–1, **photo 7**
Mayonnaise
    Browned Shallot Mayonnaise,
        164
    Jalapeño Mayonnaise, 190
    Wasabi Mayonnaise, 147,
        photo 8
Meringue
    Chocolate-dipped Meringue
        Kisses, 106–7, **photo 7**
Mexican Three Kings Bread,
    130–31, **photo 6**
Midnight Supper menu, 150–55
Mince
    Apple-Mince Tartlets, 31–32,
        photo 11
Miniature Cookie Houses, 33–37,
    photo 2
Mint Buttercream Filling, 30
Mocha
    Chocolate-Marzipan-Mocha
        Layered Bars, 28–29
    Mocha Silk Frosting, 54
    Mocha Truffles, 99
More Gift Ideas from the
    Christmas Kitchen, 239
Morning Coffee Gift, 232
Mousse
    Almond Chocolate Mousse, 59
Mueller, Marnie, 236
Mulled Cider, 162
Mulled Wine, 162
Mushrooms
    Chicken with Mushrooms in
        Sherried Cream Sauce, 217,
        218
    Mushroom and Roast Pepper
        Frittata, 191–92

Wild Rice with Mushrooms and
    Onions, 171, **photo 10**
Mustard
    Honey Mustard Sauce, 147,
        photo 8
    Mustard-and-Maple-glazed
        Ham, 179–80
    Tarragon Mustard, 239

No-Fail Flan, 209
Nora's Plum Puddings, 174–75,
    photo 10
Nuts
    Bittersweet Chocolate-Nut
        Sauce, 231
    Brandy-baked Apples with Nuts
        and Raisins, 155
    checklist for, 87
    Nut Shortbread, 21
    Spiced Nuts, 242, **photo 13**
    toasting, method for, 40
    See also specific nuts

Old-fashioned Burnt-Sugar
    Gingerbread with Double
    Cream Topping, 73–75
Old-fashioned Chocolate Pecan
    Fudge, 108–9, **photo 7**
Old-fashioned Lemon Curd, 230,
    photo 9
Onions
    Apple-Onion Chutney, 234,
        photo 13
    Marinated Onion and Red
        Pepper Relish, 238,
        photo 13
    Wild Rice with Mushrooms and
        Onions, 171, **photo 10**
Open House menu, 176–83

Oranges
  Black Bean Salad with Oranges,
    Avocado and Coriander, 207
  Cranberry-Orange Tartlets,
    31–32, **photo 2**
  Fresh Orange Relish, 232,
    photo 13
  garnishes, 178
  Orange-Almond Filling, 128
  Orange-Chocolate Chip
    Shortbread, 21
  Orange Glaze, 118
  Orange-Hazelnut Cake, 85
  Orange Truffles, 99
  Sliced Oranges in Light Lemon
    Syrup, 160, **photo 9**
Organization for baking, 133
Ornaments
  cookie, 15–16, 21, 24–25
  herb and spice, 101
  natural, 150
Oven-baked French Toast, 161,
  photo 9

Panettone di Natale (Italian
  holiday bread), 134–35,
  photo 6
Parsley
  Blue Cheese Parsley Butter, 240
  Parsley Pesto, 241
Parsnips
  Individual Packets of Winter
    Vegetables, 172–73, **photo 10**
Party menus, 184
  Caroling Party, 194–201
  Christmas Fiesta Buffet, 202–9
  Saturday Night Gala, 186–93
  Super-Easy Smorgasbord for
    Christmas Eve Guests, 143–49

tips and guidelines for preparing,
  185
Yuletide Open House, 176–83
Pasta
  dressings for, 224
  sauces for, 224–27
Pastel Peppermint Patties, 112–13,
  photo 7
Peaches
  Marnie's Dried Peach and
    Apricot Chutney, 236
Peanuts
  Dark Chocolate Raisin-Peanut
    Clusters, 96
Pears
  Chocolate-dipped Apricots and
    Pears, 110–11
  Spiced Pear and Cherry Kuchen,
    119–20, **photo 5**
  Winter Pear Butter, 233
Pecans
  Buttermilk-Pecan Fruitcakes,
    92–93, **photos 3 and 11**
  Ginger-Nut Loaves, 127
  Honey-Pecan Crescents, 121–22,
    photo 5
  Old-fashioned Chocolate Pecan
    Fudge, 108–9, **photo 7**
  White Chocolate Coconut-Pecan
    Clusters, 97
Peppermint
  Pastel Peppermint Patties,
    112–13, **photo 7**
Peppers
  Corn Pudding with Hot Peppers,
    182
  Crunchy Vegetables with Crisp
    Garlic, 193
  Jalapeño Mayonnaise, 190

Marinated Onion and Red
  Pepper Relish, 238, **photo 13**
Mushroom and Roast Pepper
  Frittata, 191–92
Persimmons
  Salad of Persimmon and
    Grapefruit Slices with Lime
    Dressing, 141–42, **photo 11**
Pesto
  Parsley Pesto, 241
Pies, 48
  decorations for, 67
  Pumpkin Pies with Walnut-
    Crumb Crusts, 54–55
  tips and guidelines for baking, 49
Pineapple
  Carrot-Pineapple Fruitcakes, 81
Piping methods of cookie
  decoration, 19, 46
Plum puddings
  Nora's Plum Puddings, 174–75,
    photo 10
Poached Chicken Breasts, 212–13
Popcorn
  Caramel Popcorn Balls, 103
  Popcorn and Pretzel Snacks, 241
Pork
  Crown Roast of Pork with
    Savory Fruit Stuffing, 169–70,
    photo 10
Potatoes
  Holiday Potato Salad, 149,
    photo 8
Poultry
  Chicken Enchilada Stacks,
    205–6
  Chicken with Mushrooms in
    Sherried Cream Sauce, 217,
    218

Poultry (*continued*)
  Poached Chicken Breasts, 212–13
  Roast Turkey, 165–68
  Spicy Yogurt Chicken with Vegetables, 214–15, **photo 12**
Pound cakes
  pound cake desserts, 66
  Rich Holiday Pound Cake, 66–67
Pretzels
  Popcorn and Pretzel Snacks, 241
Prunes
  Brandied Prune Fruitcakes, 84
  Prune-Apricot Custard Tart with Sweet Lemon Crust, 70–72, **photo 4**
Puddings
  Corn Pudding with Hot Peppers, 182
  Individual Baked Pumpkin Puddings, 200–1, **photo 14**
  Nora's Plum Puddings, 174–75, **photo 10**
Pumpkins
  Individual Baked Pumpkin Puddings, 200–1, **photo 14**
  Pumpkin Pies with Walnut-Crumb Crusts, 54–55
Punch
  ice rings for, 187
  White Wine Punch, 186
Put-together parties, tips on, 139

Quick and Easy
  Decorations for Baked Cookies, 25
  Decorations for Cakes, Pies and Tarts, 67

Decorations for Unbaked Cookies, 32
  Do-It-Yourself Gift Assortments, 232
  More Decorations for Baked Cookies, 39
  Natural Ornaments, 150
  Sampler Gifts, 235
Quick Takes
  Food for Cocktail Parties, 199
  Mix-and-Match Menus, 144
  More Menus Using Braised Beef Cubes, 220
  More Menus Using Poached Chicken Breasts, 217
  Pound Cake Desserts, 66

Radish garnishes, 178
Raisins
  Brandy-baked Apples with Nuts and Raisins, 155
  Couscous with Raisins and Walnuts, 216, **photo 12**
  Dark Chocolate Raisin-Peanut Clusters, 96
Red and Green Supper menu, 144
Relishes
  Fresh Orange Relish, 232, **photo 13**
  Marinated Onion and Red Pepper Relish, 238, **photo 13**
Rice
  Shrimp Jambalaya with White Rice, 140–41, **photo 11**
  Wild Rice with Mushrooms and Onions, 171, **photo 10**
Rich Holiday Pound Cake, 66–67
Roast Turkey, 165–66

Rolled Sugar Cookies, 24–26, **photos 1 and 2**
Rum
  Rum Buttercream Frosting, 58
  Rum-Walnut Balls, 107

Salad Lover's Gift, 232
Salads
  Beet Salad, 148, **photo 8**
  Black Bean Salad with Oranges, Avocado and Coriander, 207
  Christmas Chopped Salad, 198–99, **photo 14**
  Cucumber Salad, 148, **photo 8**
  Holiday Potato Salad, 149, **photo 8**
  Persimmon and Grapefruit Slices with Lime Dressing, 141–42, **photo 11**
  Vinaigrette sauces for, 176
Salmon
  Gravlax with Condiments, 146–47, **photo 8**
Salsa
  Winter Salsa, 237, **photo 13**
Sanchez, Liz, 22, 29
Santa Lucia Buns, 132–33, **photo 5**
Saturday Night Gala menu, 186–93
Sauces
  Bittersweet Chocolate-Nut Sauce, 231
  Caramel Sauce, 62
  Creamy Spinach and Herb Sauce, 227
  Fluffy Apricot Sauce, 91
  Green Sauce, 206
  hard sauces, 80

Sauces (*continued*)
   Honey Mustard Sauce, 147,
      photo 8
   for pasta, 224–27
   Savory Tomato Eggplant Sauce,
      225–26
   Sherried Cream Sauce, 218
   Vinaigrette Sauce, 176
   Warm Custard Sauce, 201
Sausage Stuffing, 167
Savory Butters, 240
Savory Fruit Stuffing, 170,
   photo 10
Savory Toast, 166
Savory Tomato-Eggplant Sauce,
   225–26
Scandinavian-style decorations,
   145
Seafood
   Gravlax with Condiments,
      146–47, **photo 8**
   Shrimp Jambalaya with White
      Rice, 140–41, **photo 11**
Shallots
   Browned Shallot Mayonnaise,
      164
   Shallot Vinaigrette Sauce, 176
Sherry
   Sherried Cream Sauce, 218
   Sherry Fruitcakes with Fluffy
      Apricot Sauce, 90–91, **photo 3**
Shortbread
   Chocolate Chip Shortbread, 21
   Christmas Shortbread, 20–21,
      photo 2
   Lemon Shortbread, 21
   Nut Shortbread, 21
   Orange-Chocolate Chip
      Shortbread, 21

Shrimp Jambalaya with White
   Rice, 140–41, **photo 11**
Simple Piping, 19, 46
Simple Sponge Cake, 69
Simple Wraps for Gift
   Assortments, 237
Skewered fruit, 214
Sliced Oranges in Light Lemon
   Syrup, 160, **photo 9**
Smorgasbord menu, 143–49
Snacks with friends, tips for, 131
Snider, Jenny, 221
Soups
   from chicken broth, 151
   Creamy Carrot and Leek Soup,
      152
Spice
   Buttermilk-Spice Cupcakes with
      Brown Butter Frosting, 63–65,
      photo 4
   herb and spice ornaments, 101
   Lightly Spiced Dark Fruitcakes,
      86–87
   Spice Cookies, 26
   Spiced Hard Sauce, 80
   Spiced Nuts, 242, **photo 13**
   Spiced Pear and Cherry Kuchen,
      119–20, **photo 5**
   Spicy Yogurt Chicken with
      Vegetables, 214–15, **photo 12**
Spinach
   Creamy Spinach and Herb
      Sauce, 227
Sponge cake, 69
Spritz cookies, 18–19
Start with Store-Bought
   Ice Cream, 57
   Pasta, 224
   Put-Together Parties, 139

Wreaths, 111
Stew
   Jenny's Beer Stew, 220, 221
Stocking stuffers
   for kids, 110
   for chefs, 240
Stollen (German holiday bread),
   117–18
Storage
   of cakes, 71
   of cookies, 45
Strawberries
   Strawberry Flowers (garnish), 214
Streusel Topping, 126
Stuffings
   preparation tips, 166
   Sausage Stuffing, 167
   Savory Fruit Stuffing, 170,
      photo 10
Sugar Biscuits with Currants, 25
Sugar cookies
   Rolled Sugar Cookies, 24–26,
      photos 1 and 2
Sugarplums
   Christmas Sugarplums, 102,
      photo 7
Sweet breads. *See* Breads;
   Coffeecakes
Sweet potatoes
   Individual Packets of Winter
      Vegetables, 172–73, **photo 10**

Tarragon Mustard, 239
Tarts, 48
   Apple-Mince Tartlets, 31–32,
      photo 11
   Apple Tart with Candied
      Cranberries and Caramel
      Sauce, 60–62, **photo 4**

Tarts (*continued*)
  Cranberry-Orange Tartlets,
    31–32, **photo 2**
  decorations for, 67
  Prune-Apricot Custard Tart with
    Sweet Lemon Crust, 70–72,
    photo 4
  shell, method for making, 60–61
  tips and guidelines for baking,
    49
Tea Sampler, 235
Teatime Gift, 232
Tex-Mex food, 202–9
The Christmas Pantry Checklist
  Appetizers and Hors d'Oeuvres,
    226
  Baking Equipment, 129
  Cake-baking Supplies, 52
  Cheese, 202
  Cookie-baking Supplies, 42
  Nuts and Dried Fruit, 87
  Stocking the Bar, 165
Thick Vanilla Glaze, 131
Tipsy Dark Fruitcakes, 88–89,
  photo 3
Toast
  Oven-baked French Toast, 161,
    photo 9
  Savory Toast, 166
  Welsh Rabbit on Toast, 197,
    photo 14
Toasted nuts, 40
Tomatoes
  Marinated Sun-dried Tomatoes,
    190
  Savory Tomato-Eggplant Sauce,
    225–26

Toppings
  Double Cream Topping, 75
  Streusel Topping, 126
Traditions, family, 180
Trifle
  Christmas Trifle, 68–69, **photo 4**
Truffles, chocolate, 98–99,
  photo 7
Turkey, roast, 165–66
  gravy for, 168
  stuffing for, 166, 167
Turnips
  Individual Packets of Winter
    Vegetables, 172–73, **photo 10**

Vanilla
  Cranberry Spiral Bread with
    Vanilla Glaze, 123–24,
    photo 5
  Thick Vanilla Glaze, 131
  Vanilla Custard, 69
  Vanilla Glaze, 118
  Vanilla Hard Sauce, 80
Vegetables
  Crunchy Vegetables with Crisp
    Garlic, 193
  Individual Packets of Winter
    Vegetables, 172–73, **photo 10**
  Spicy Yogurt Chicken with
    Vegetables, 214–15, **photo 12**
  See also specific vegetables
Vegetarian Treat menu, 144
Vinaigrette sauce, 176

Walnuts
  Couscous with Raisins and
    Walnuts, 216, **photo 12**

Rum-Walnut Balls, 107
  Walnut-Crumb Pie Crusts, 55
Warm Custard Sauce, 201
Wasabi Mayonnaise, 147,
  photo 8
Wassail Bowl, 194
Welsh Rabbit on Toast, 197,
  photo 14
White Chocolate Coconut-Pecan
  Clusters, 97
White Wine Punch, 186
Wild Rice with Mushrooms and
  Onions, 171, **photo 10**
Wine
  Mulled Wine, 162
  White Wine Punch, 186
Winter Fruit Compote, 103
Winter Pear Butter, 233
Winter Salsa, 237, **photo 13**
Wreaths, 111

Yeast breads, tips and guidelines
  for baking, 116
  See also Breads
Yogurt
  Spicy Yogurt Chicken with
    Vegetables, 214–15, **photo 12**
Yule Log (Bûche de Noël), 50–54,
  photo 4
Yuletide Open House menu,
  176–83

Zucchini
  Calabacitas con Elote (Zucchini
    with Corn), 208
  Spicy Yogurt Chicken with
    Vegetables, 214–15, **photo 12**